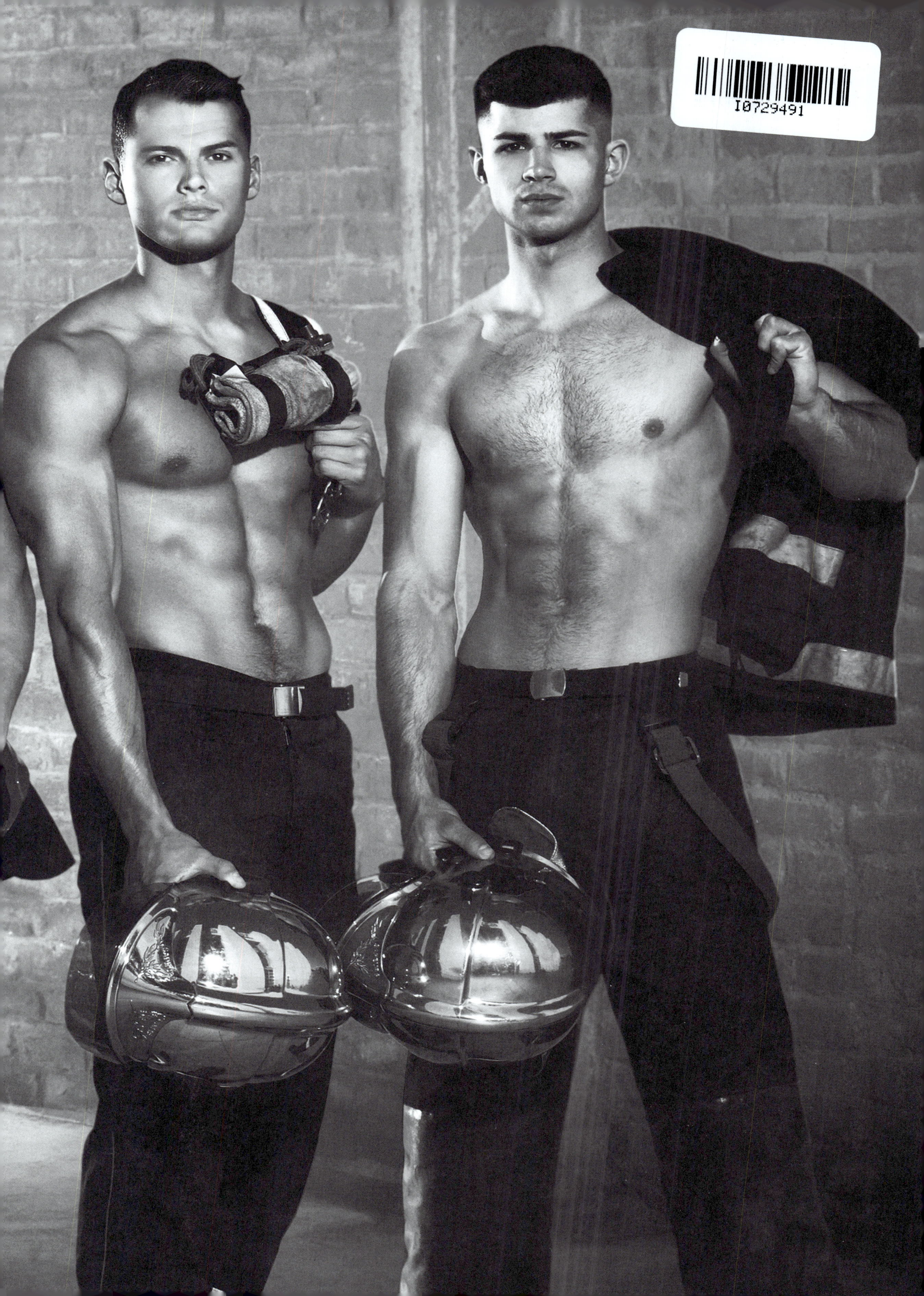
I0729491

ON FIRE

THE FIREFIGHTERS OF FRANCE

ON FIRE

THE FIREFIGHTERS OF FRANCE

Photography by
Fred Goudon

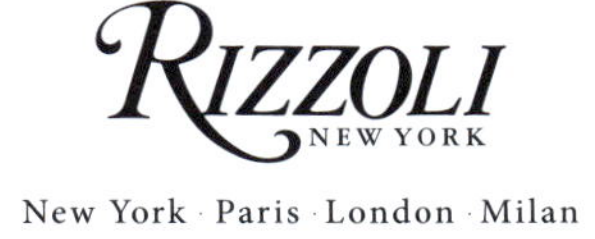

New York · Paris · London · Milan

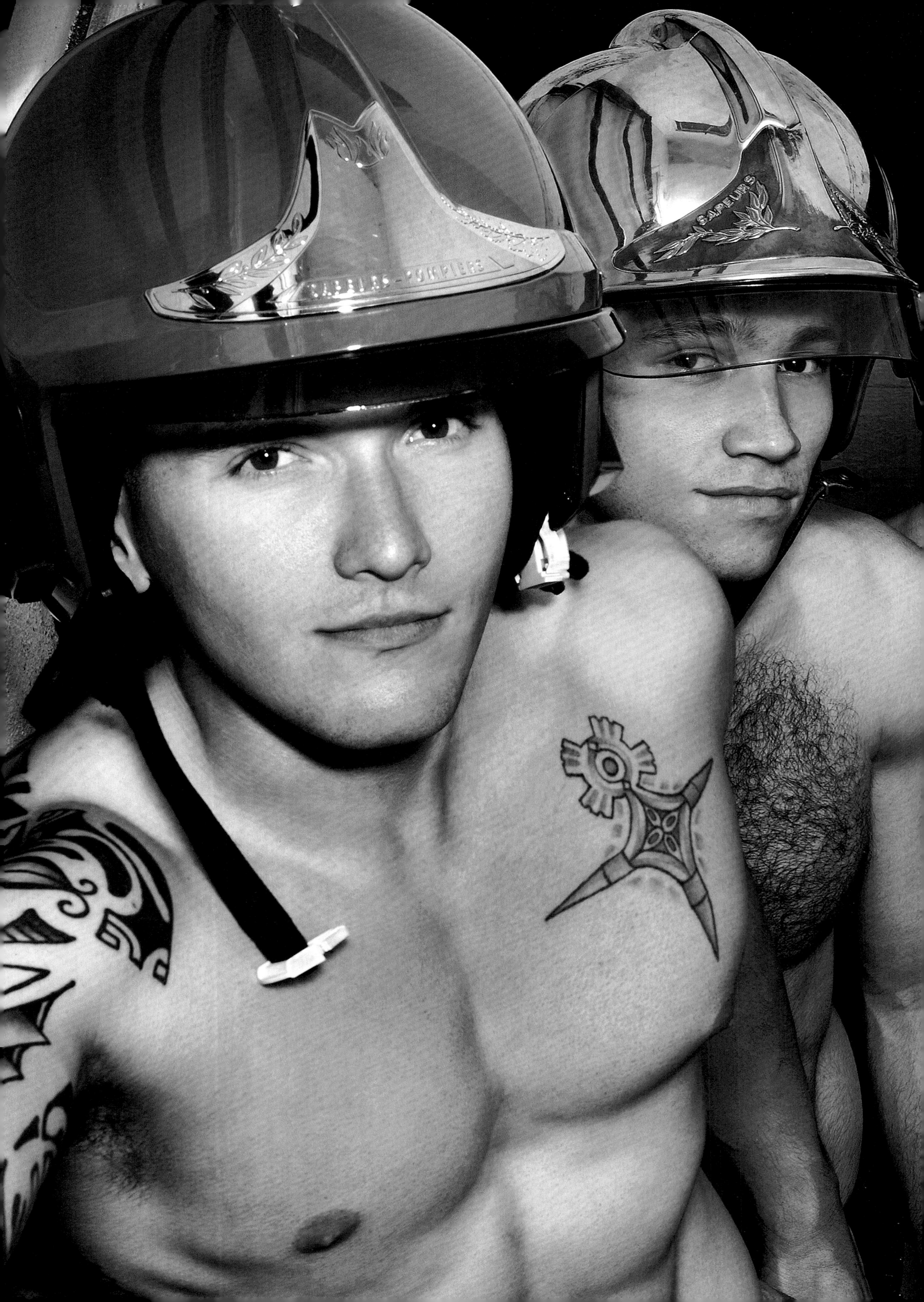

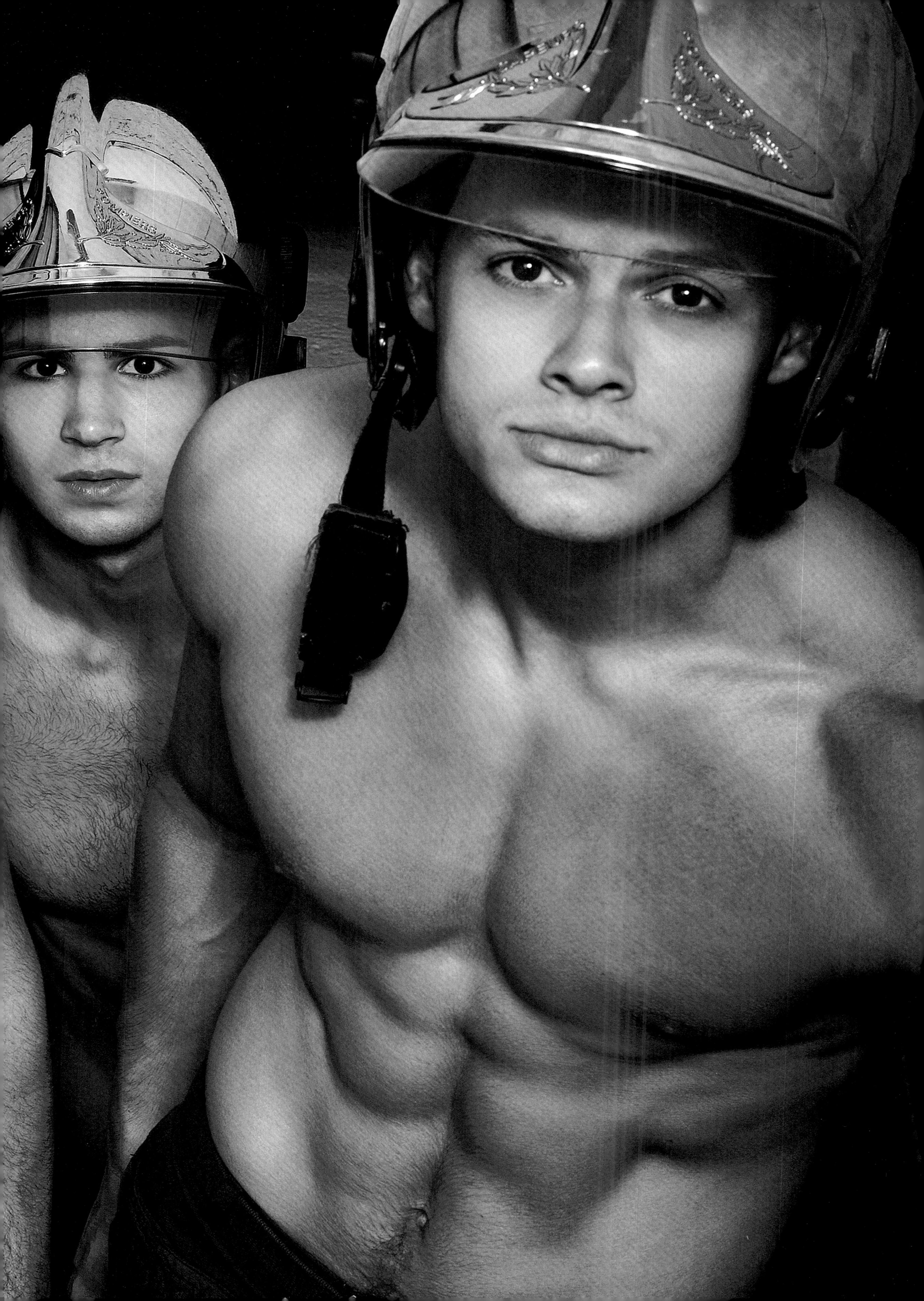

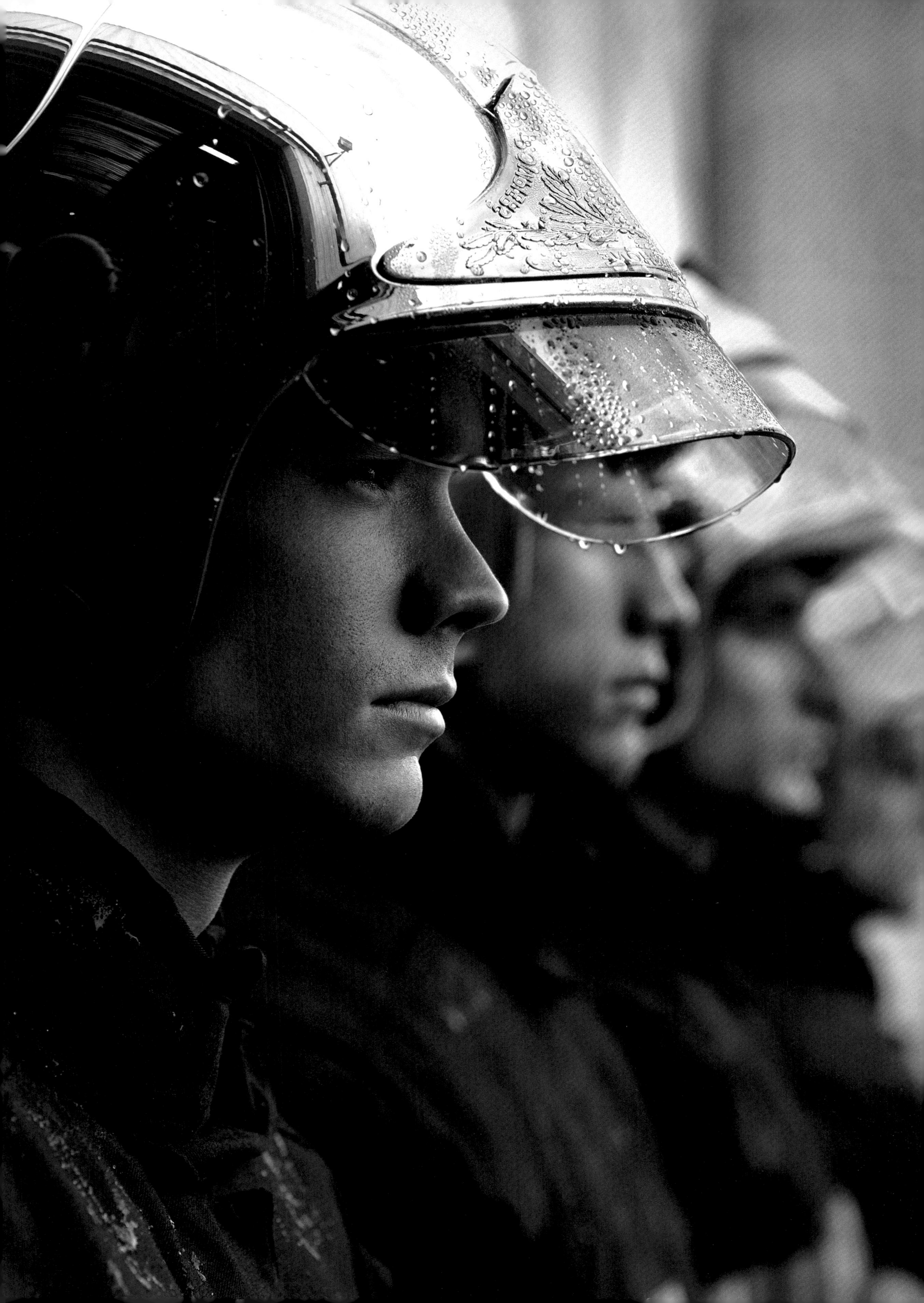

Introduction

Firefighters have always been a great inspiration to me. I've always respected these men who put their lives on the line every day—no questions asked, without any hesitation—because carved into their hearts is a message of complete devotion that I can only describe as "save or die." They follow their deep calling with unwavering resolve.

Firefighters are part of our daily lives. We see them every day, in their red fire trucks, rushing toward a new crisis. We never completely comprehend how they prepare to risk their lives for us once again.

French firefighters have a little *"je ne sais quoi,"* an attitude, a body language that allows me to pinpoint them in a crowd. There is a certain similarity between them all that's visible in the way they hold their heads high. I can tell just by the way they walk, even from behind, that they are firefighters. And I'm never wrong.

As a specialist of male artistic beauty, their athletic, brawny silhouettes inevitably catch my eye. Firefighters' physiques are highly aesthetic. Undeniably, their strong and photogenic forms are ones that I love to master through my photography. For a long time I have felt the need and desire to pay tribute to them for their bravery. And what medium does more to communicate their stories, while also exhibiting their heroism, than photography?

To better capture glimpses into their everyday lives, all the firefighters with whom I worked helped me. Each and every one of them gave me advice on how to consistently replicate the ambiance of friendship and brotherhood present in the fire stations. I would like to take this opportunity to warmly thank my first firefighters, who came filled with enthusiasm—ready to strike a pose. I owe them enormous credit for daring to participate and spreading the word to their colleagues.

Since then, a deep and special bond has formed between the French firefighters and myself. I was honored to be welcomed into their big family. Now, when an accident occurs, when a service call goes badly, or when a firefighter is injured or loses their life, I feel a sharp and visceral pain within me. It doesn't even matter if I knew them personally or not: The tragedy affects me as if I've lost a close friend.

I have taken a lot of photographs honoring great athletes, sportsmen, farmers, actors, and models over time—and I love doing so. But I have to confess that these photographs of French firefighters hold a very special place in my heart.

This book is a necessary, crucial tribute to these everyday heroes.

—**FRED GOUDON**

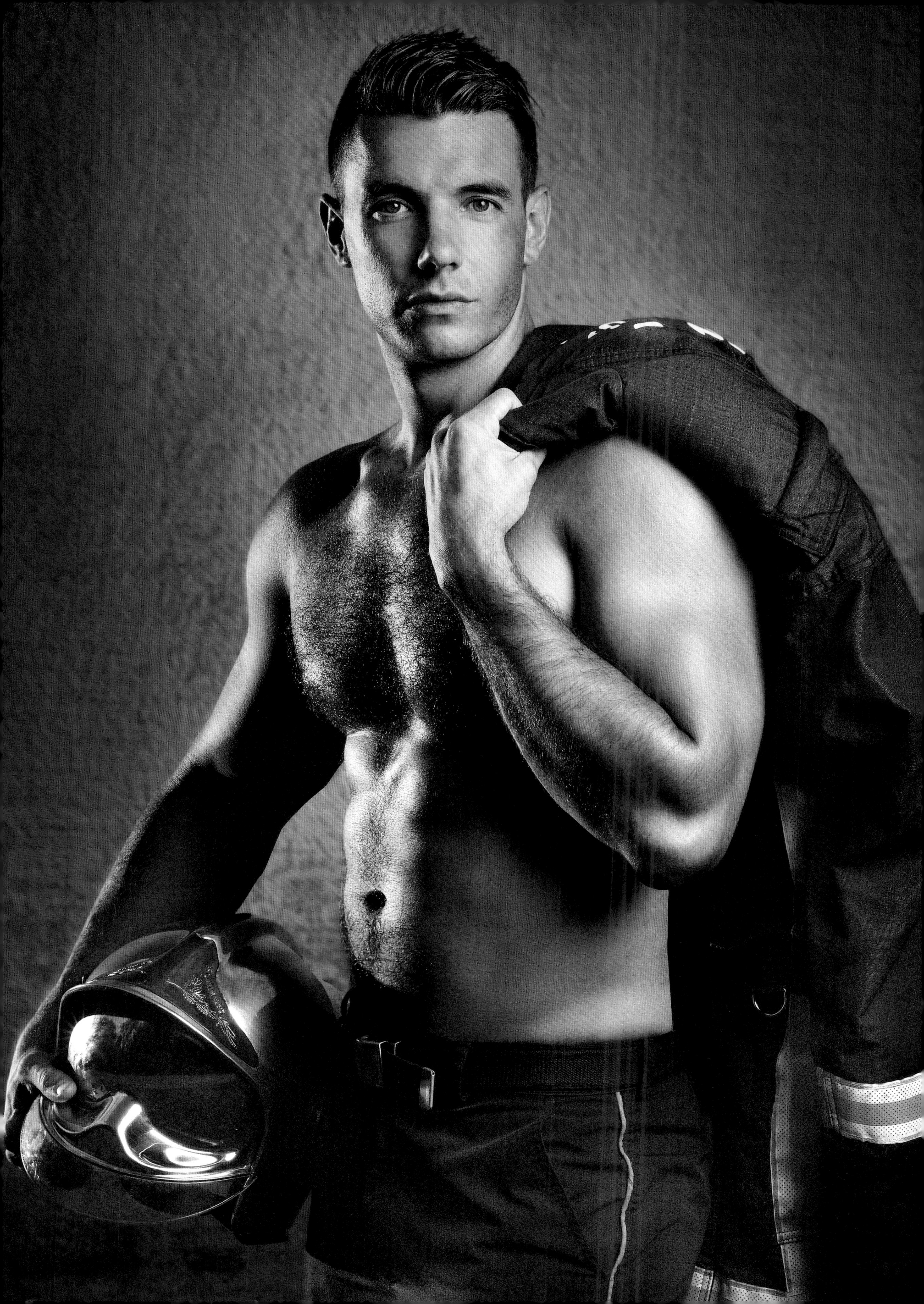

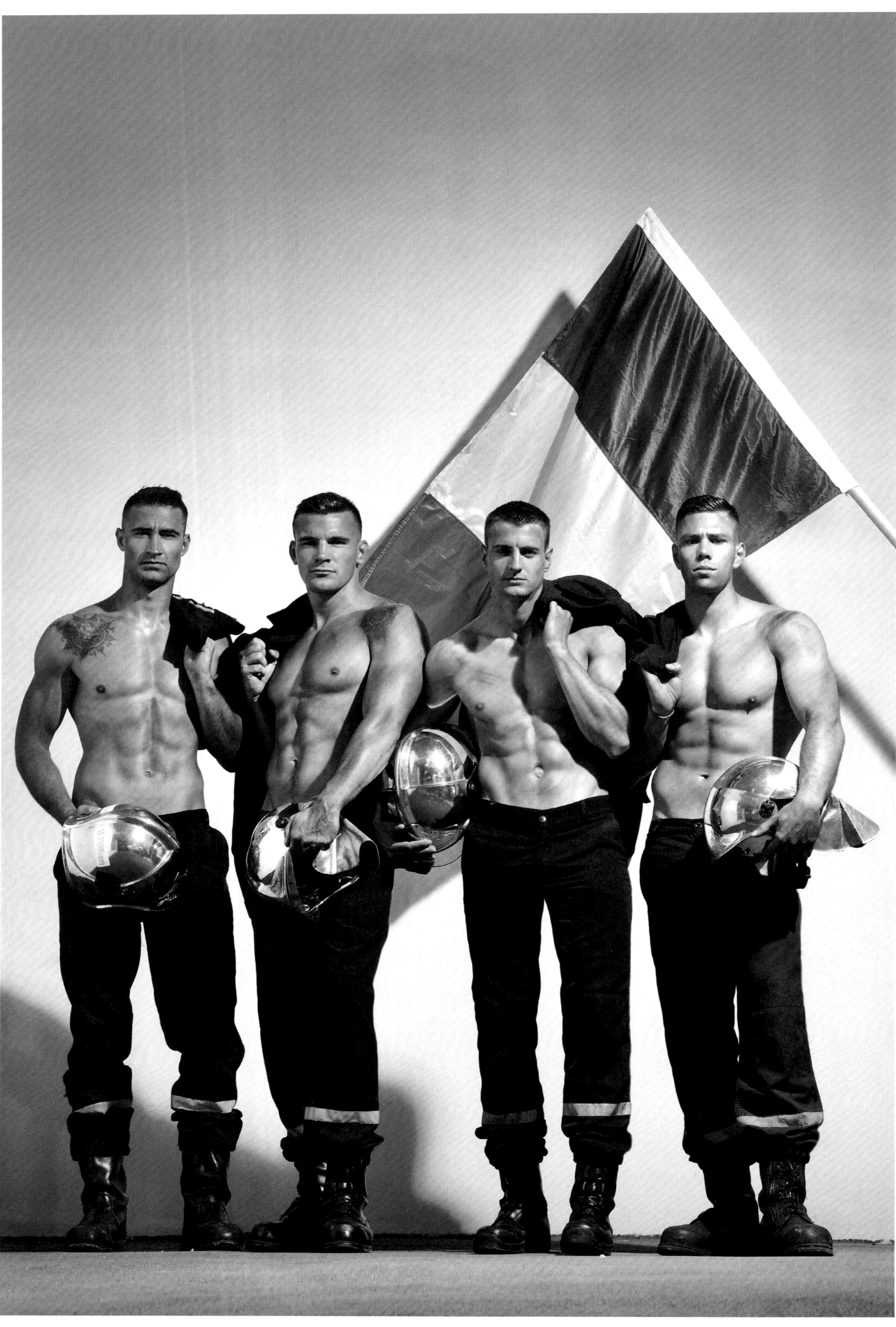

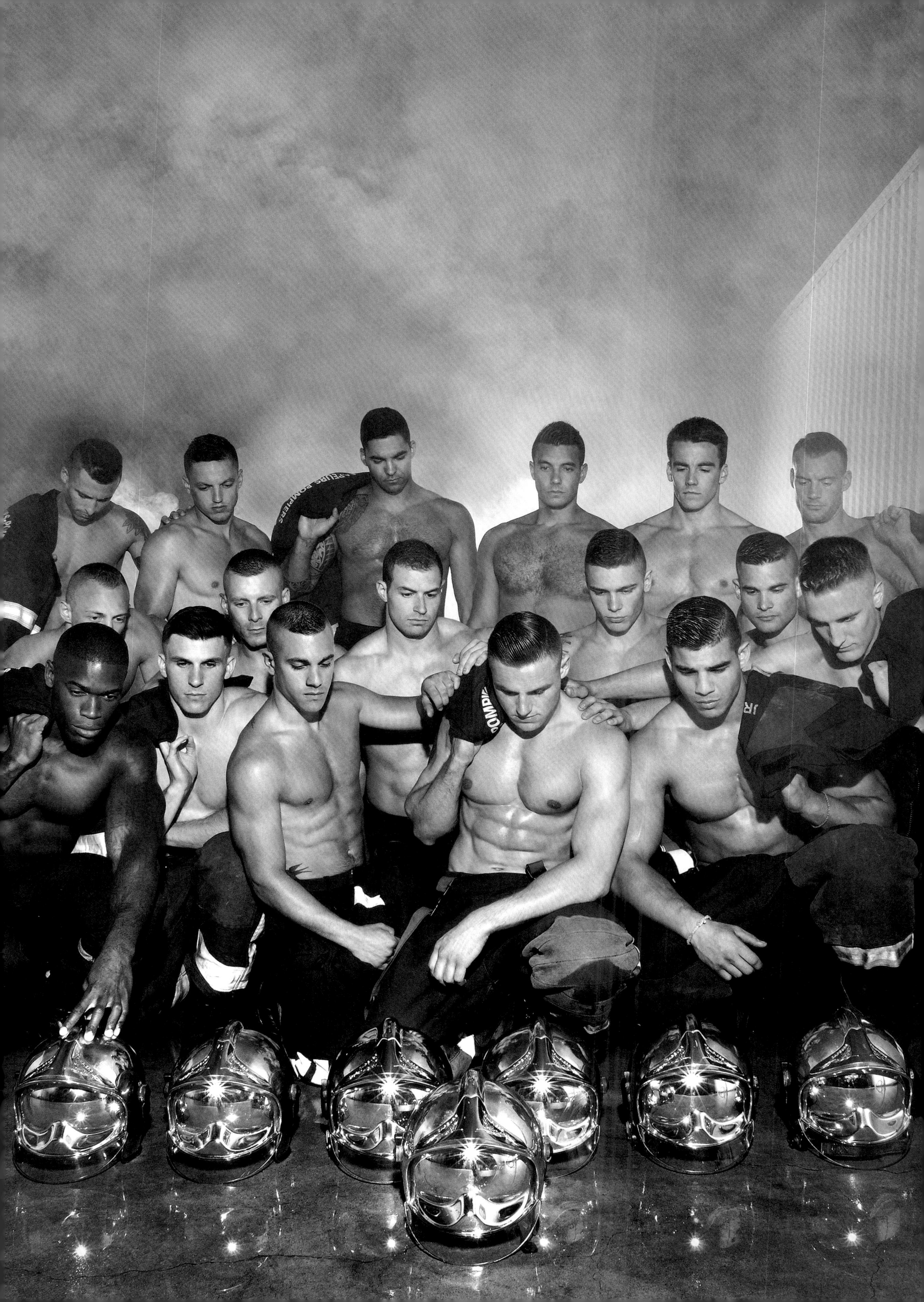

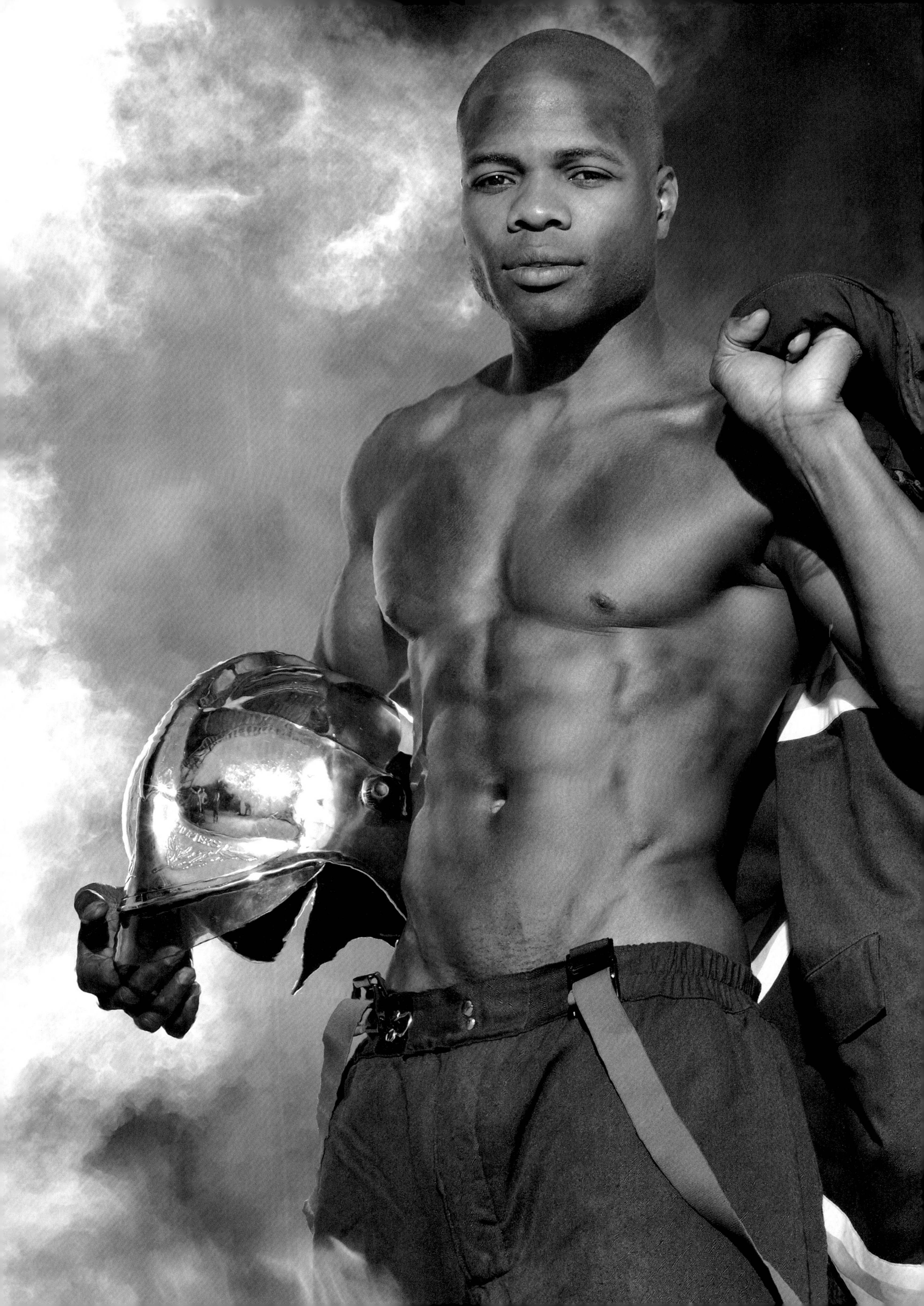

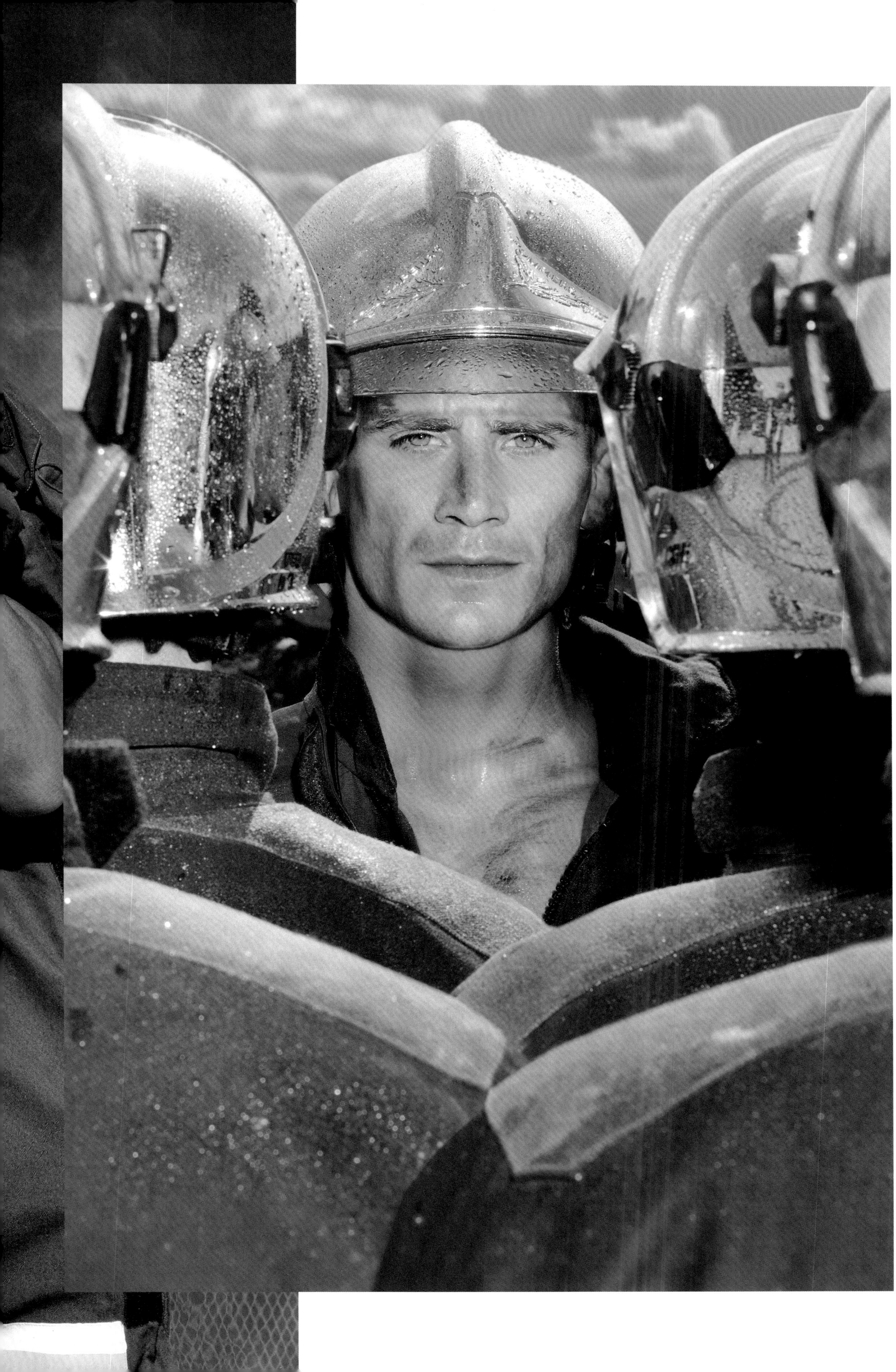

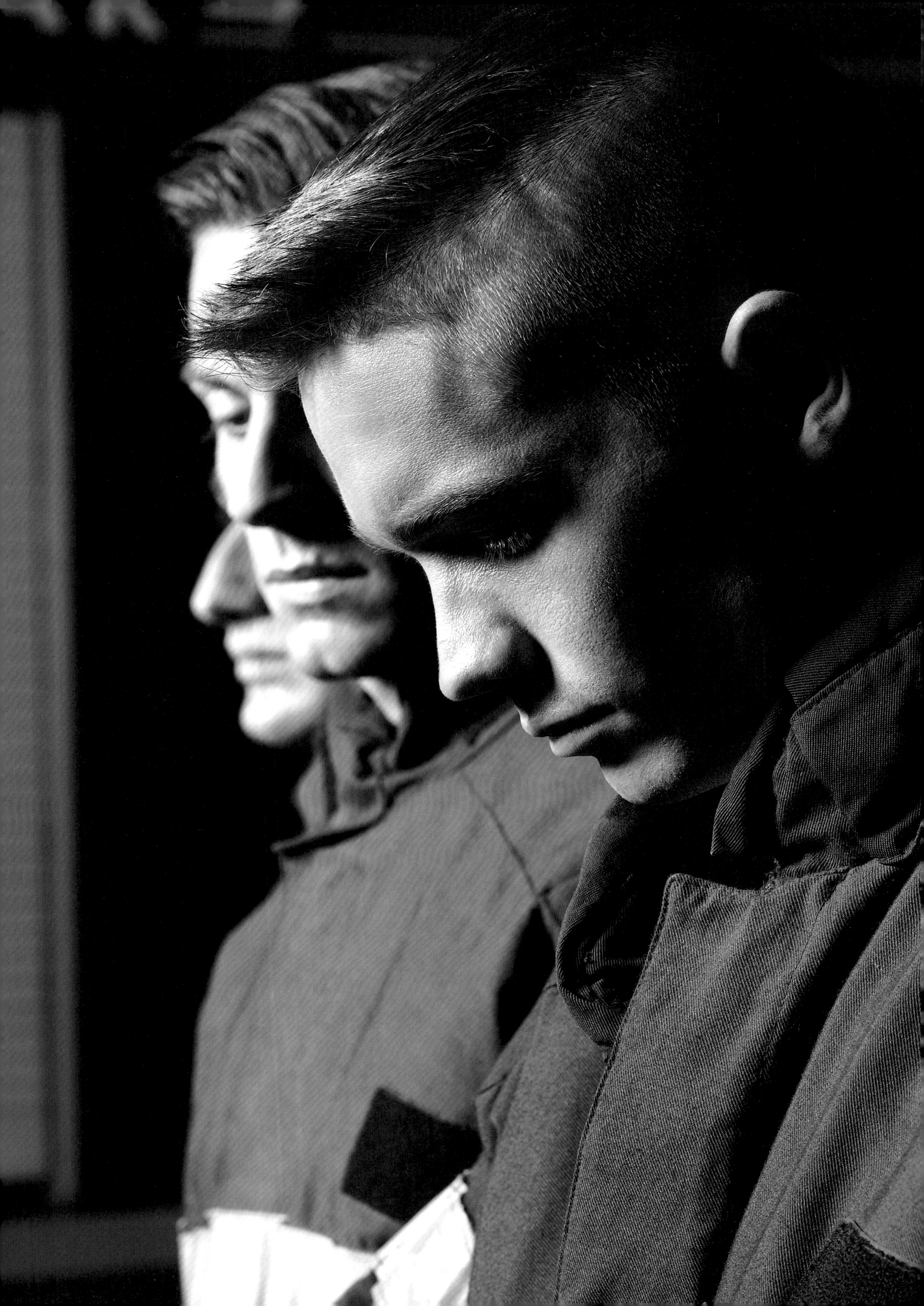

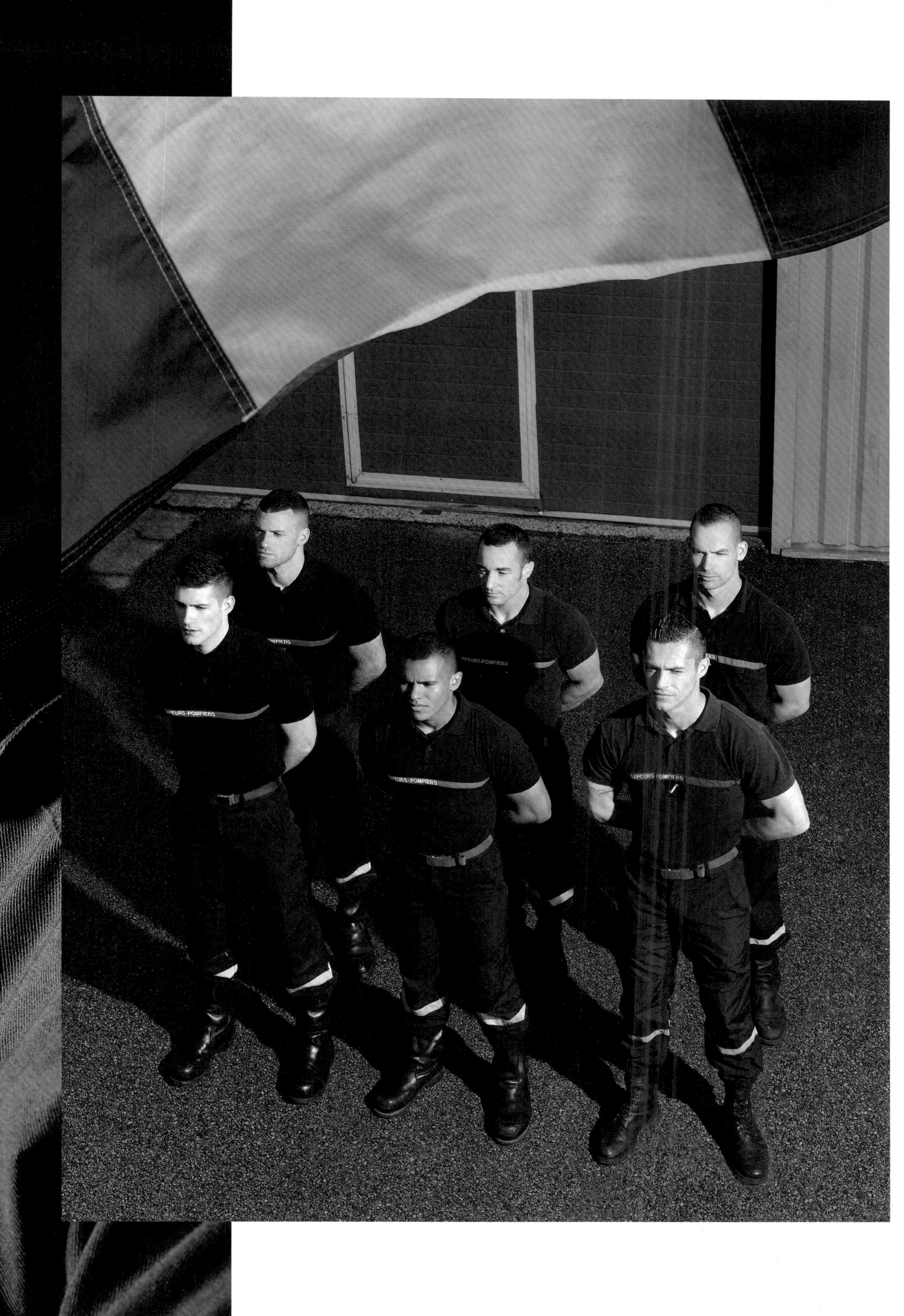

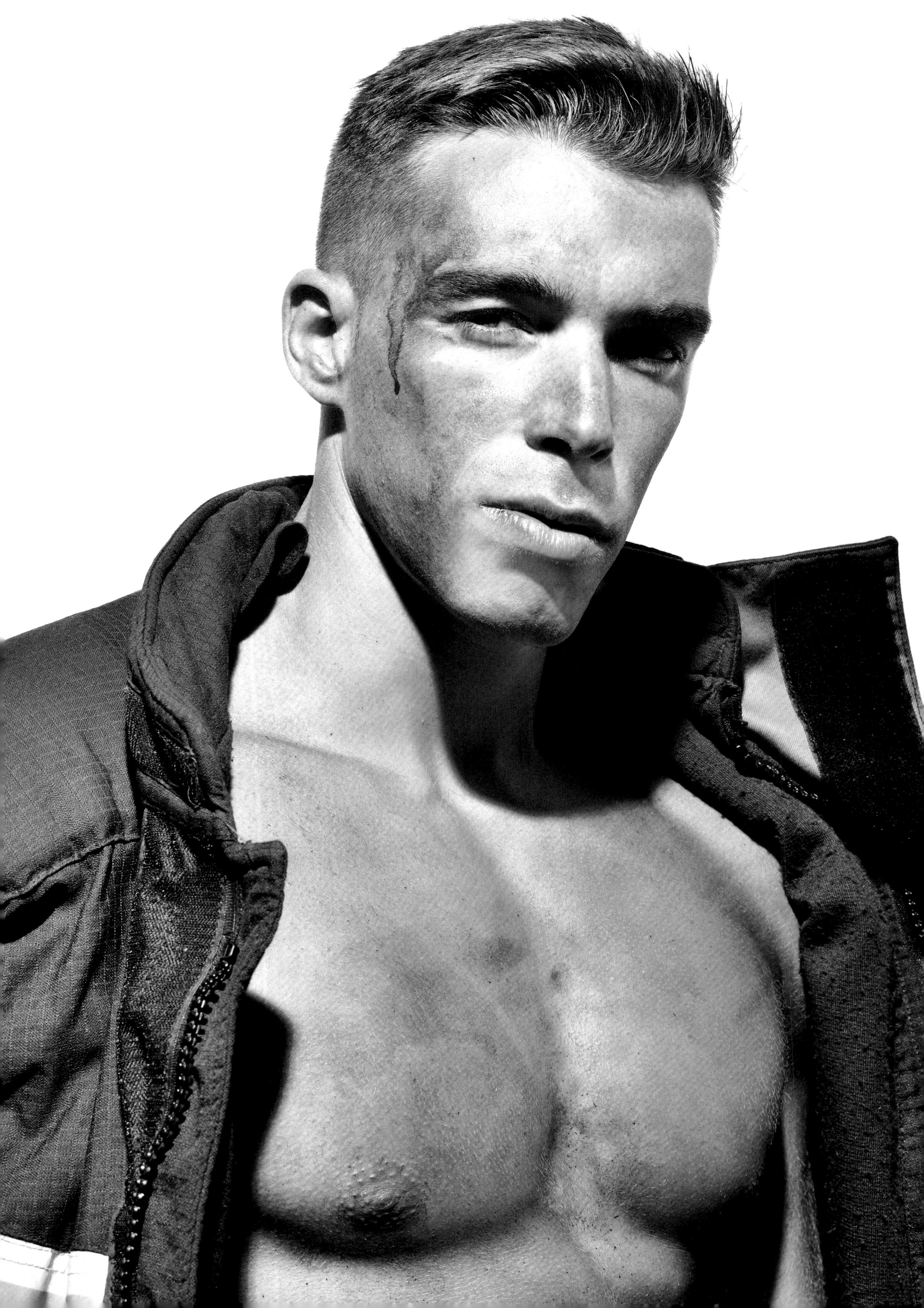

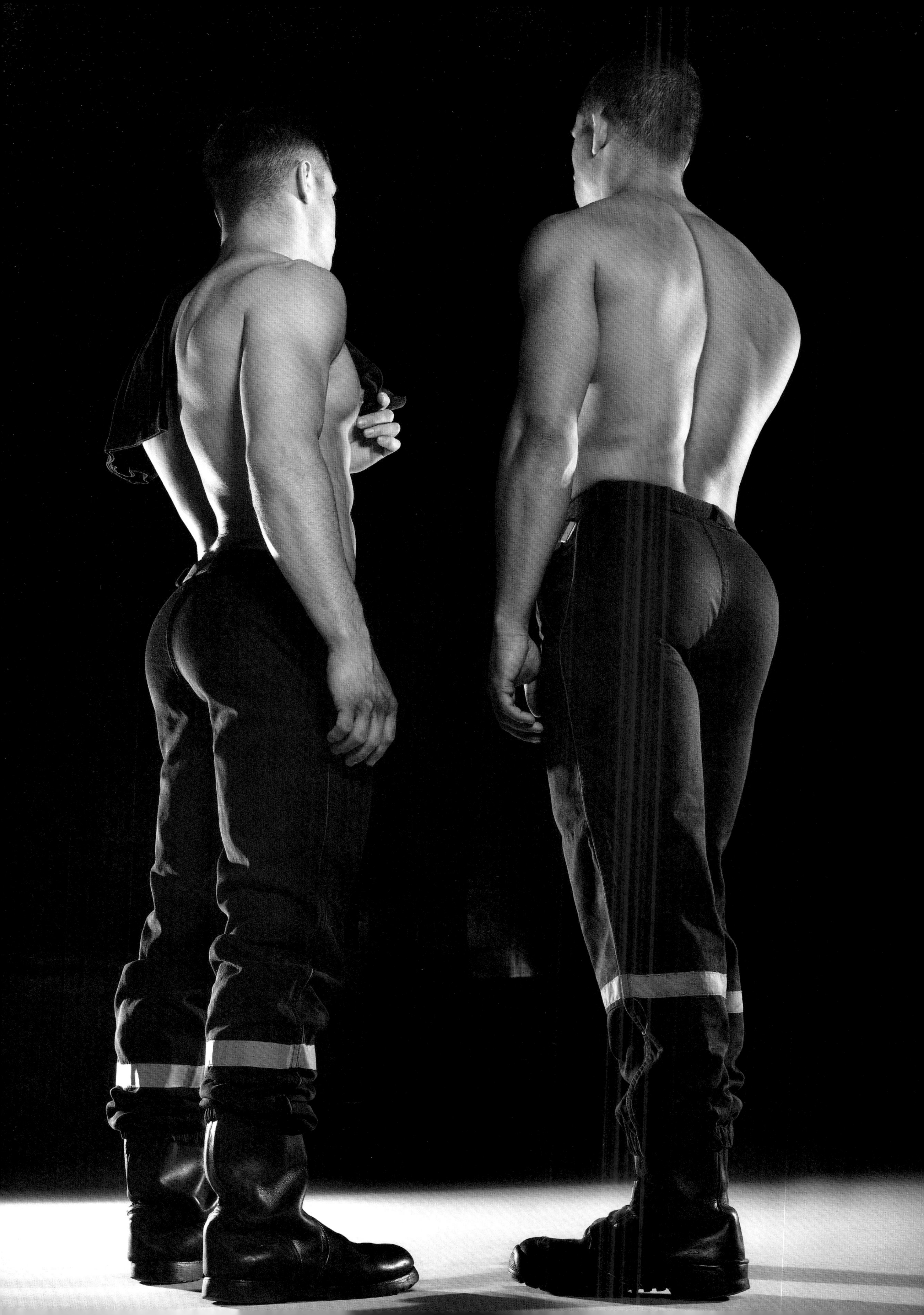

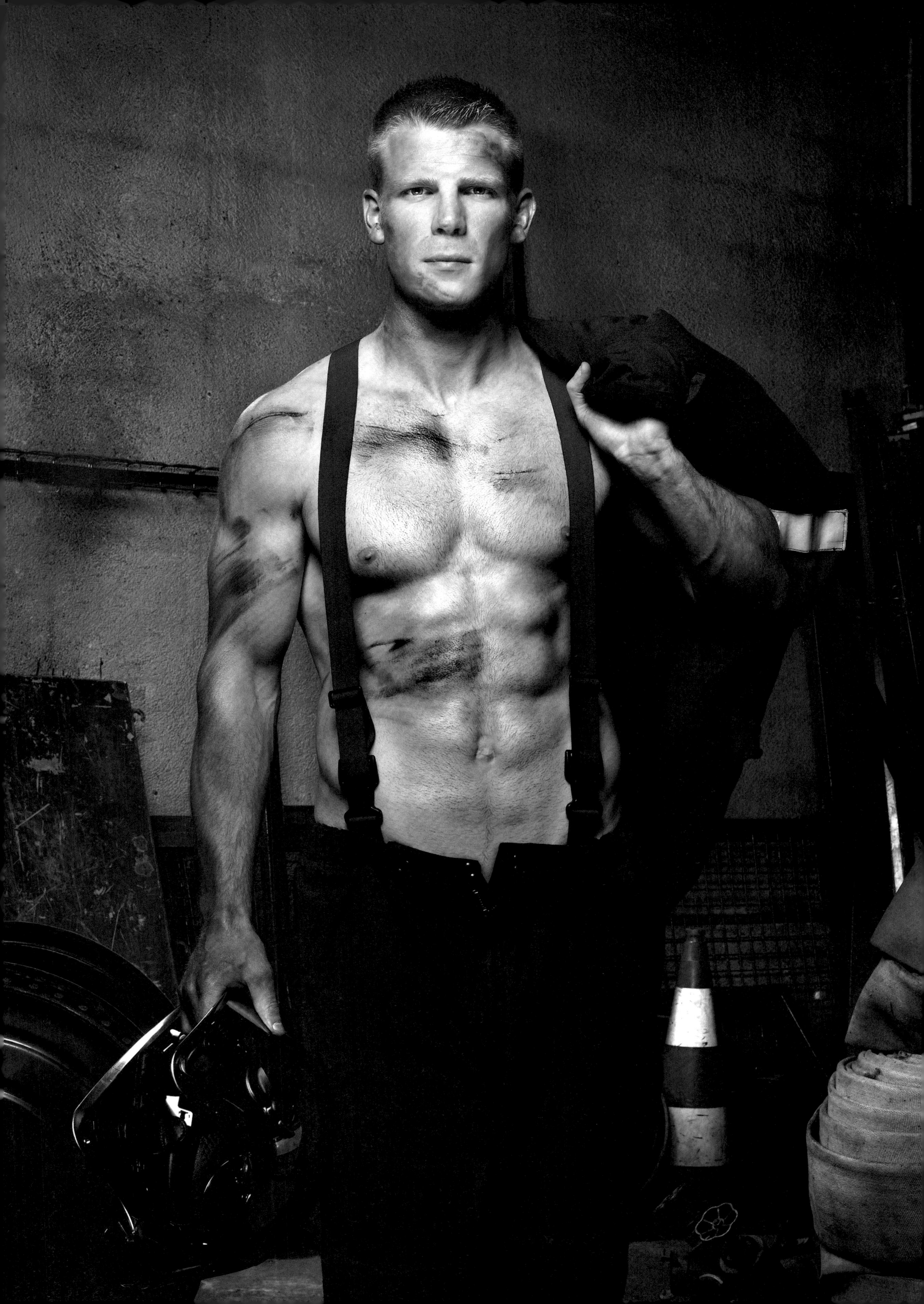

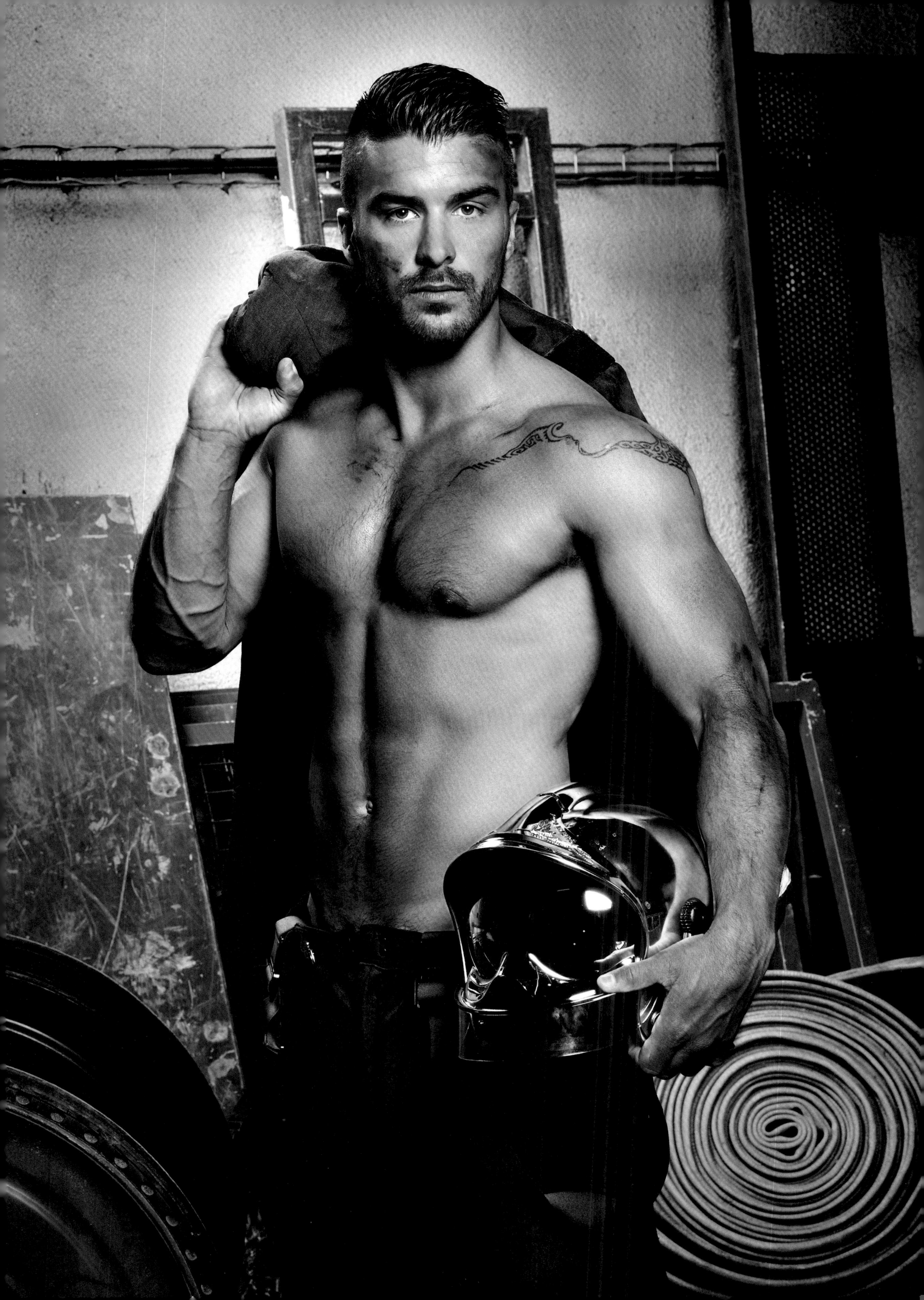

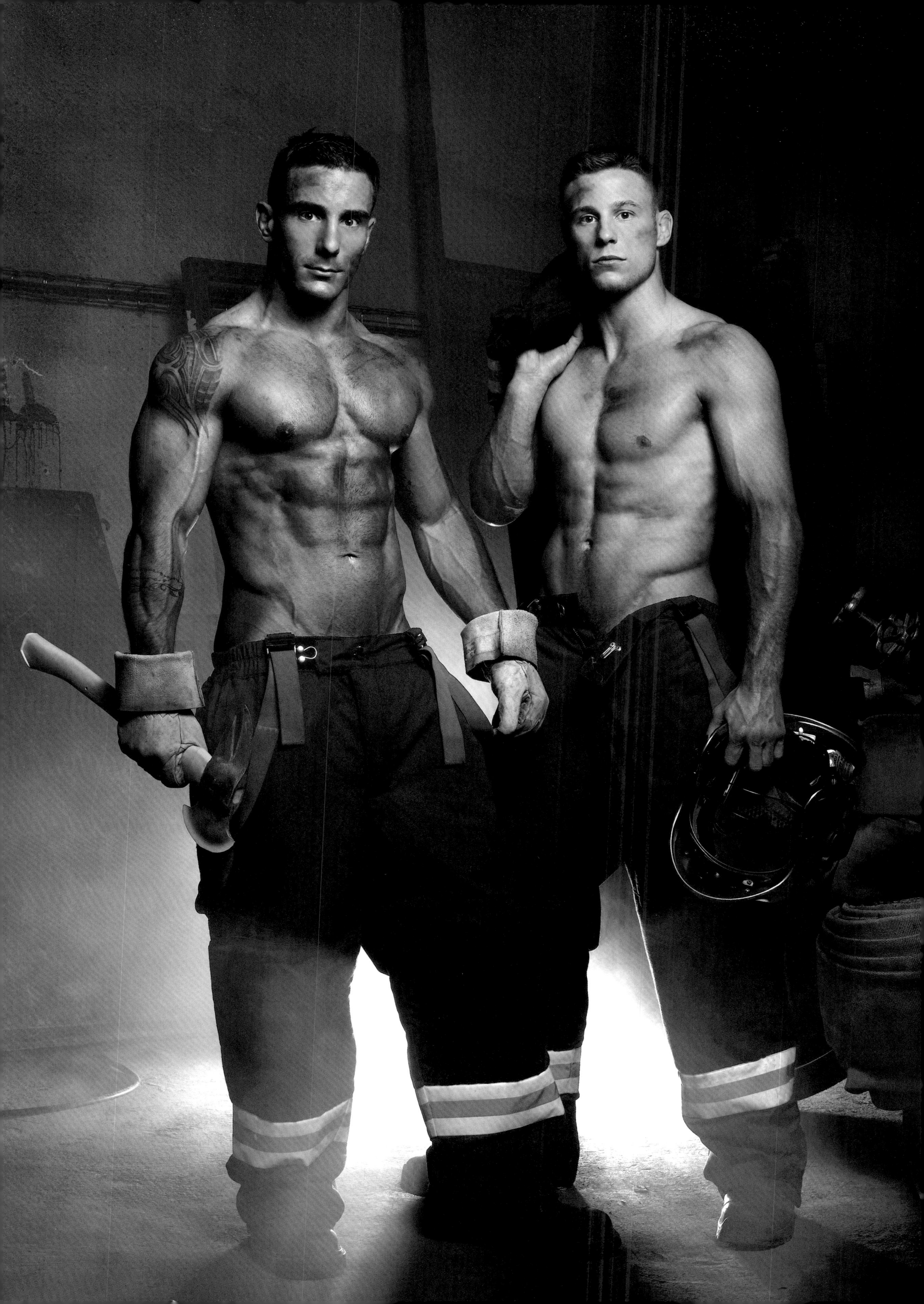

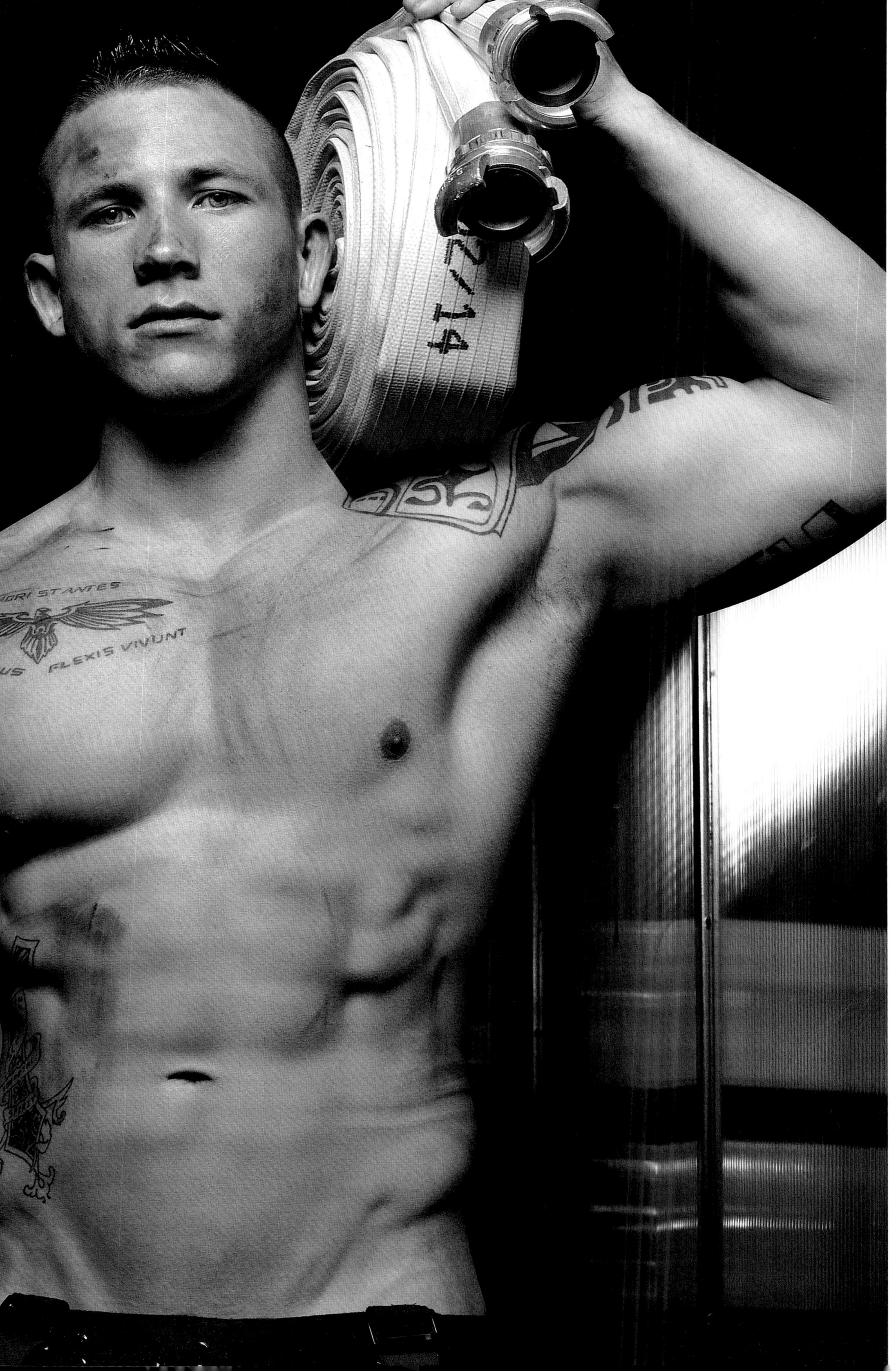
MORI STANTES
FLEXIS VIVUNT

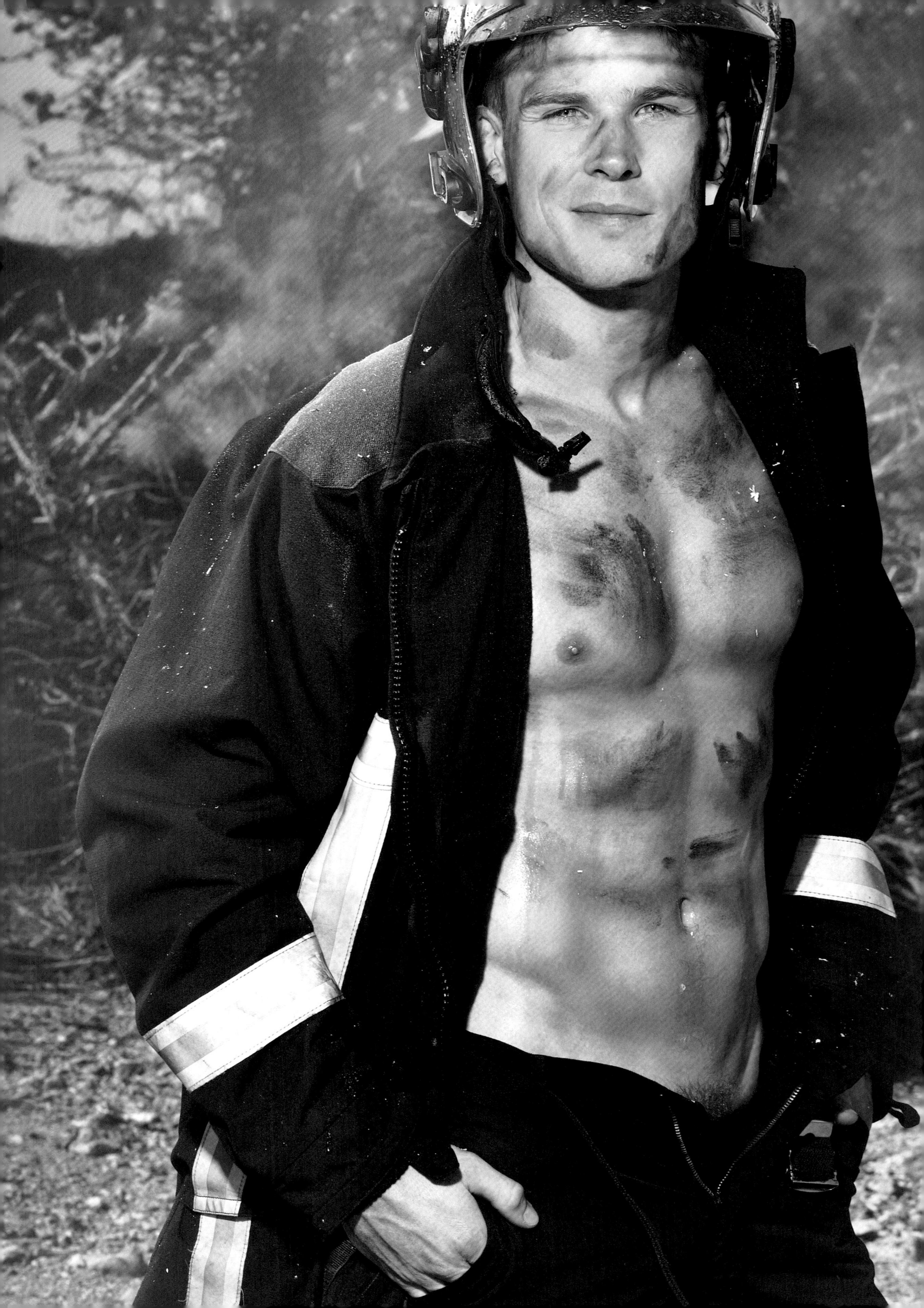

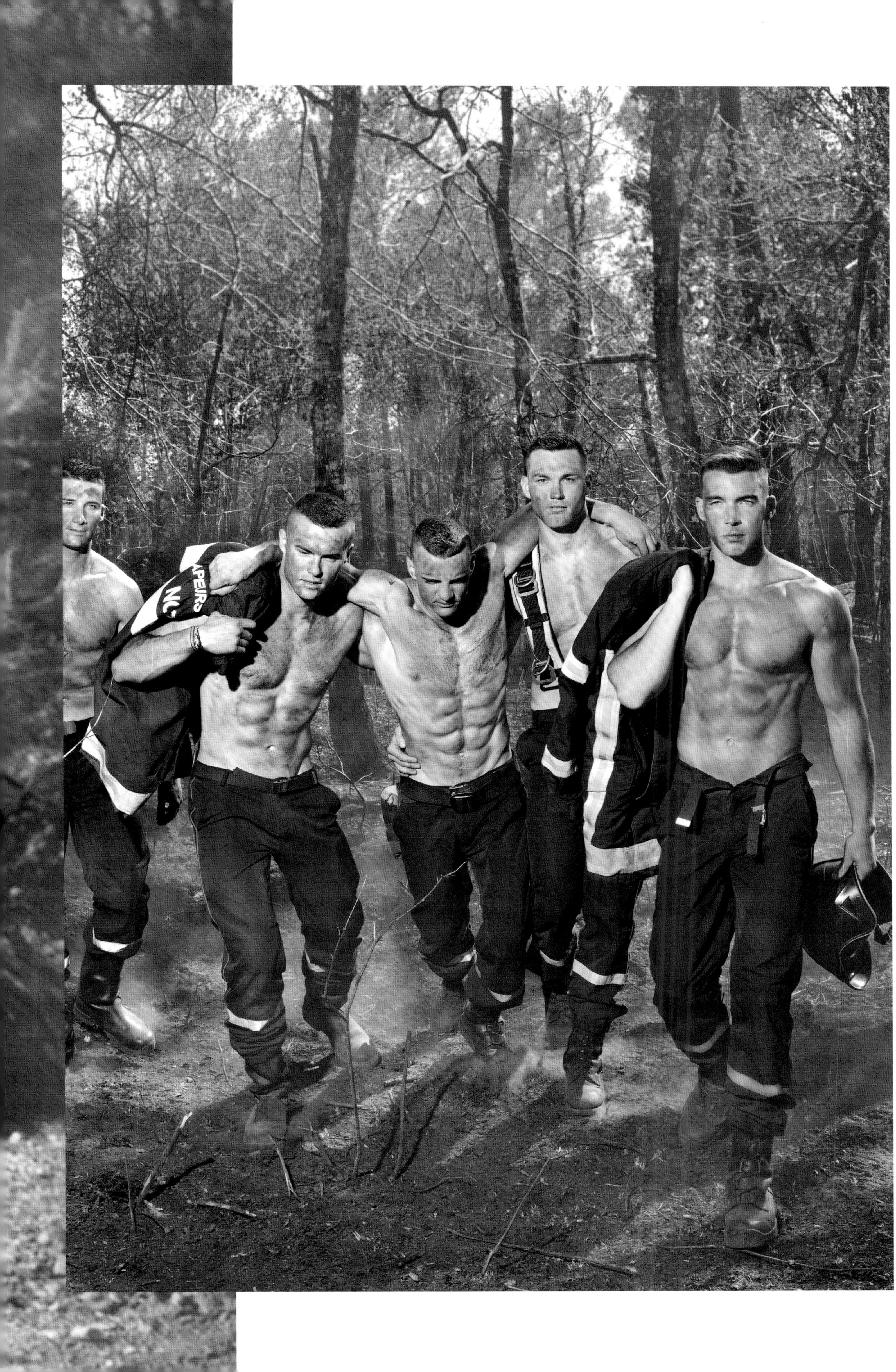

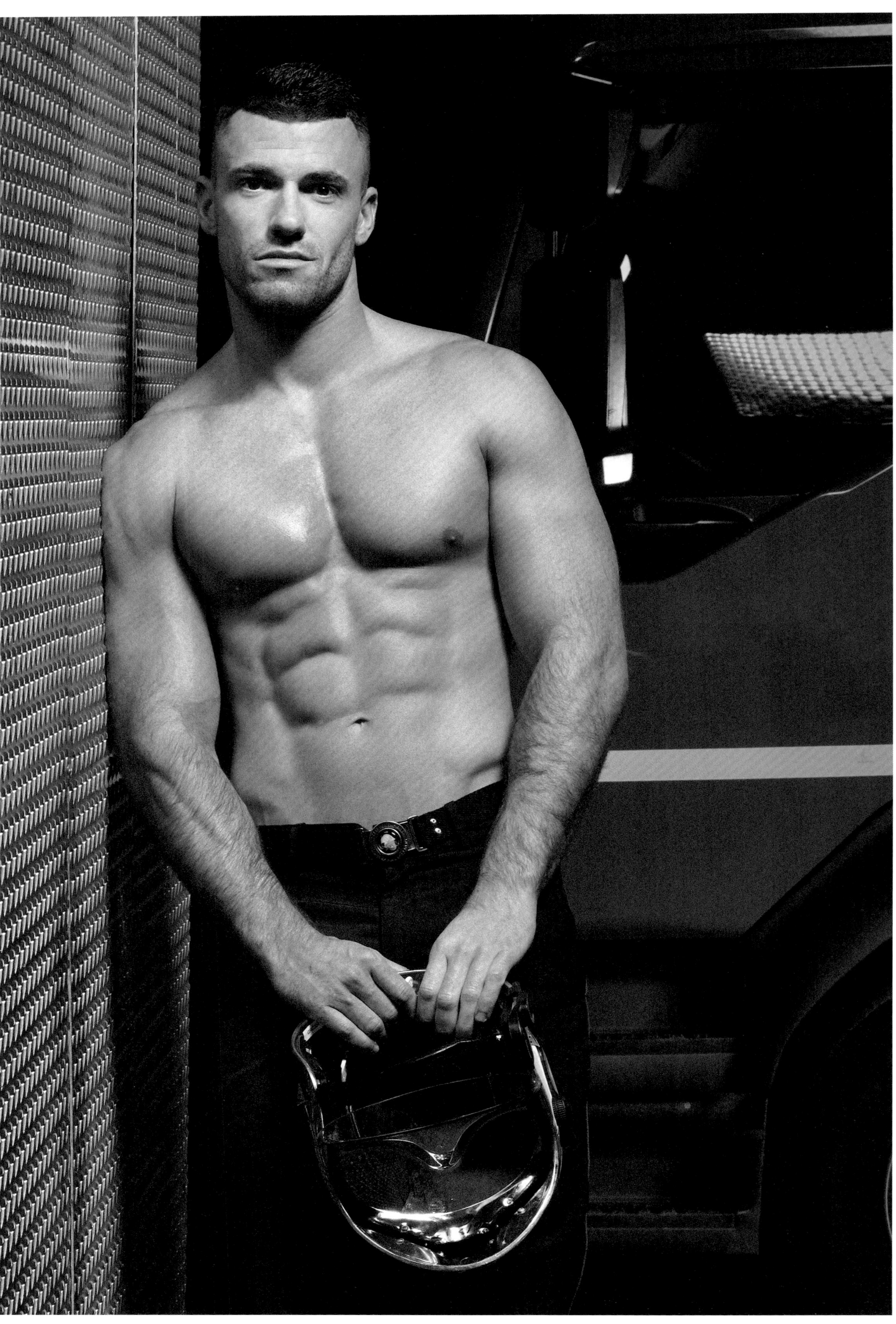

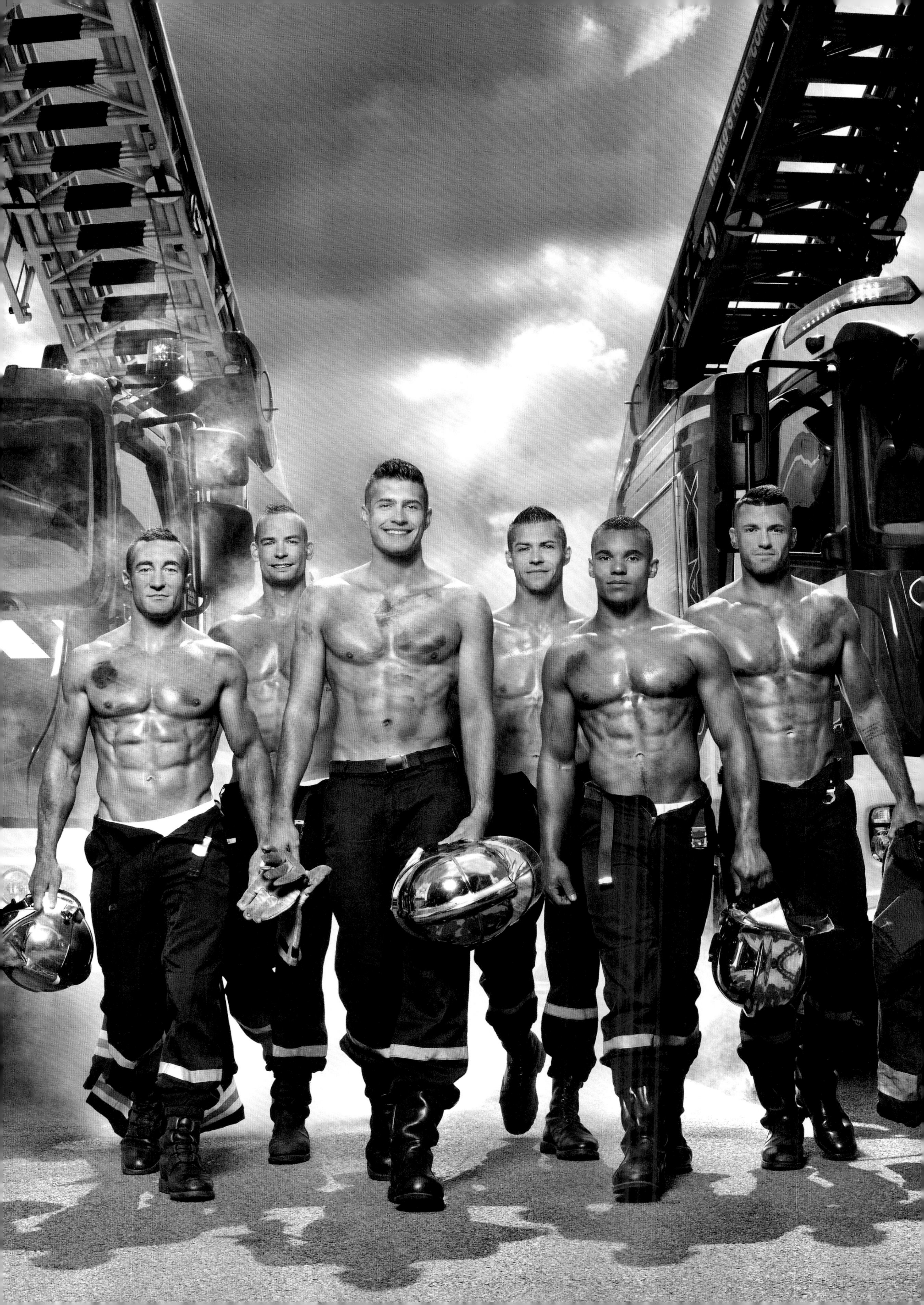

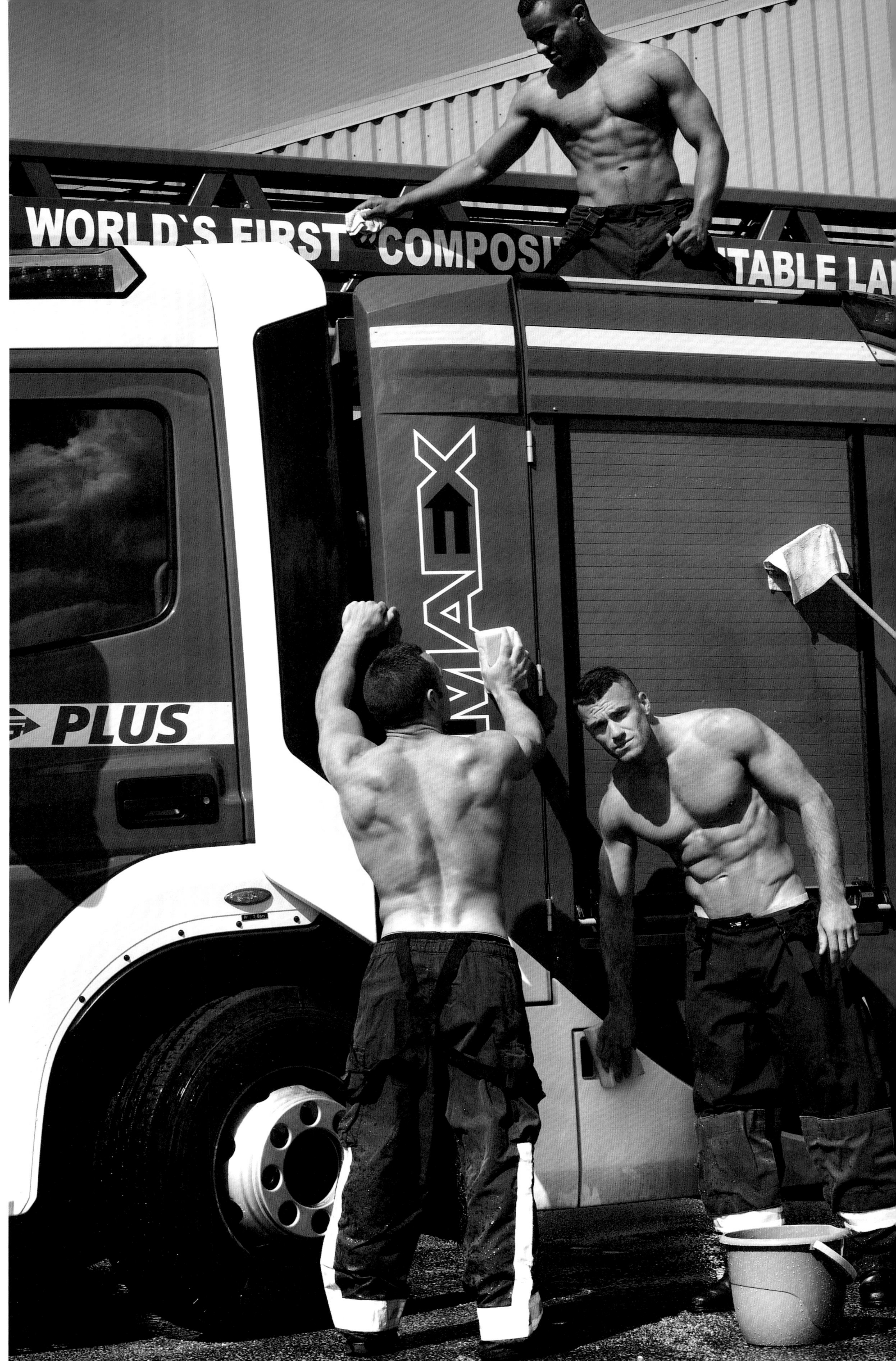

28

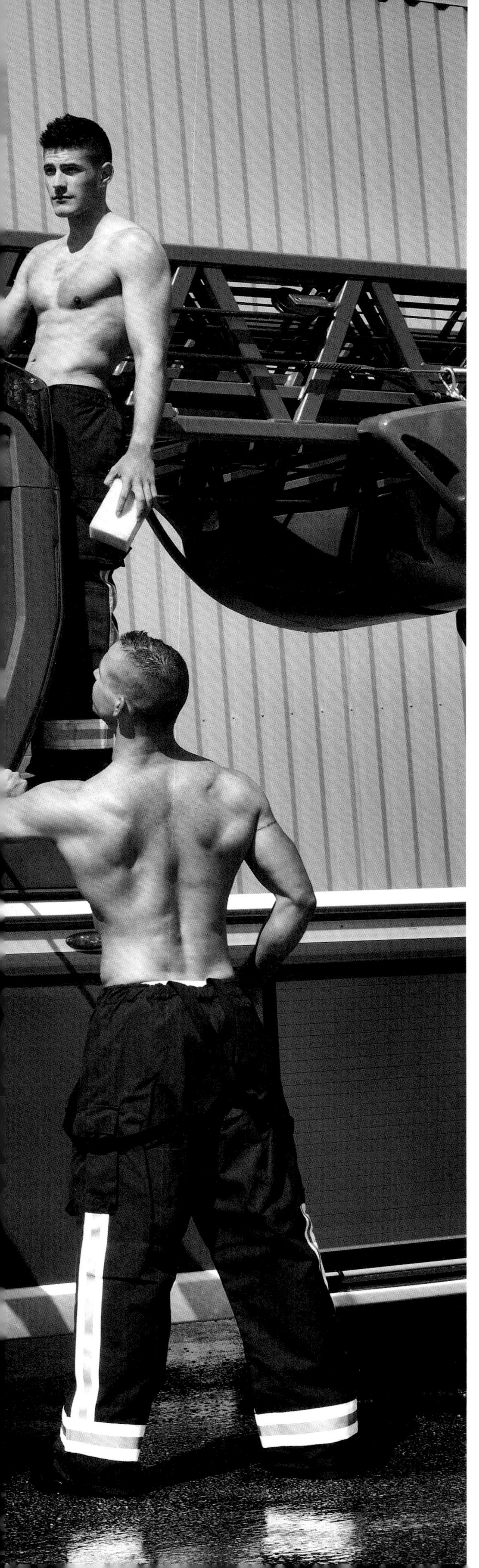

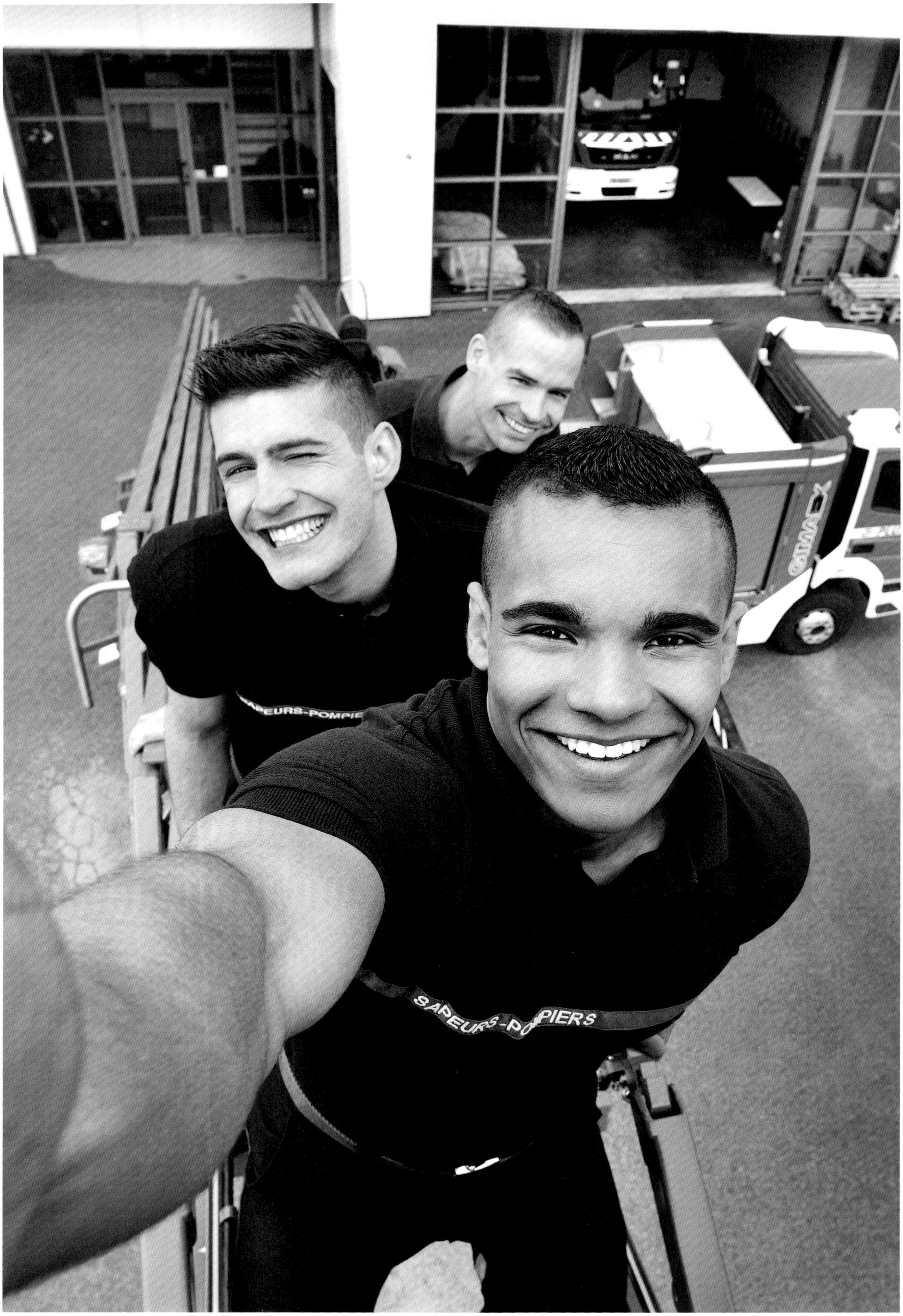

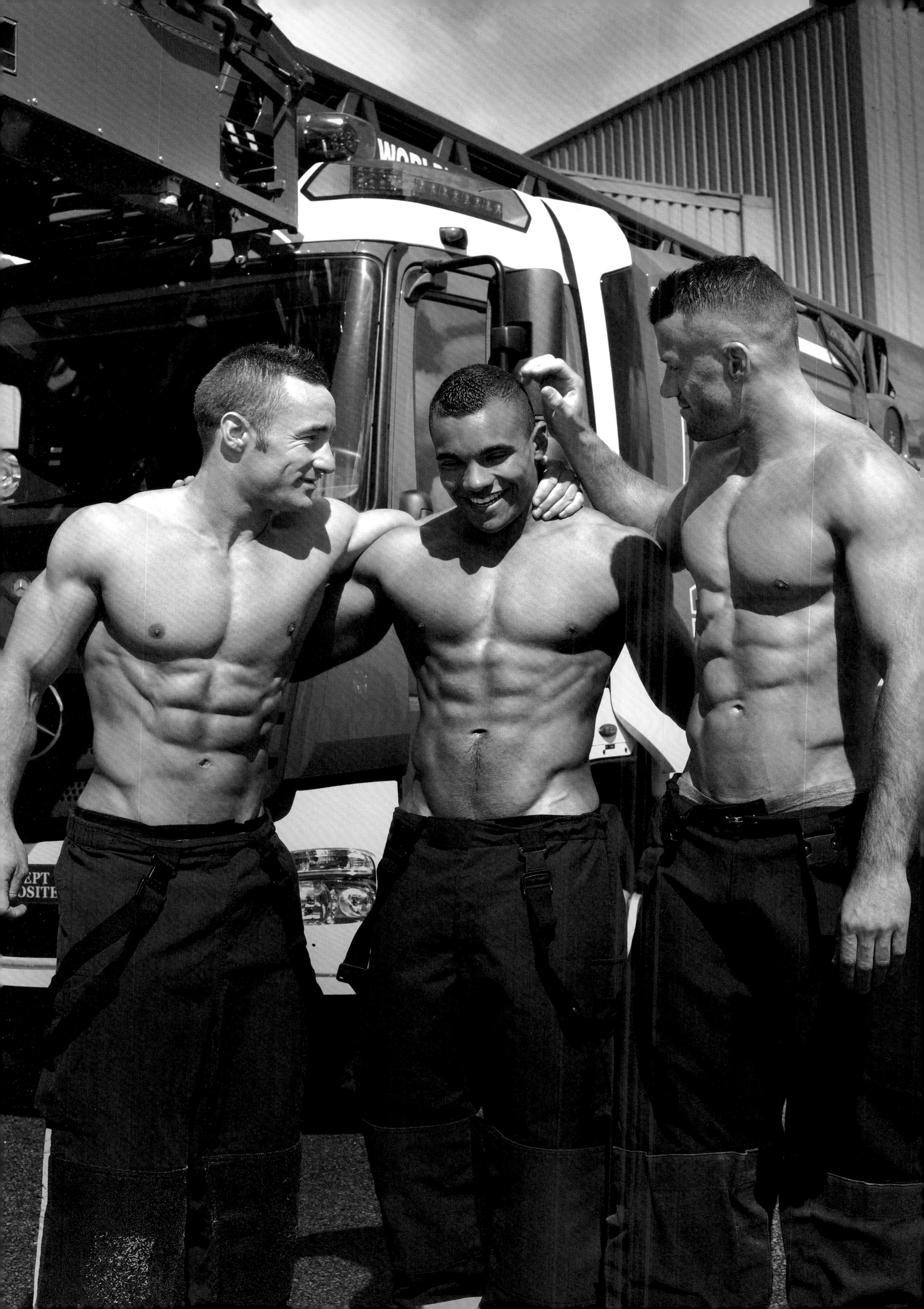

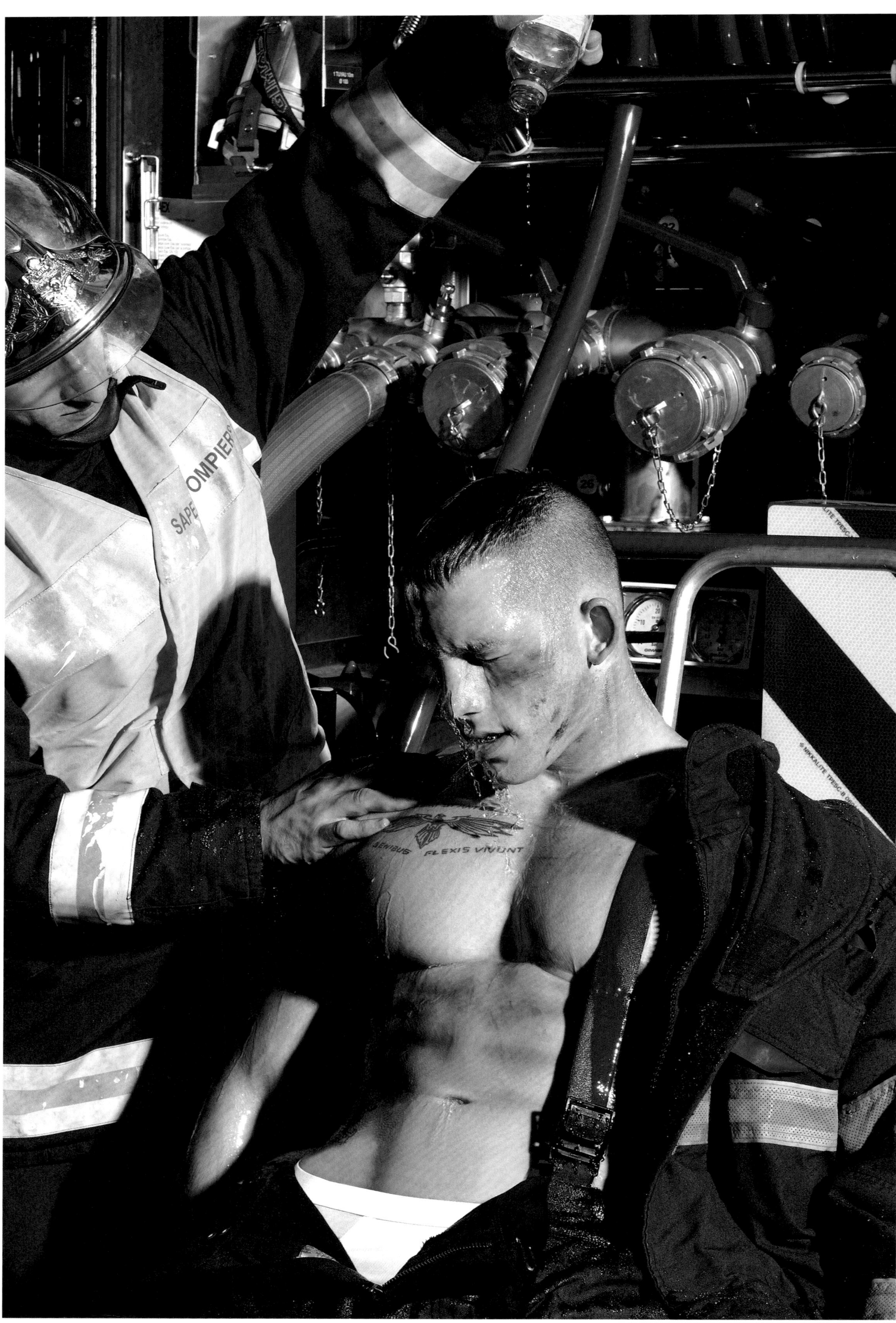
GENIBUS FLEXIS VIVUNT

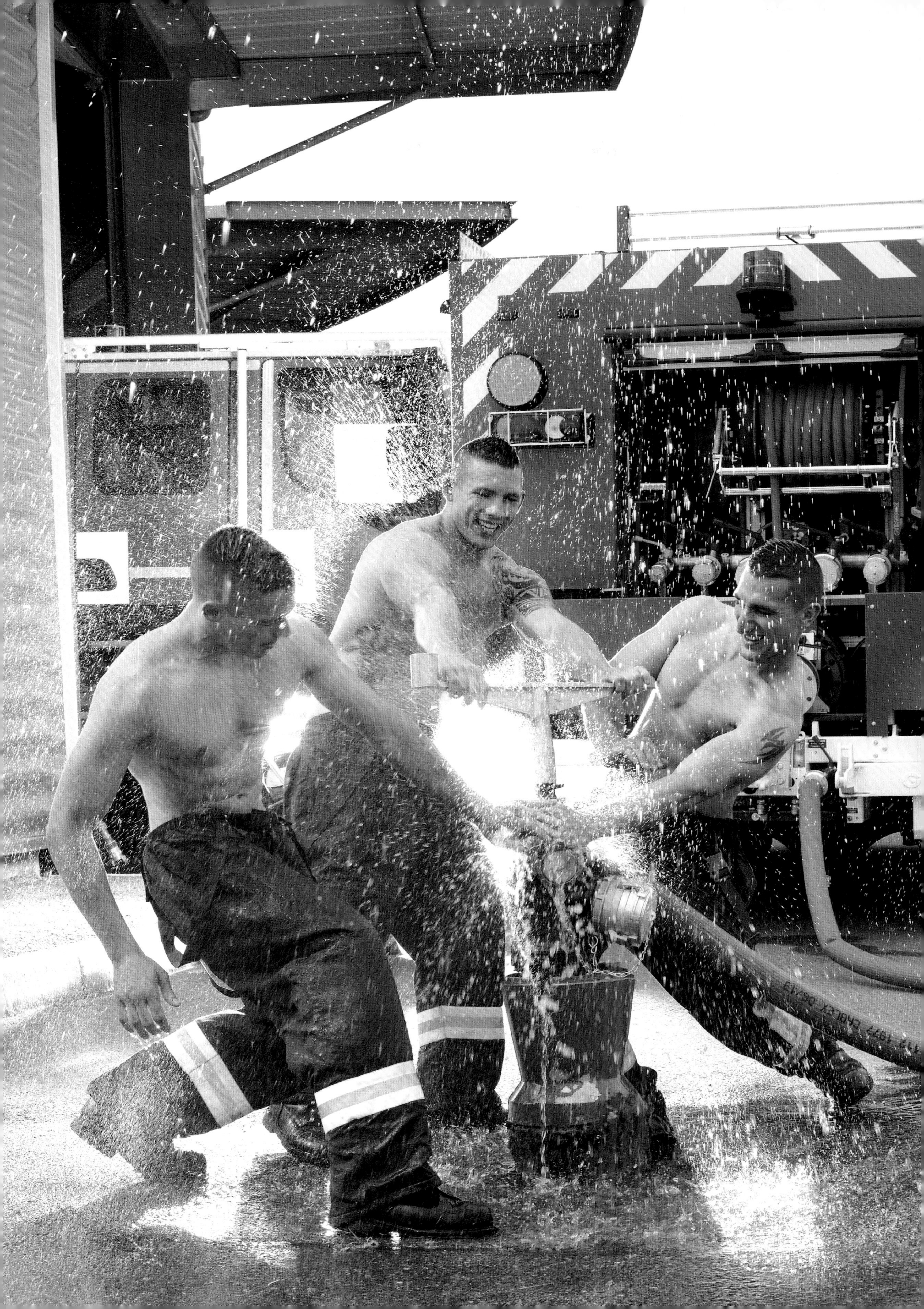

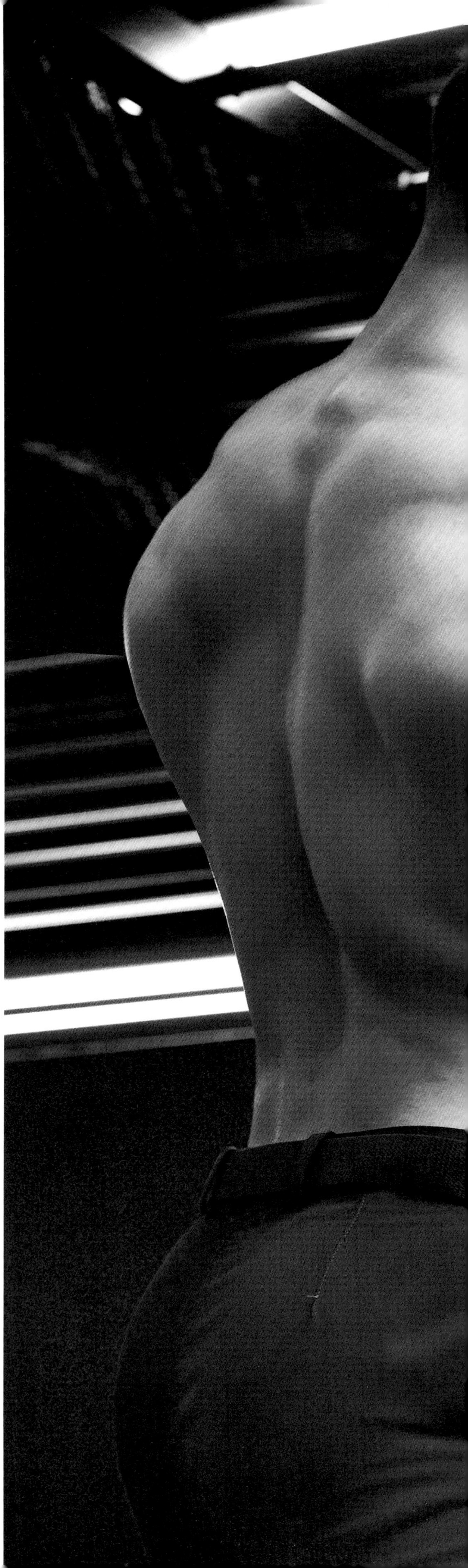

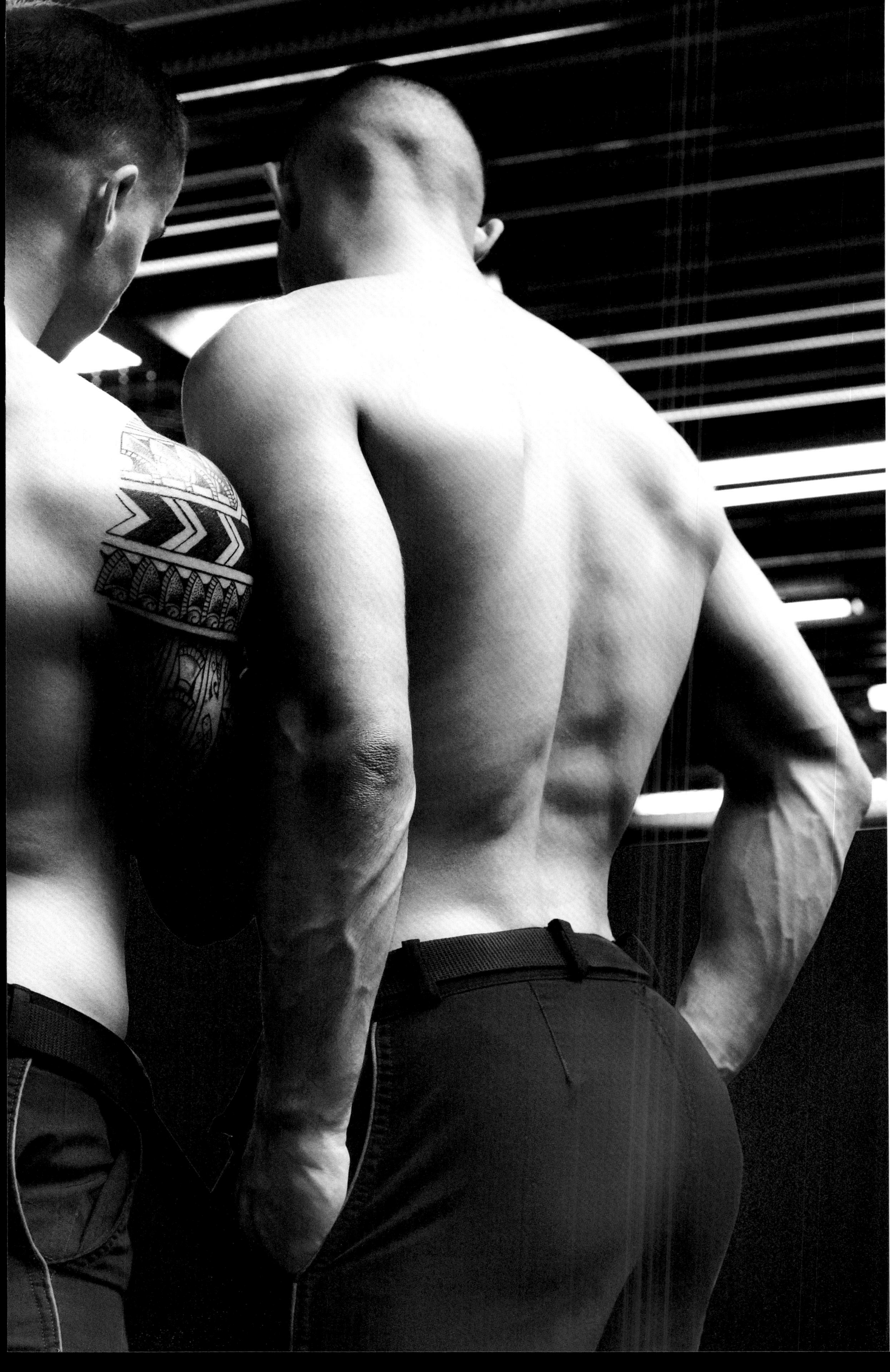

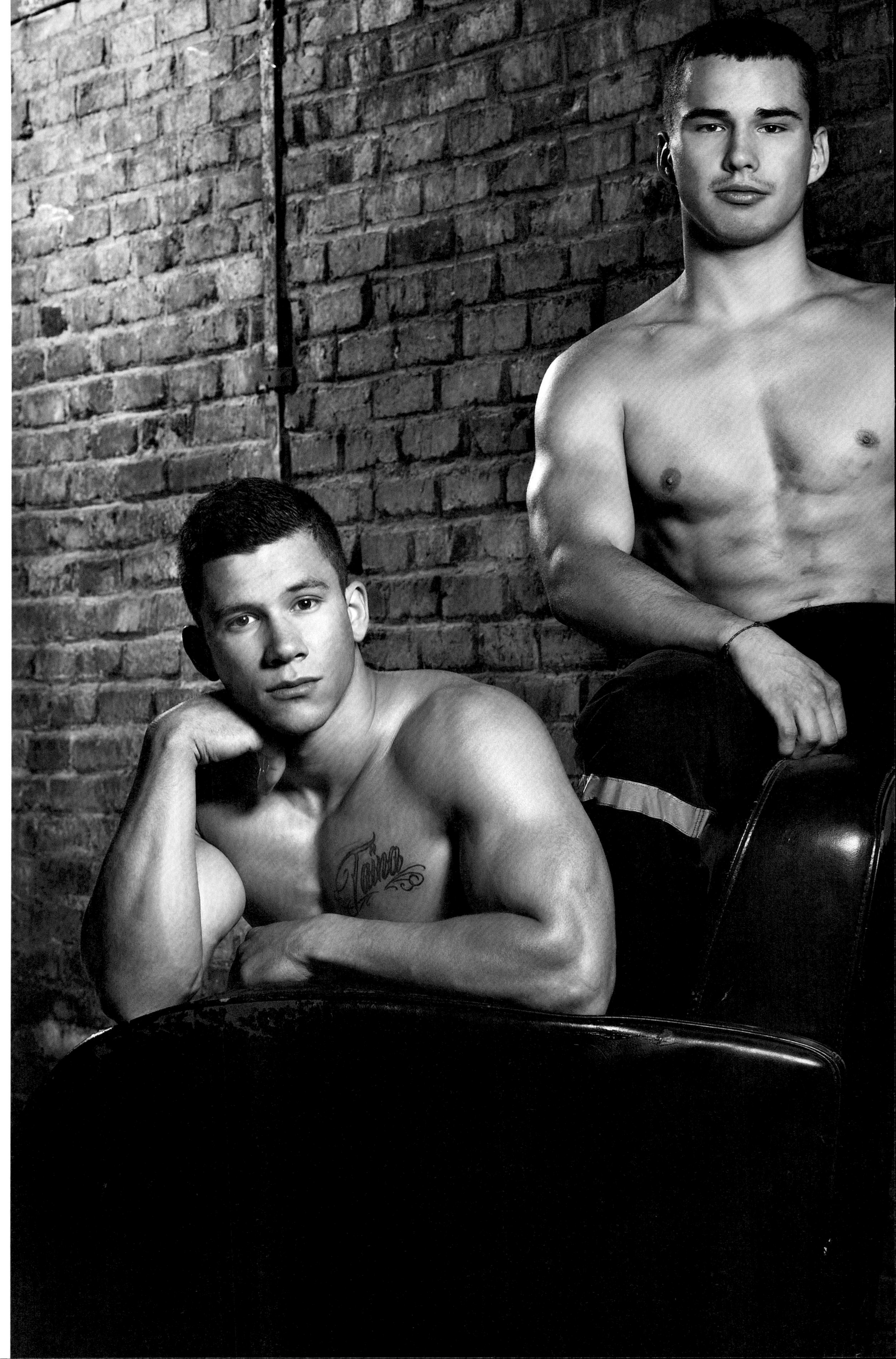

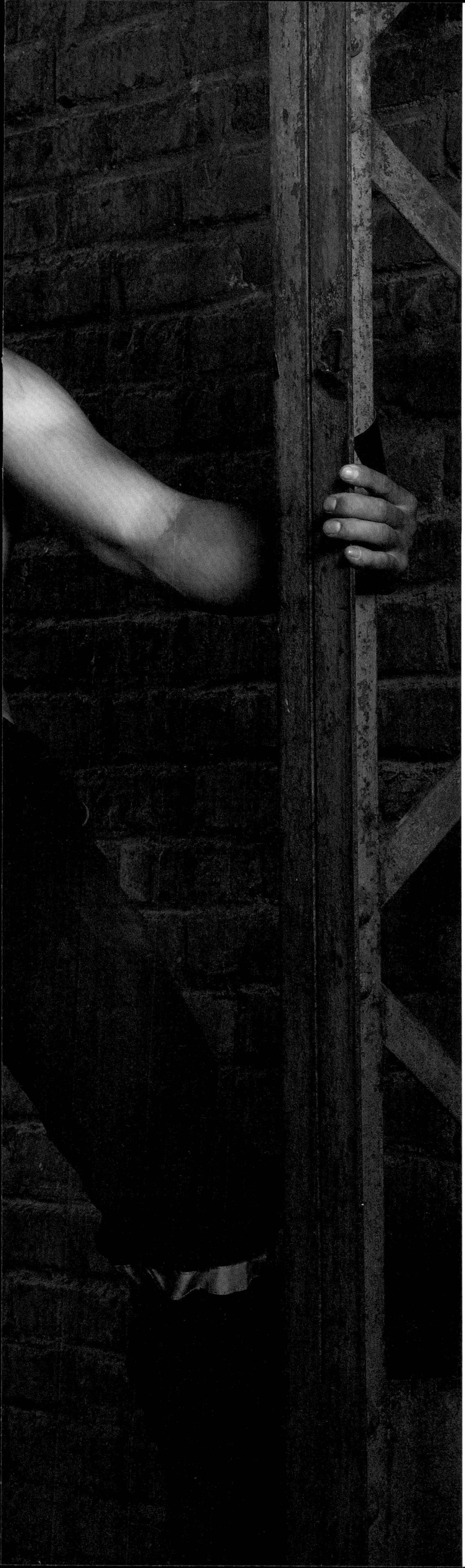

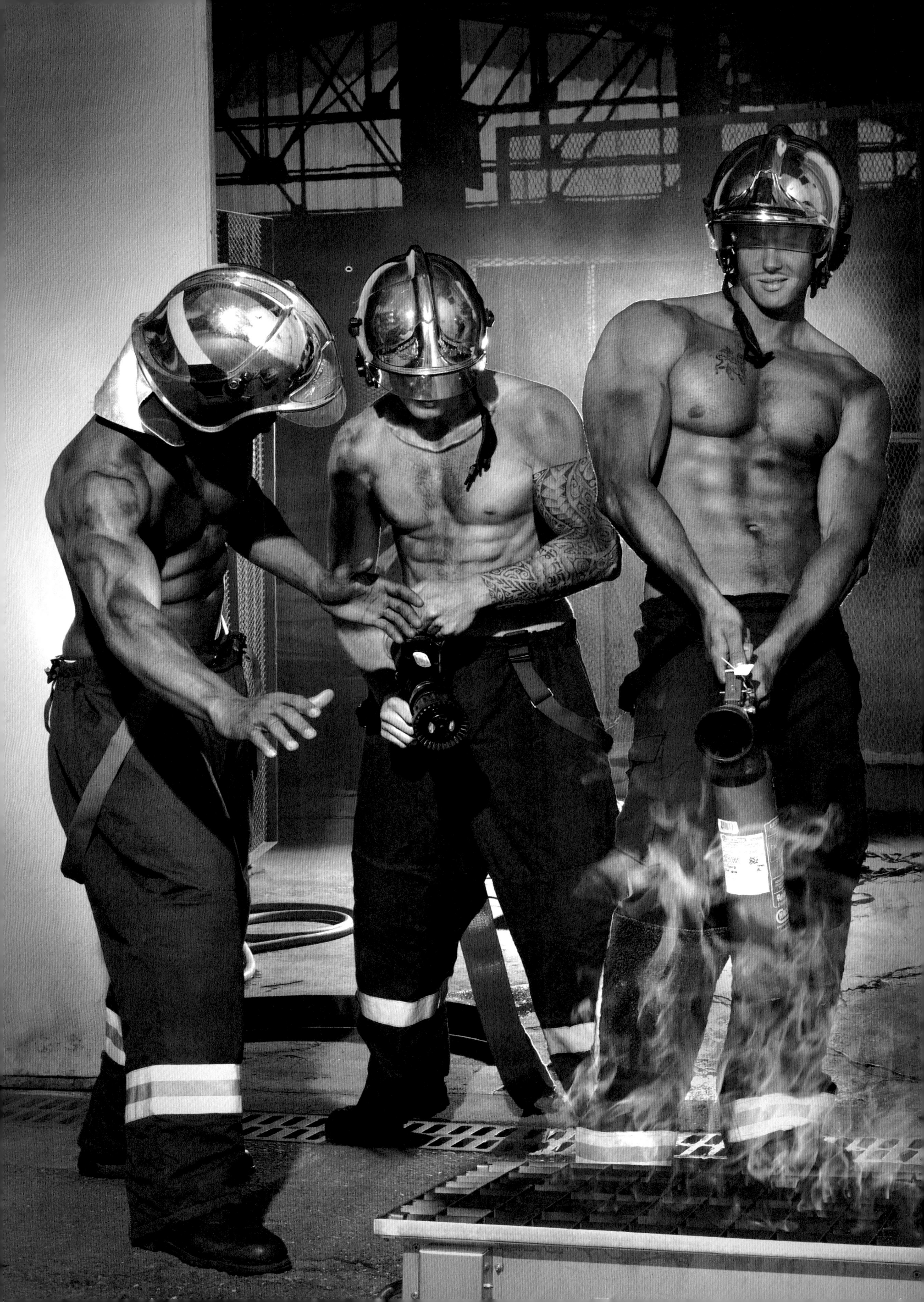

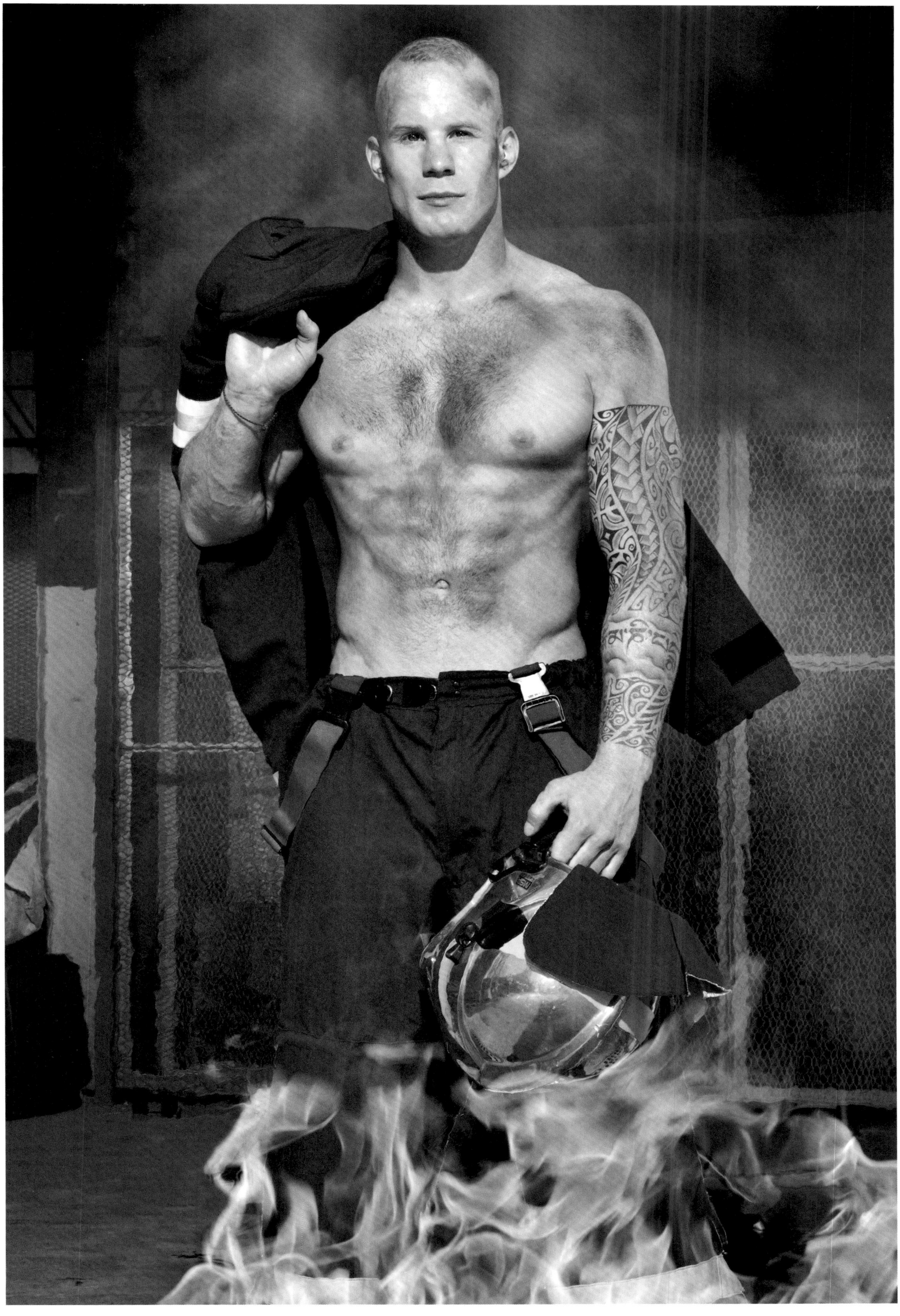

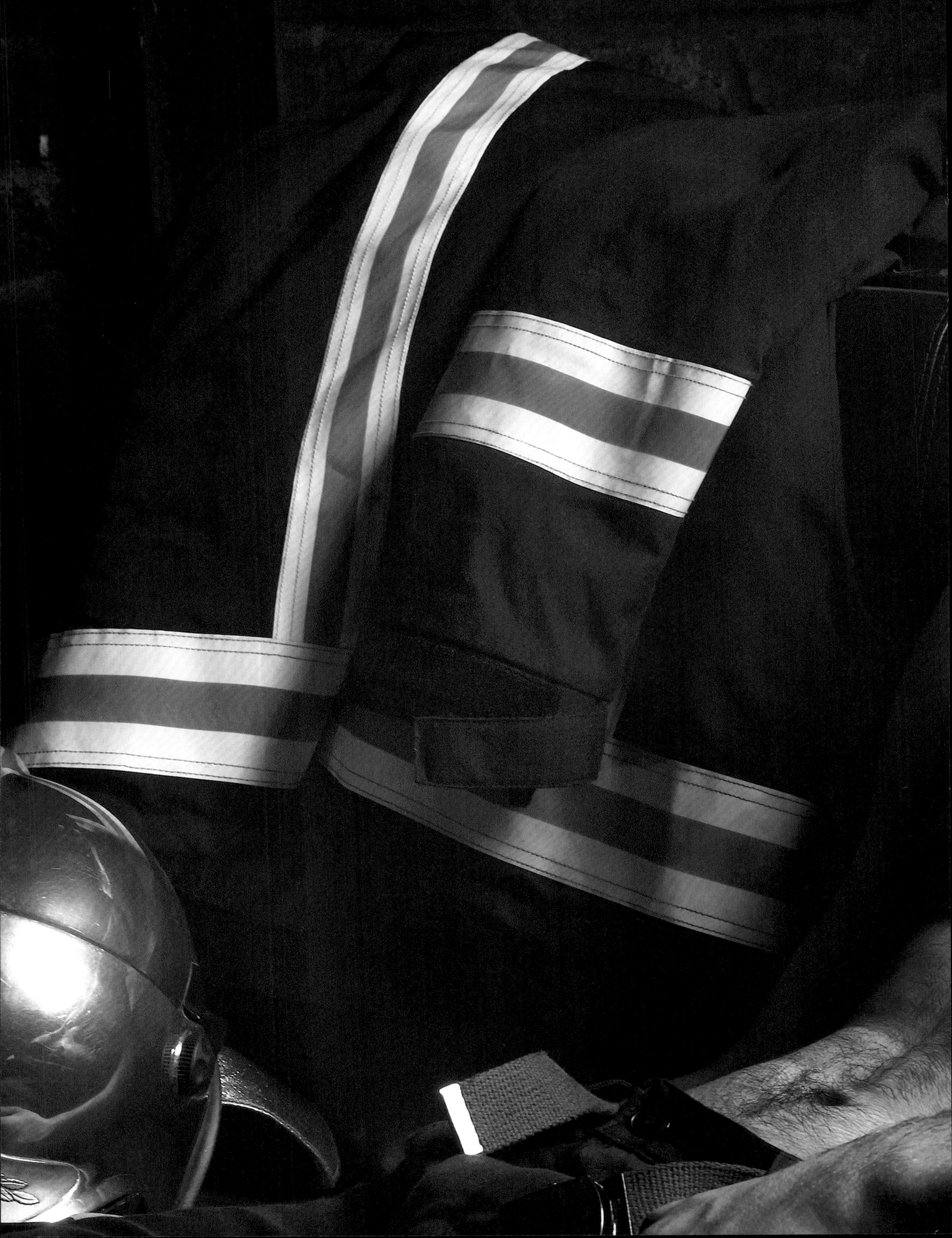

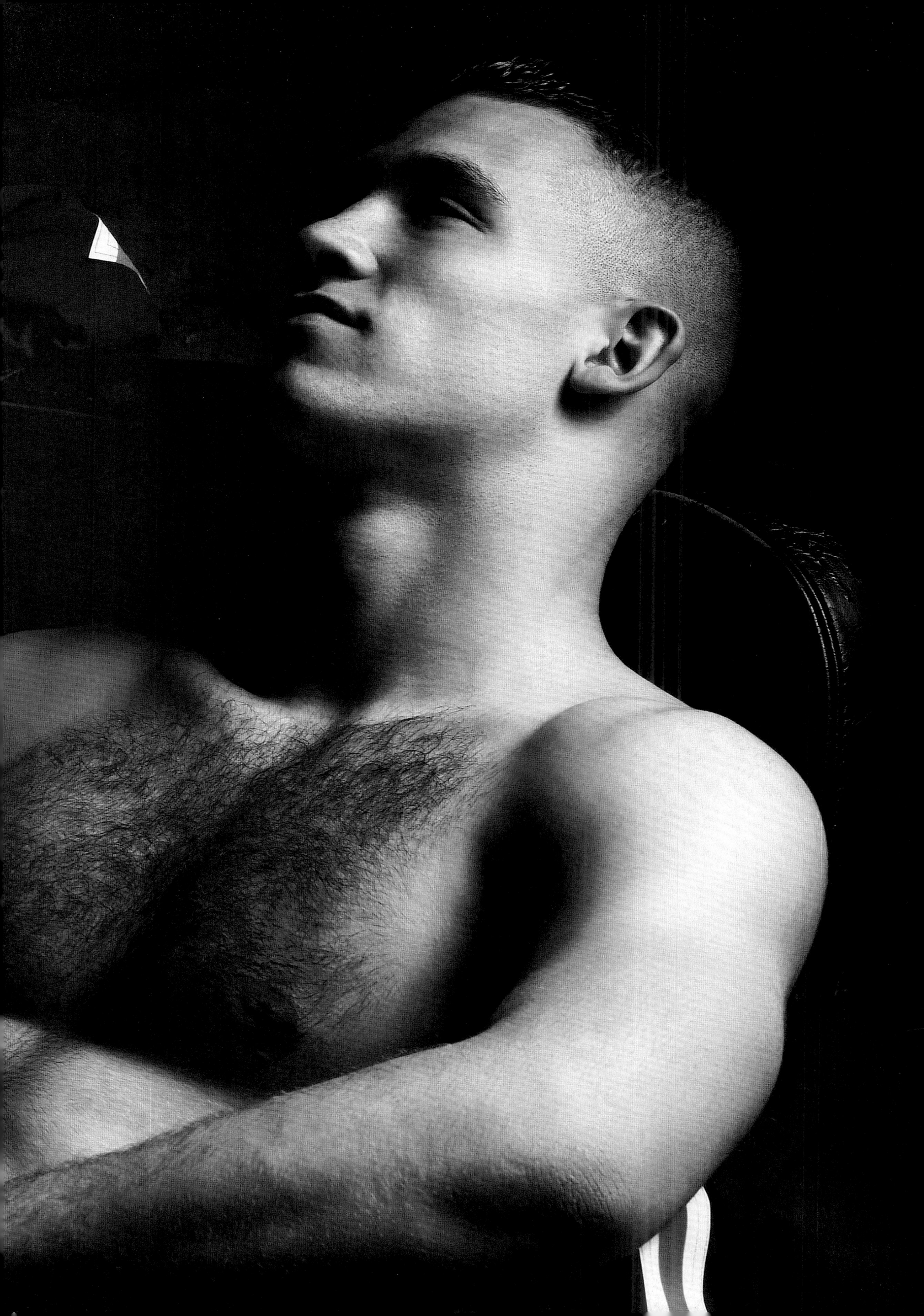

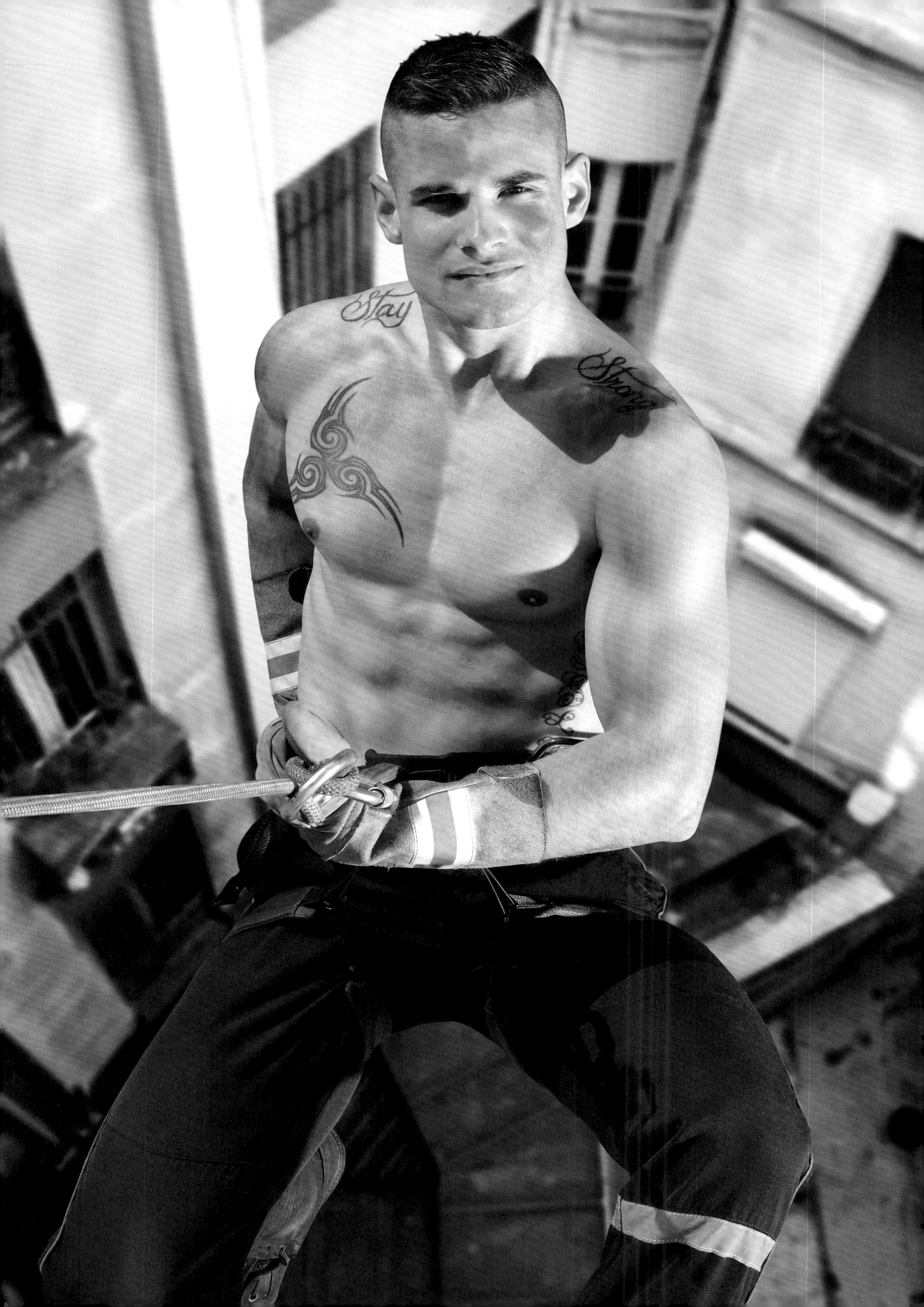
Stay
Strong

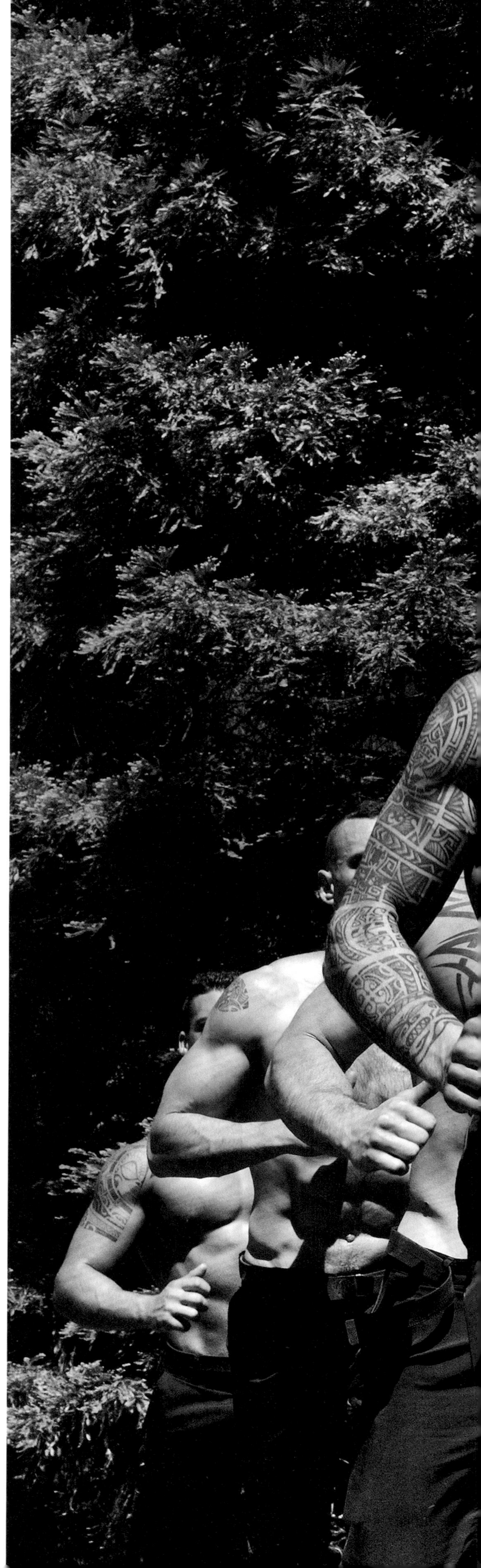

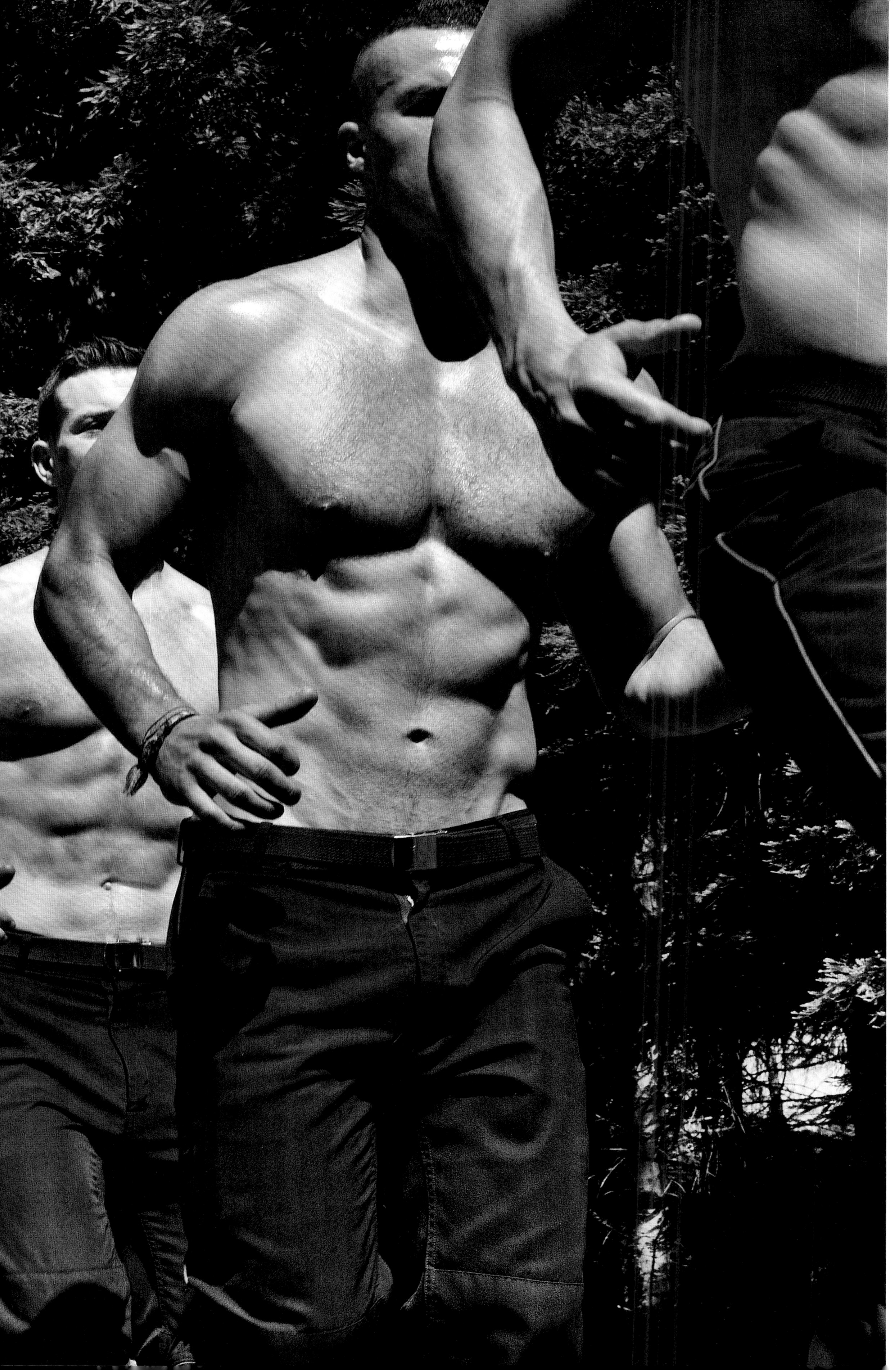

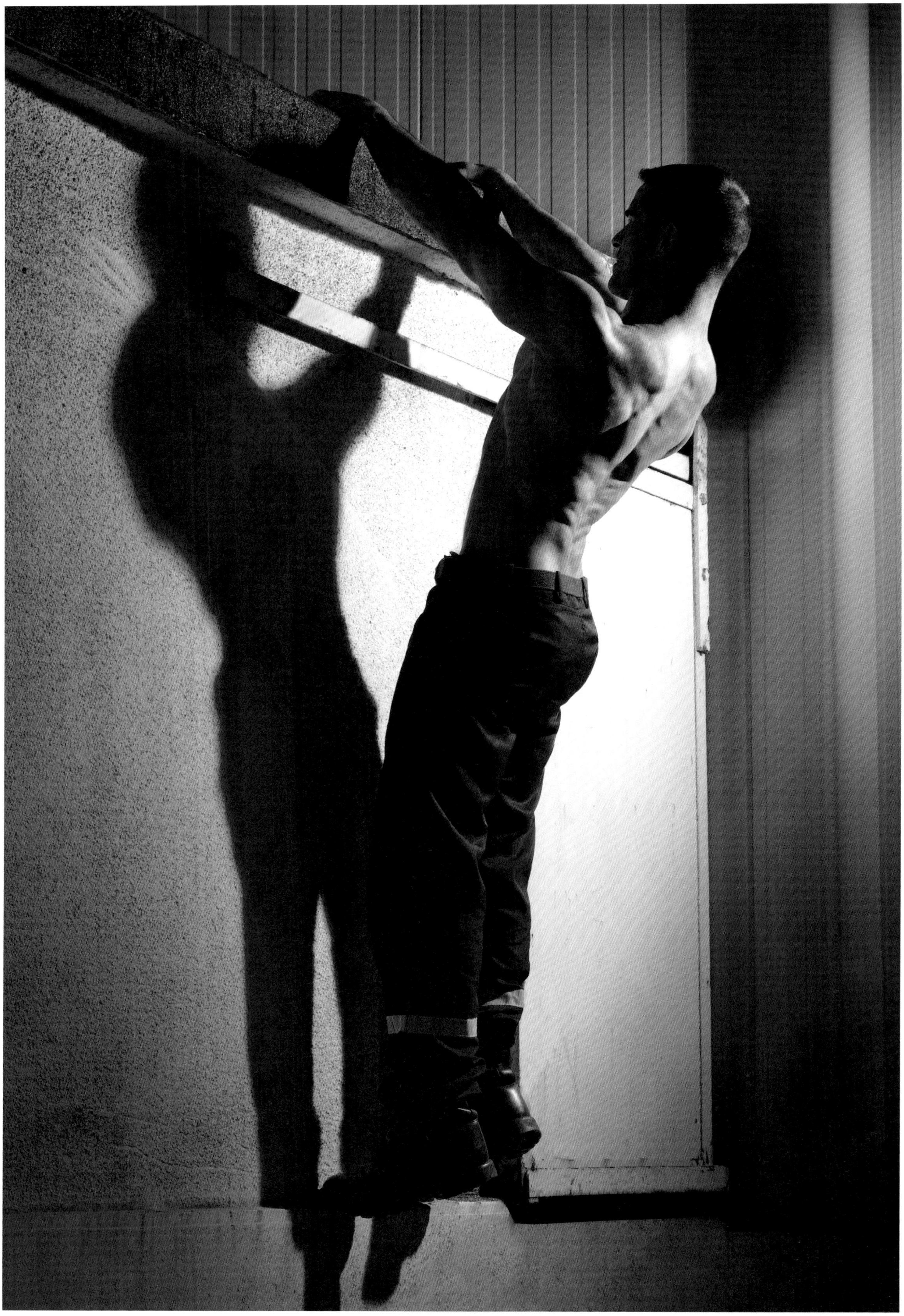

46

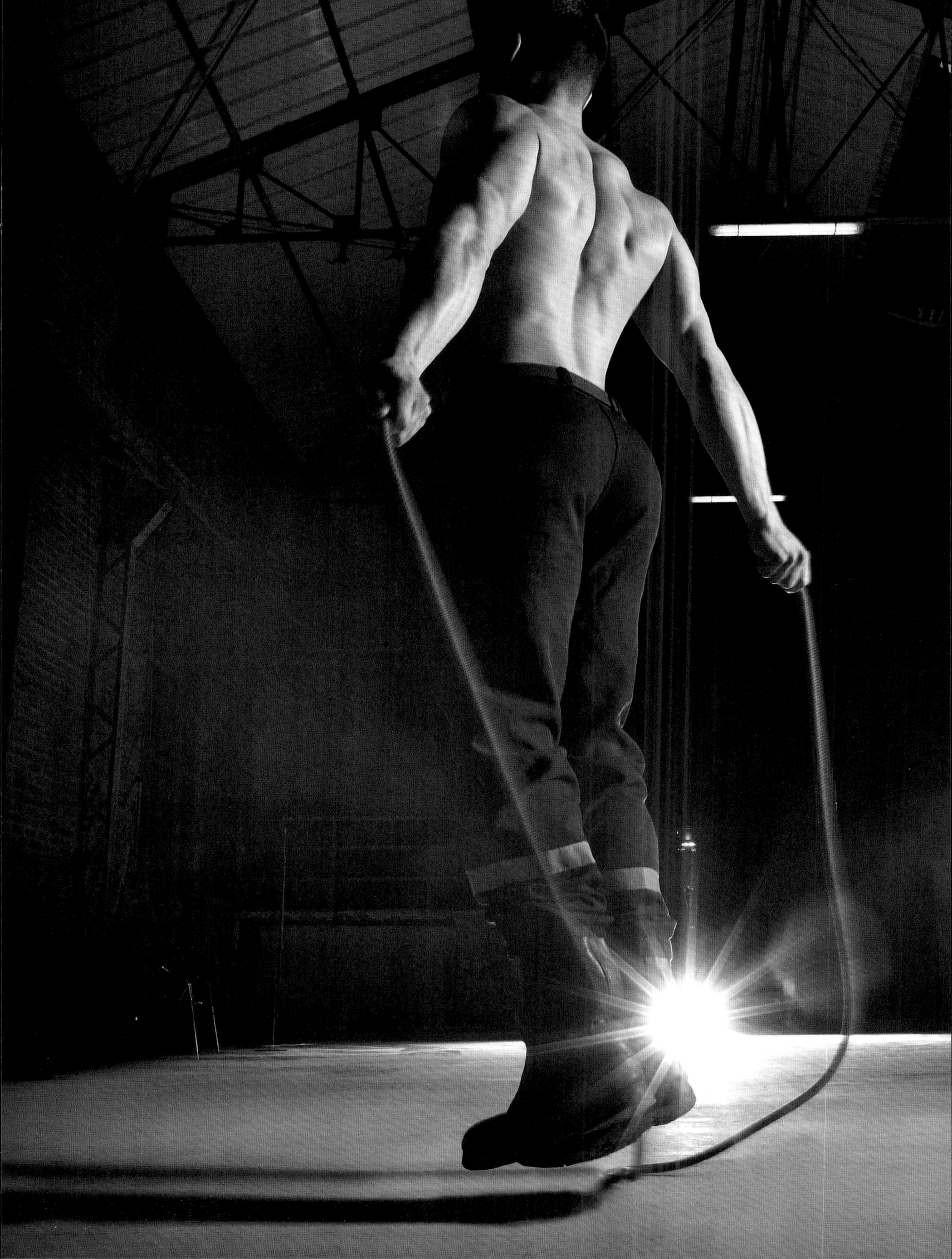

15Kg
20Kg

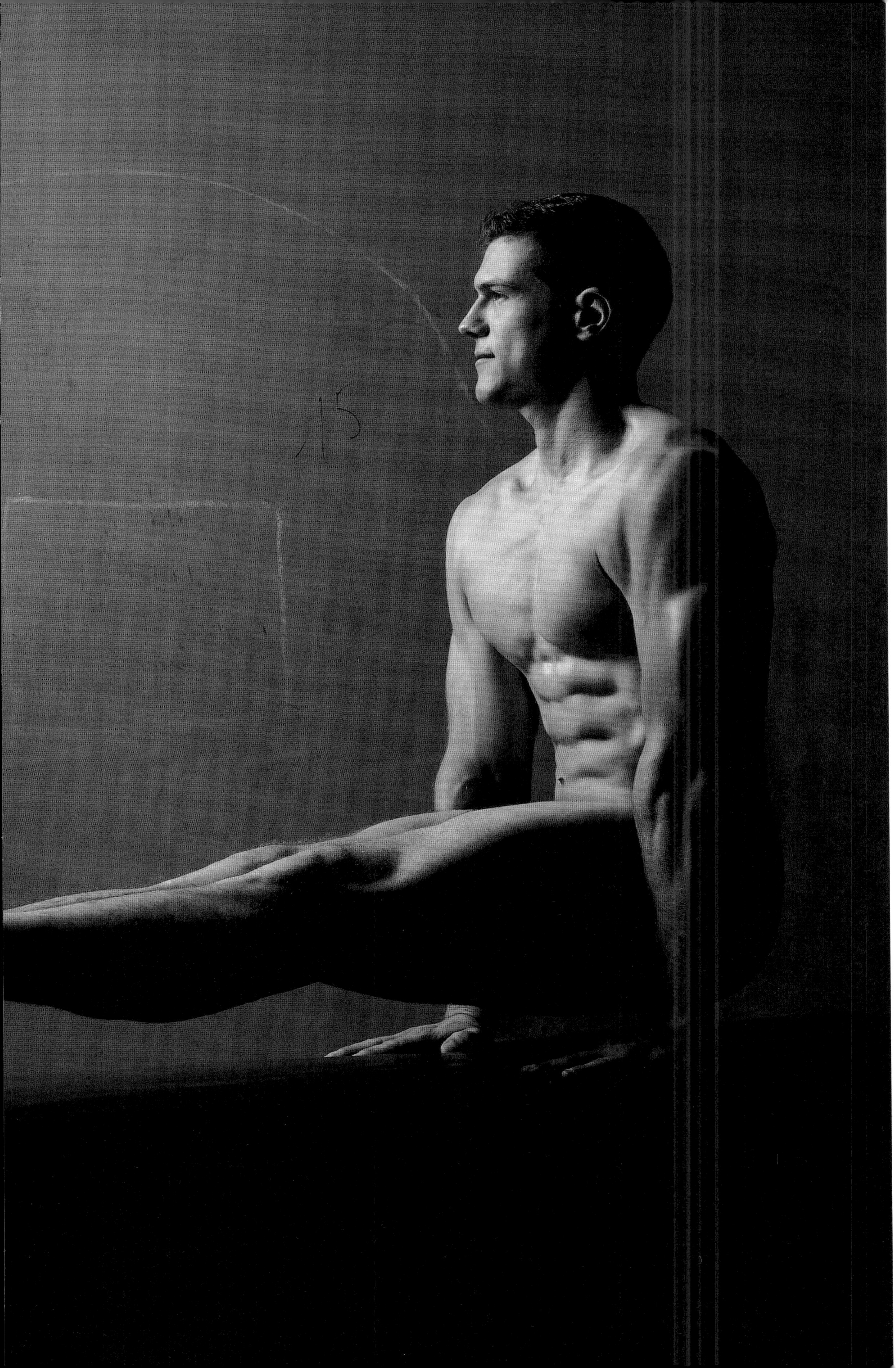

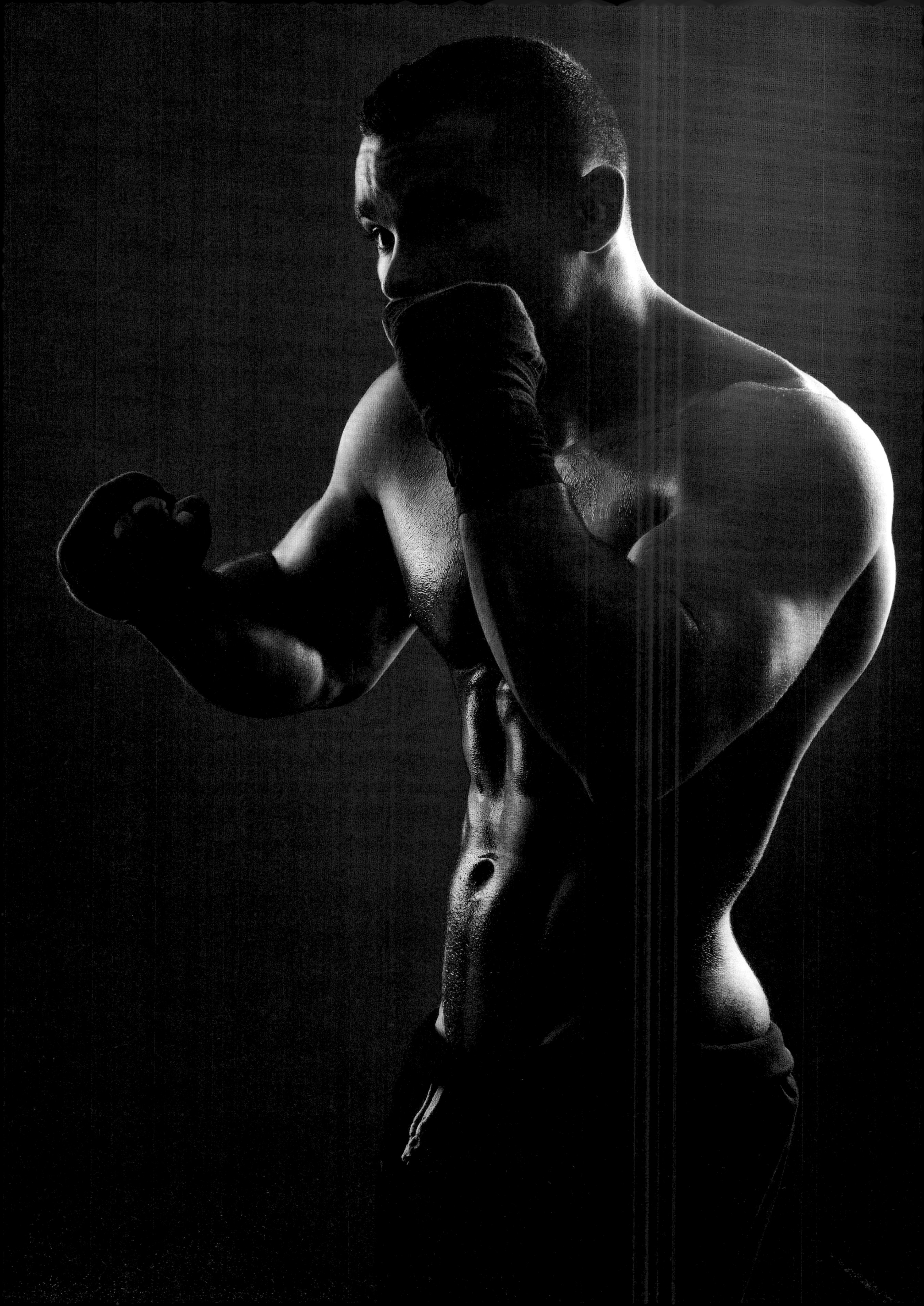

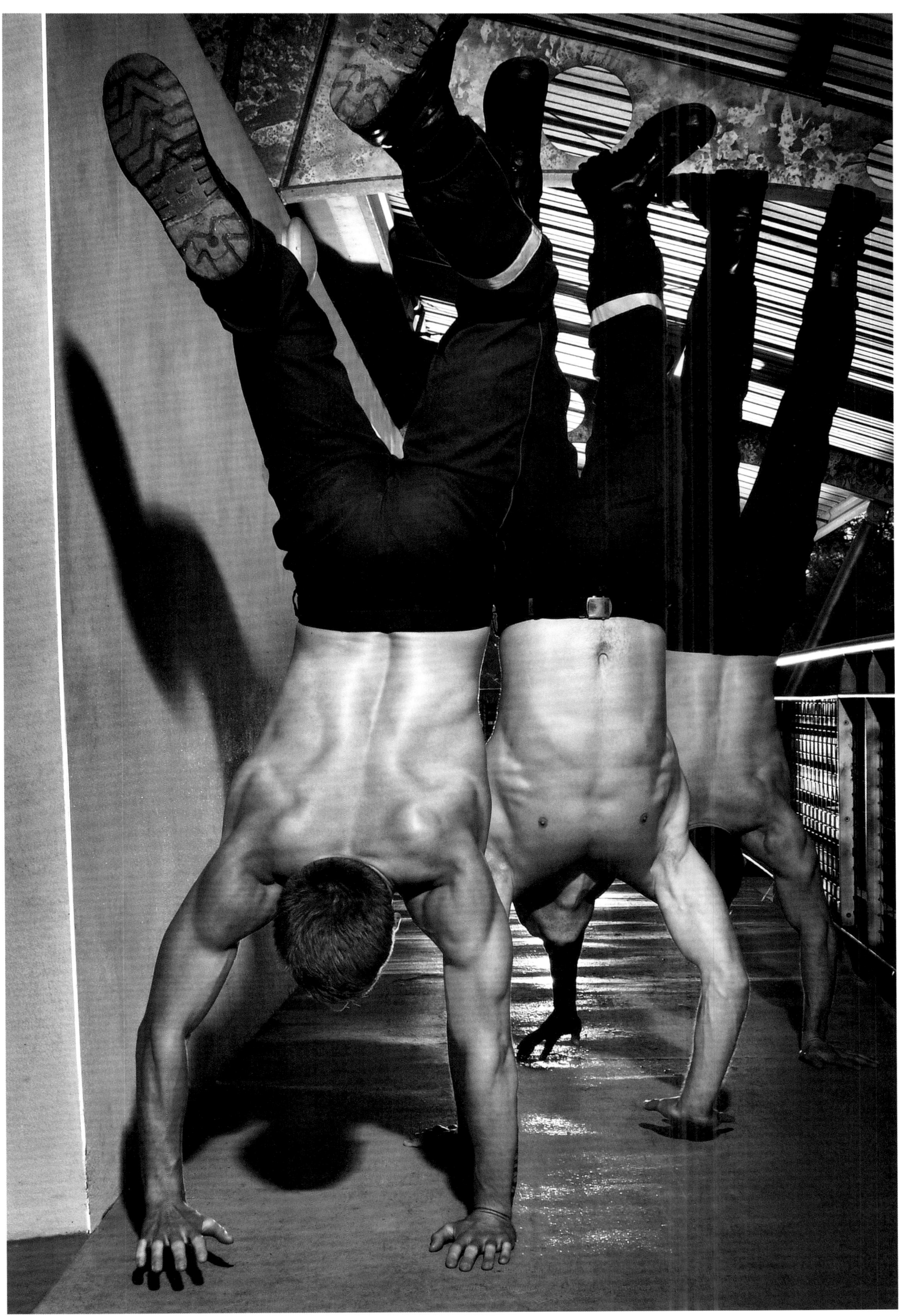

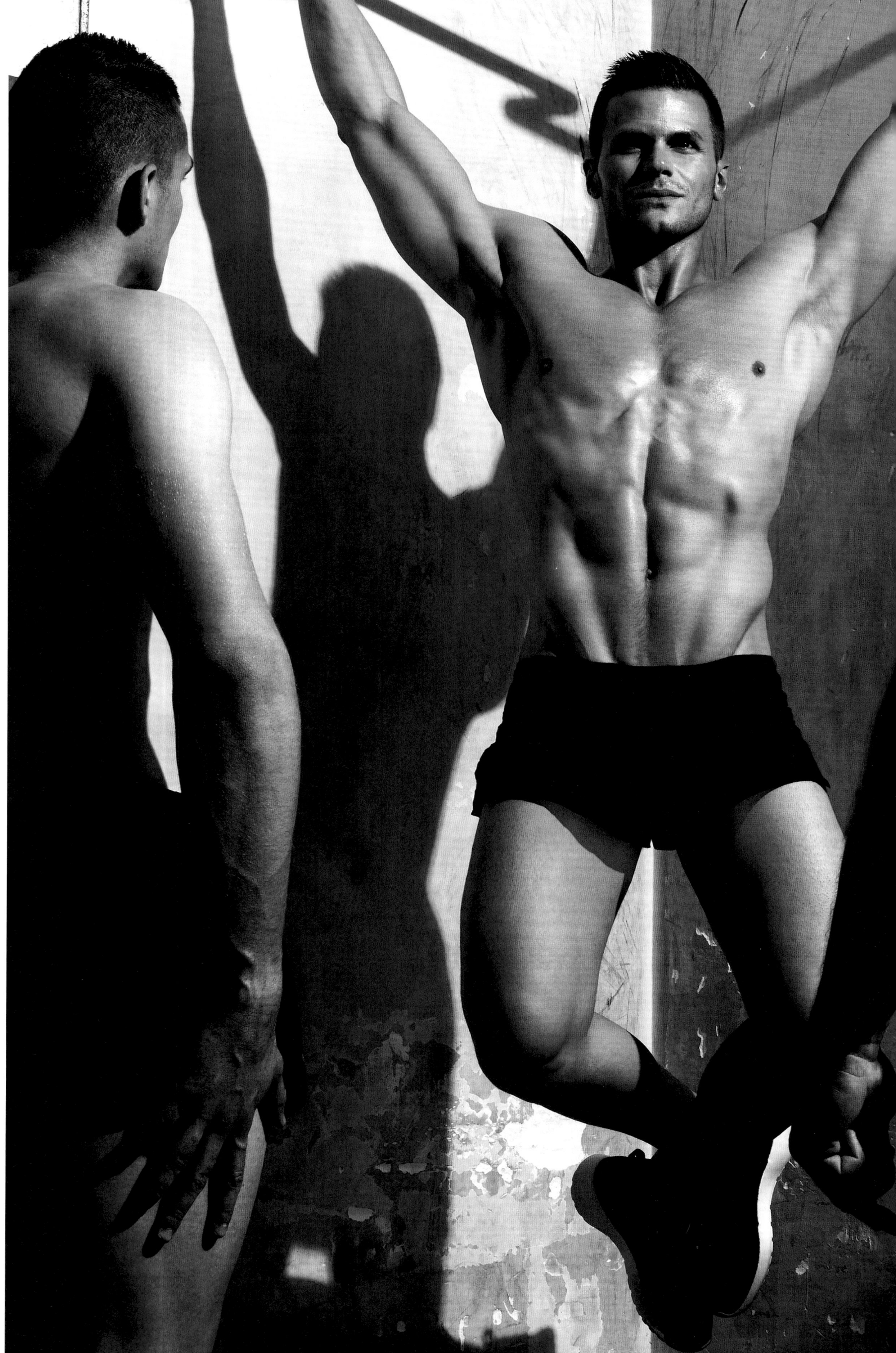

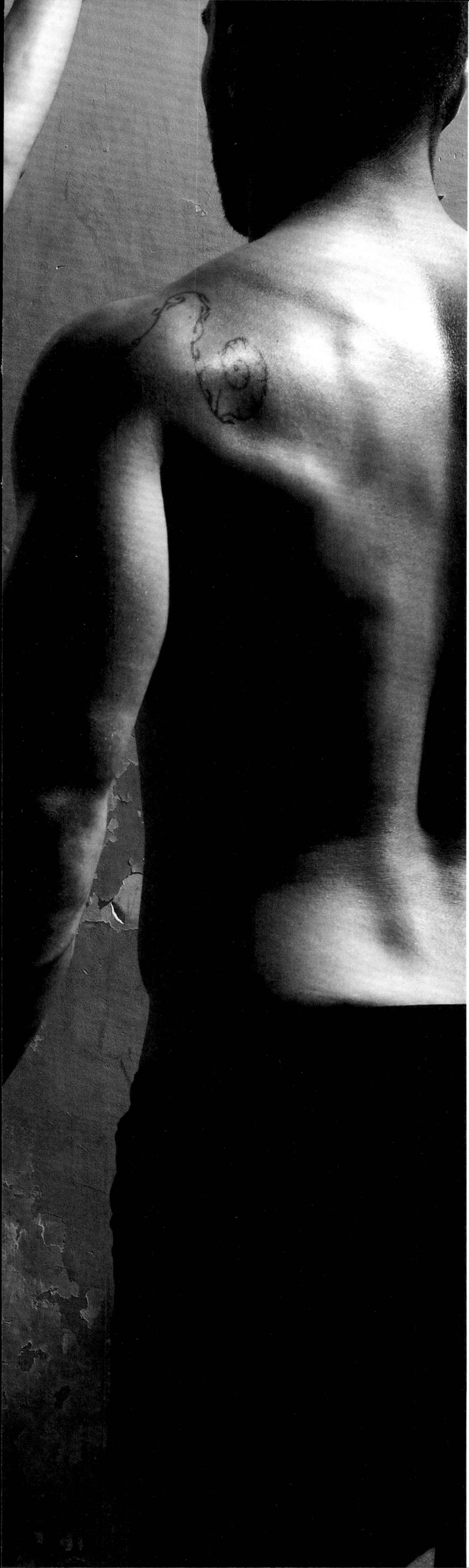

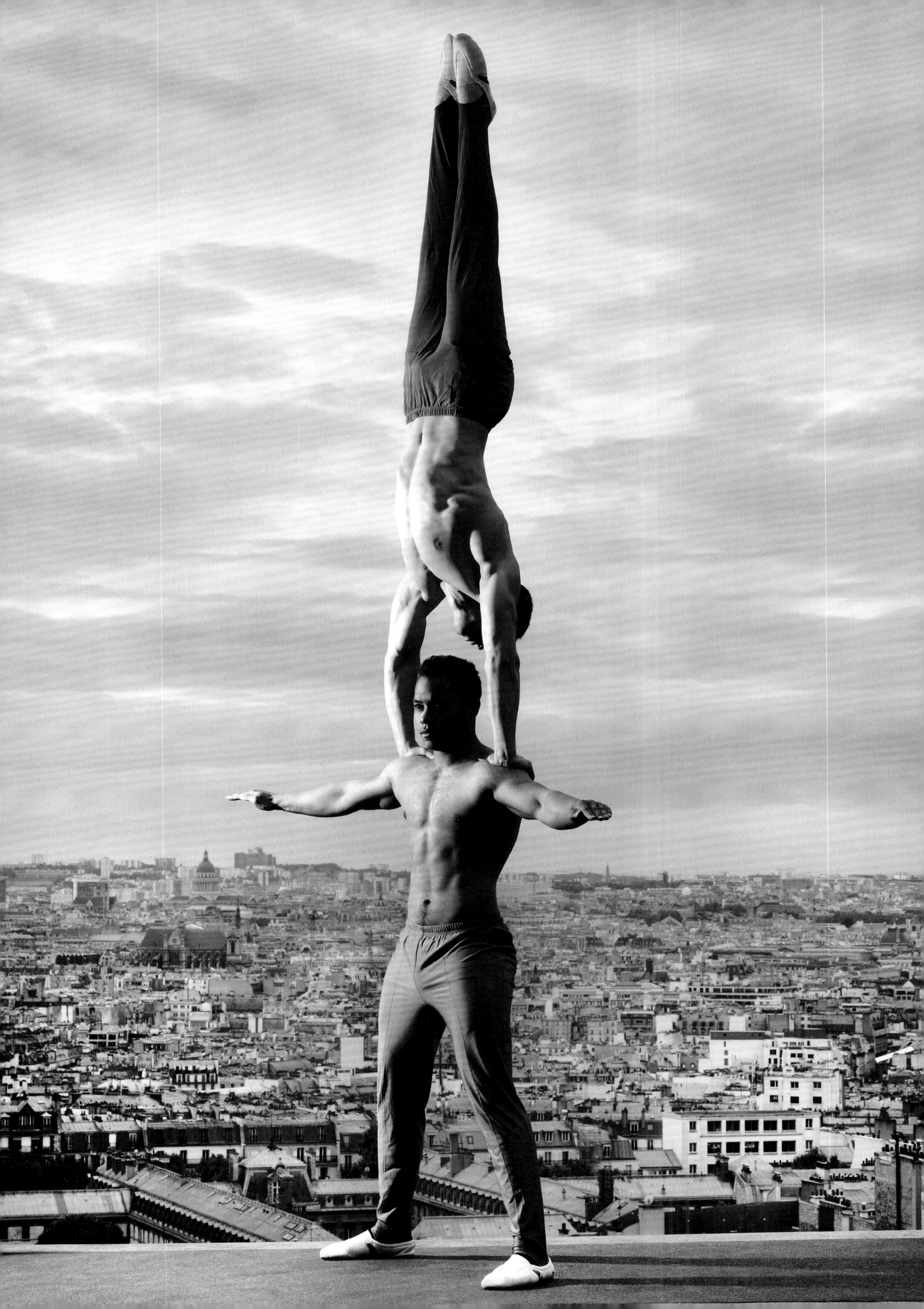

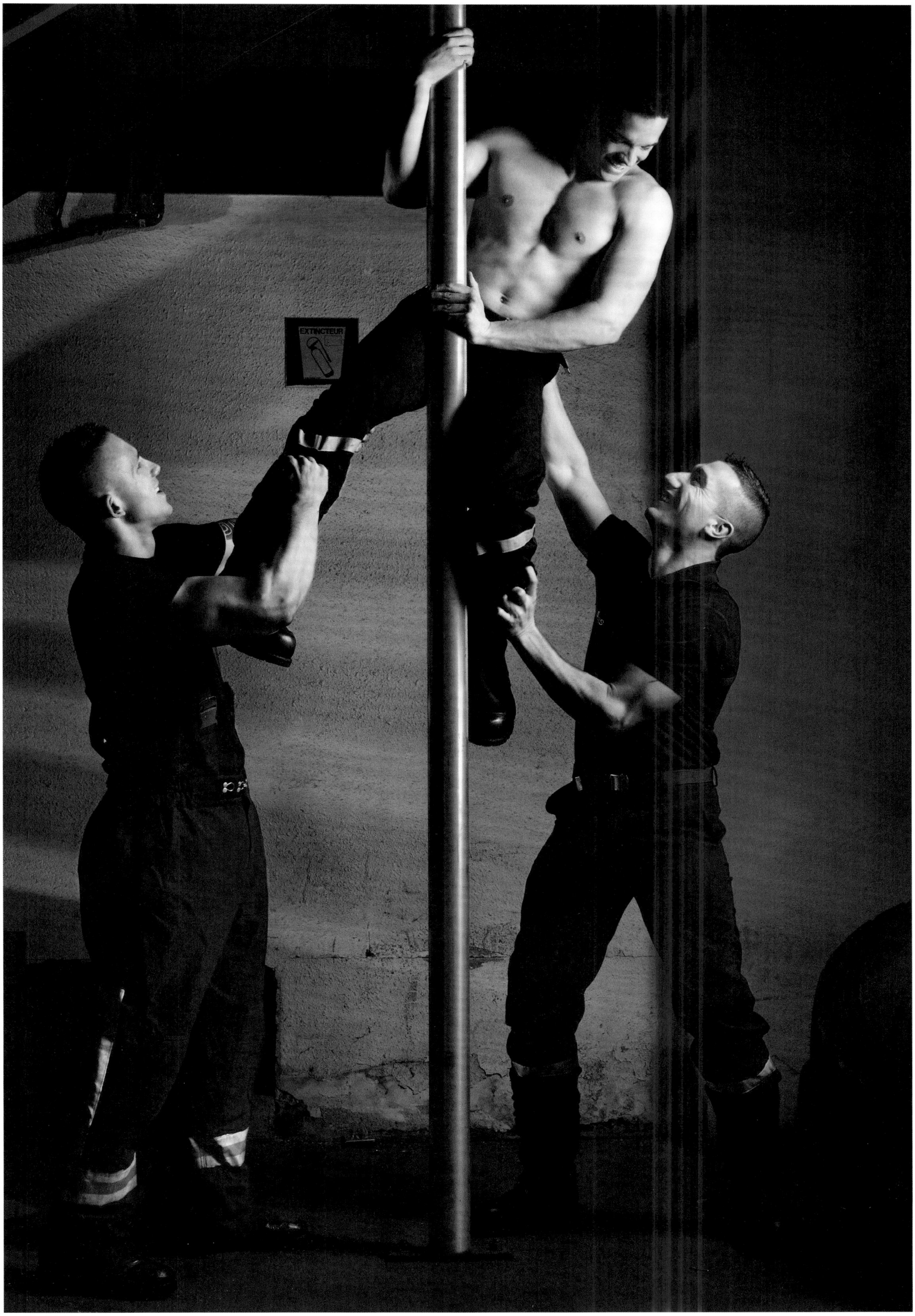

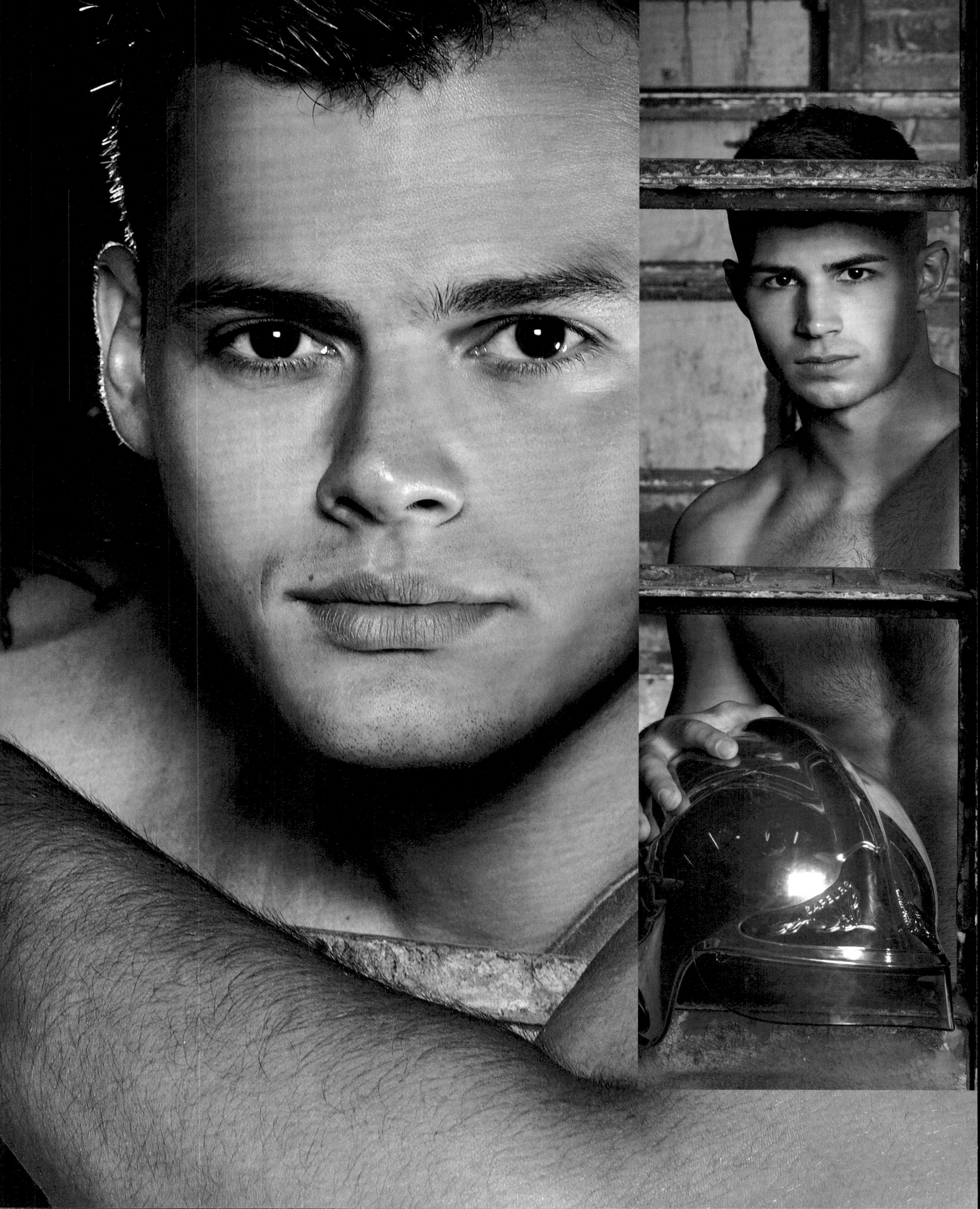

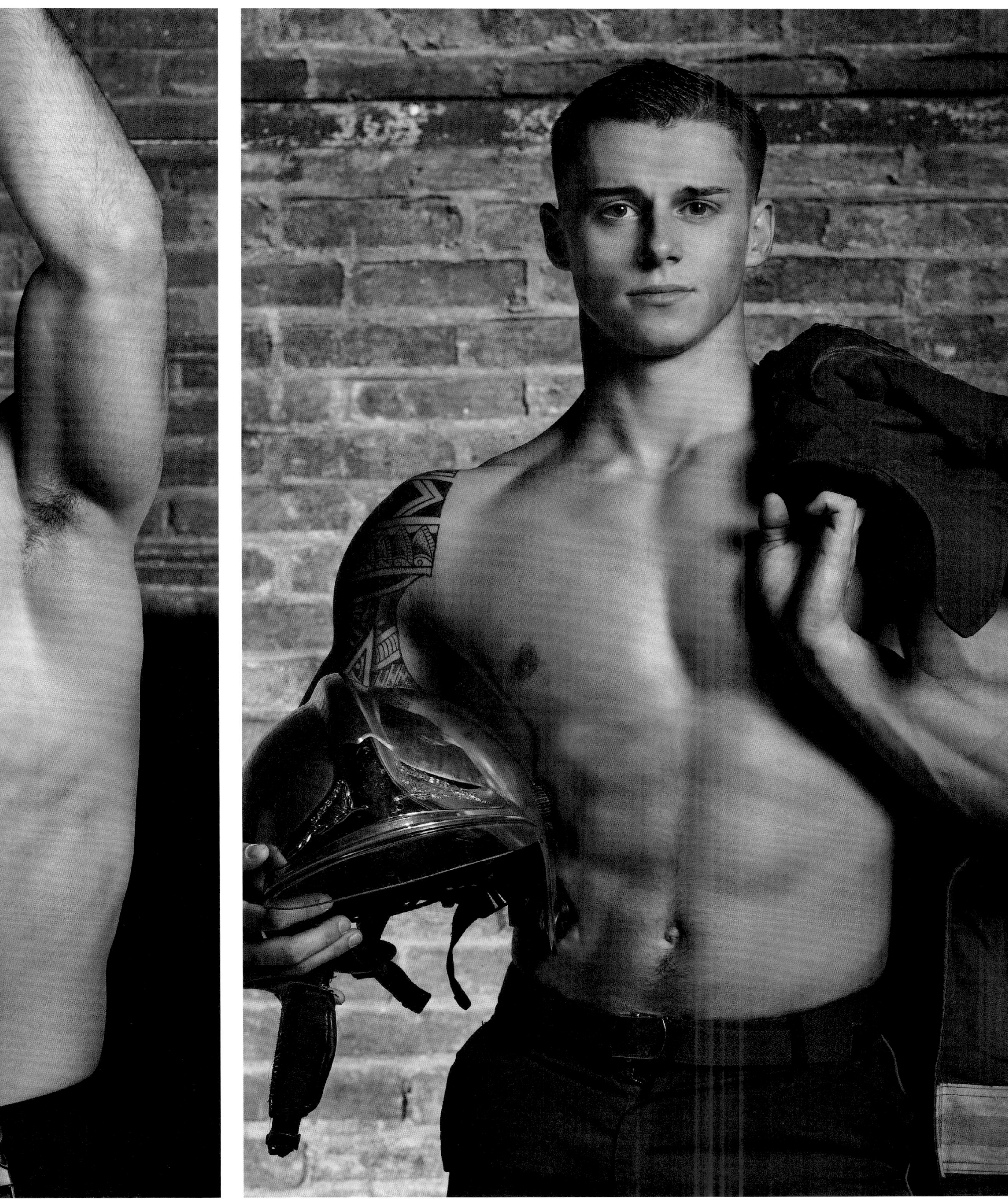

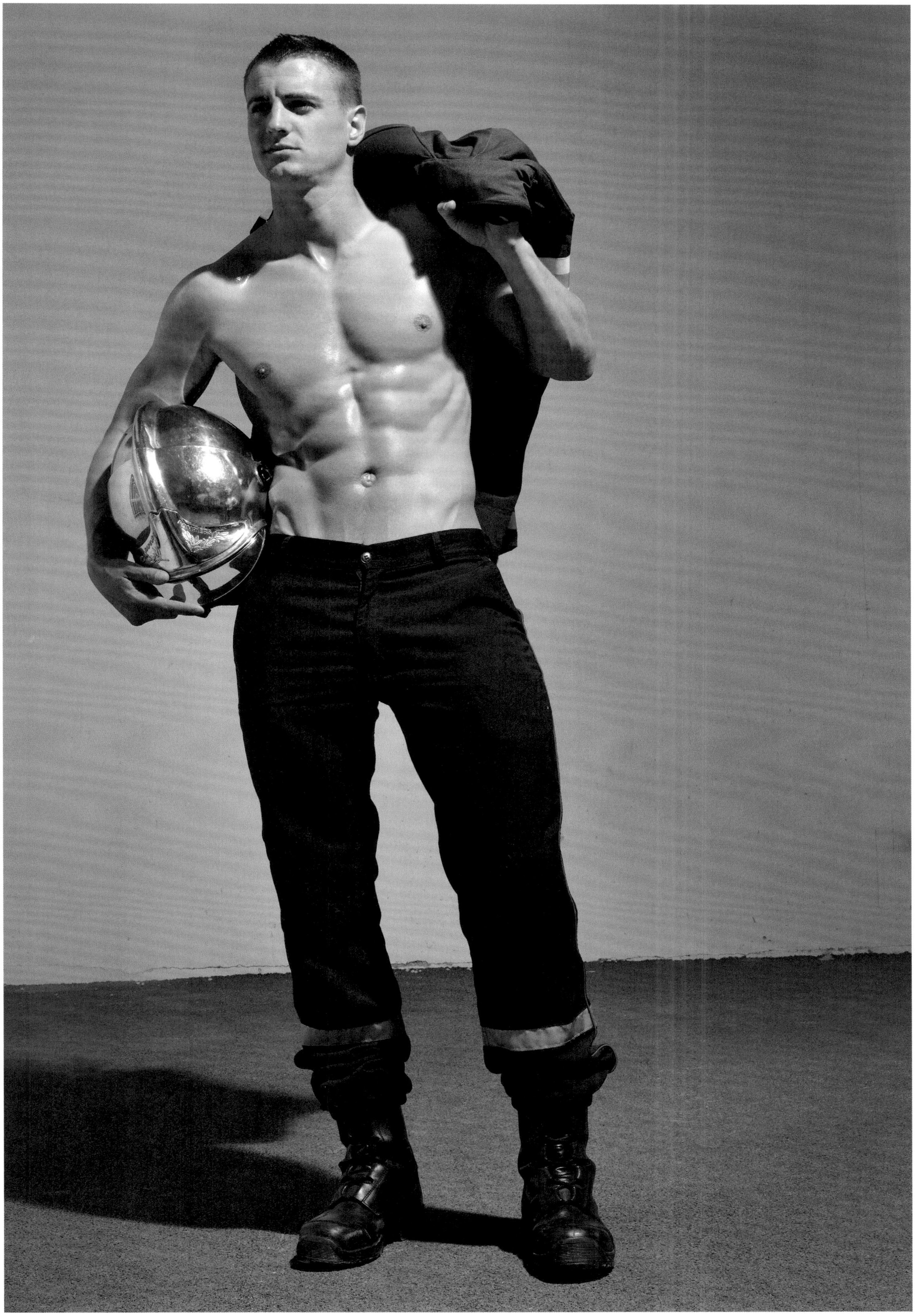

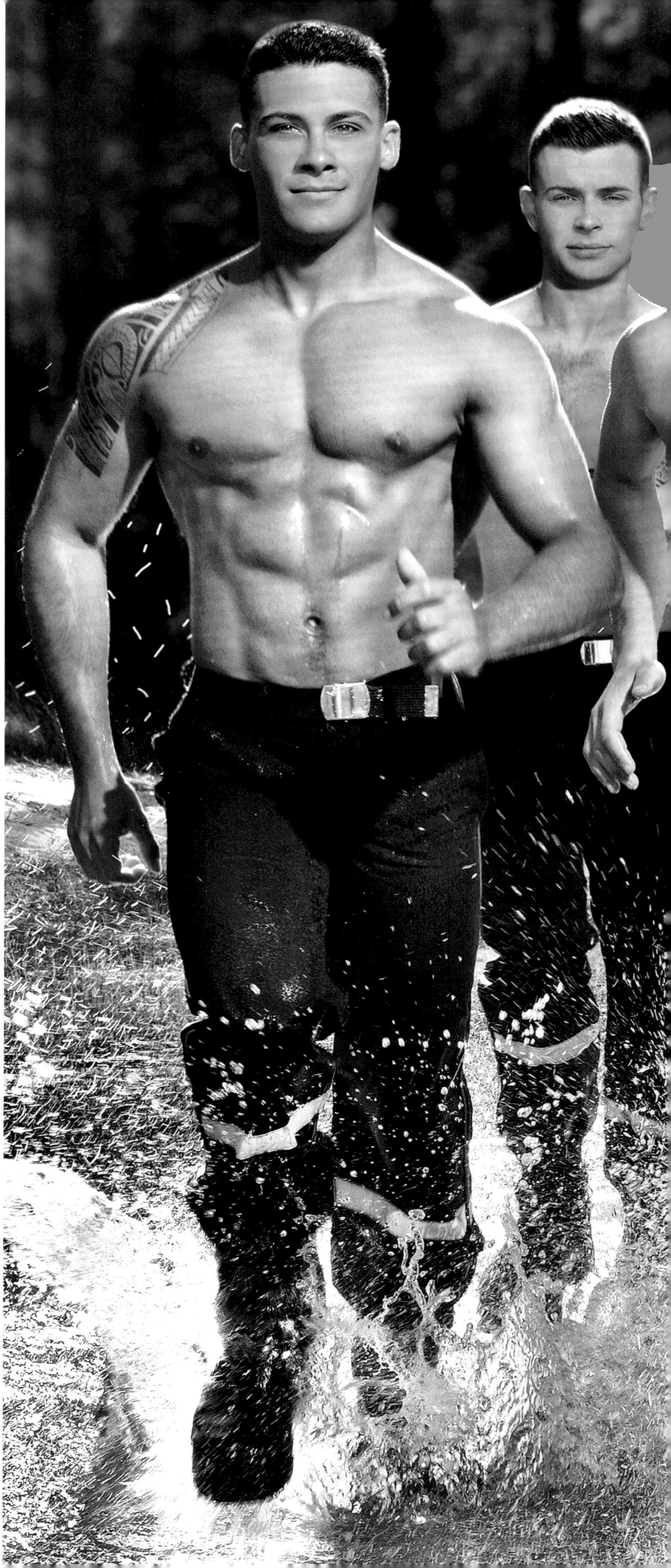

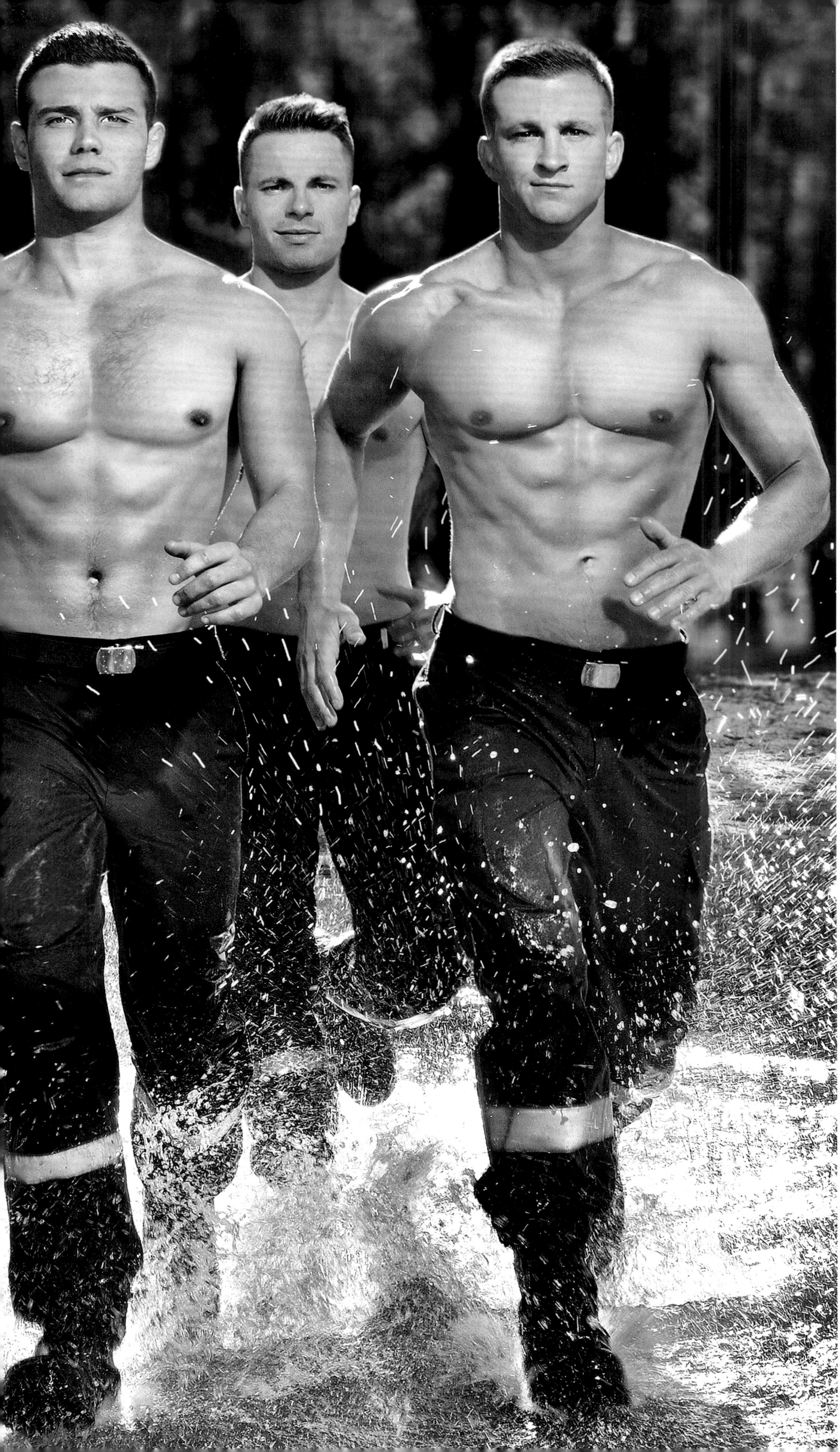

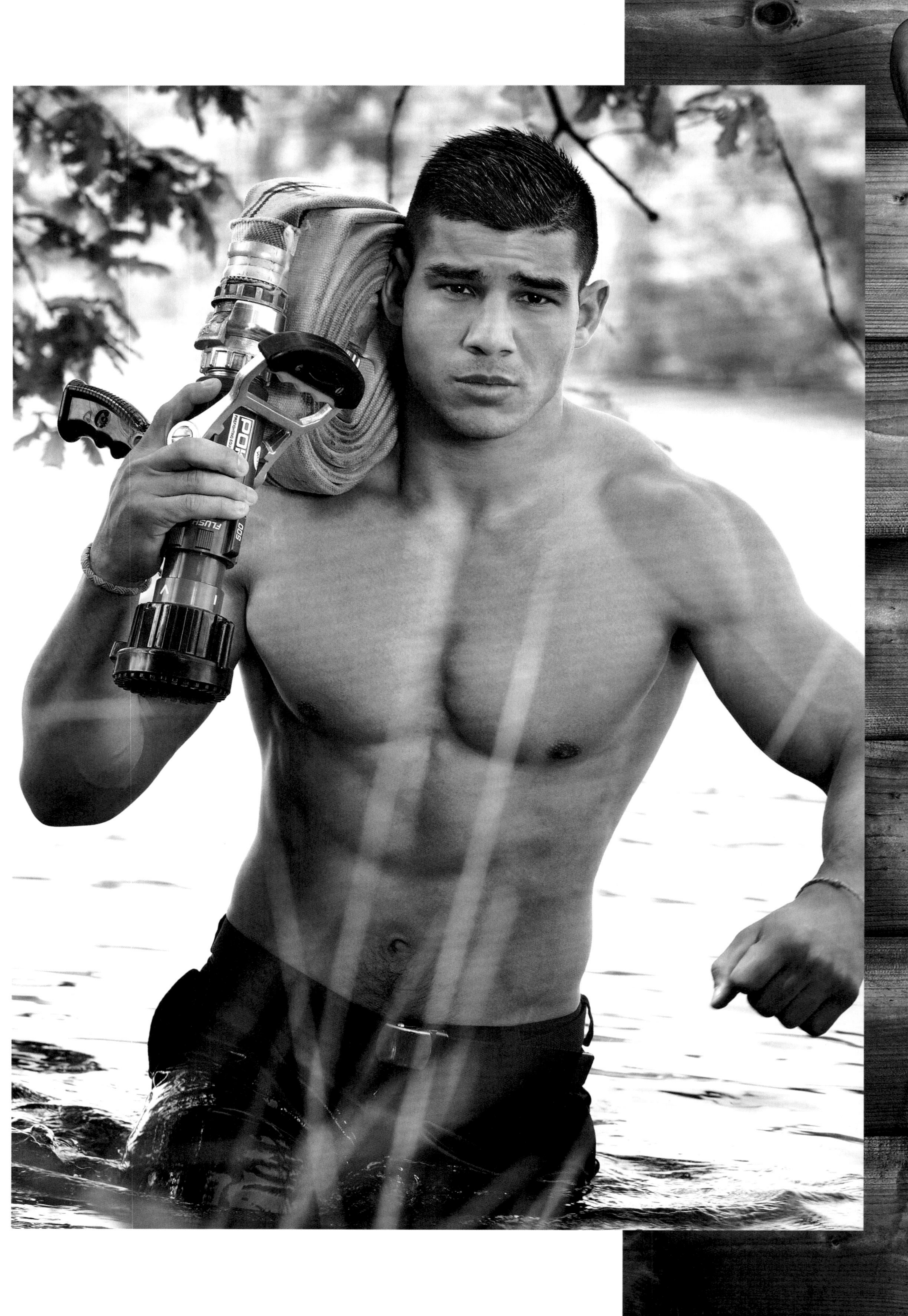

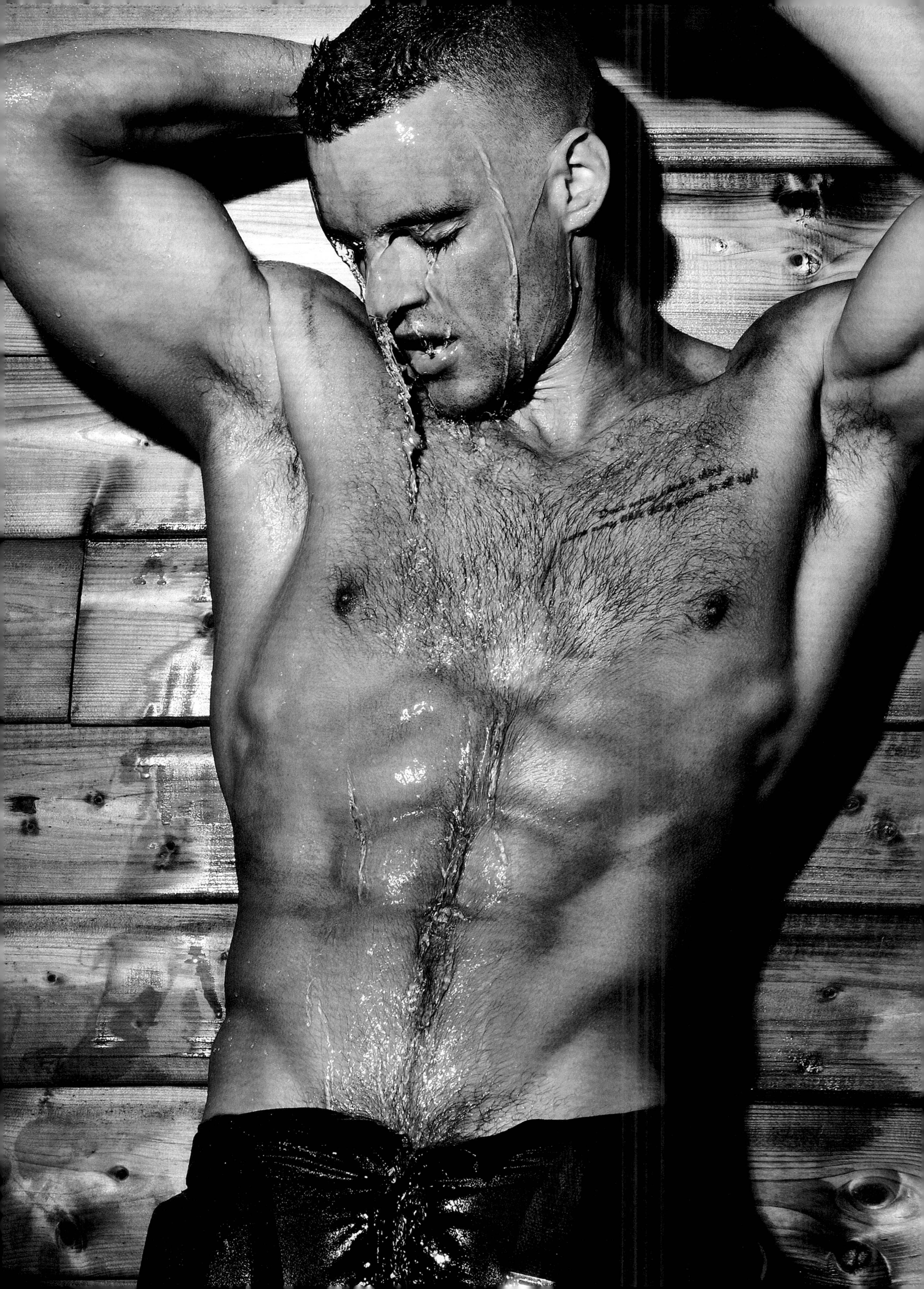

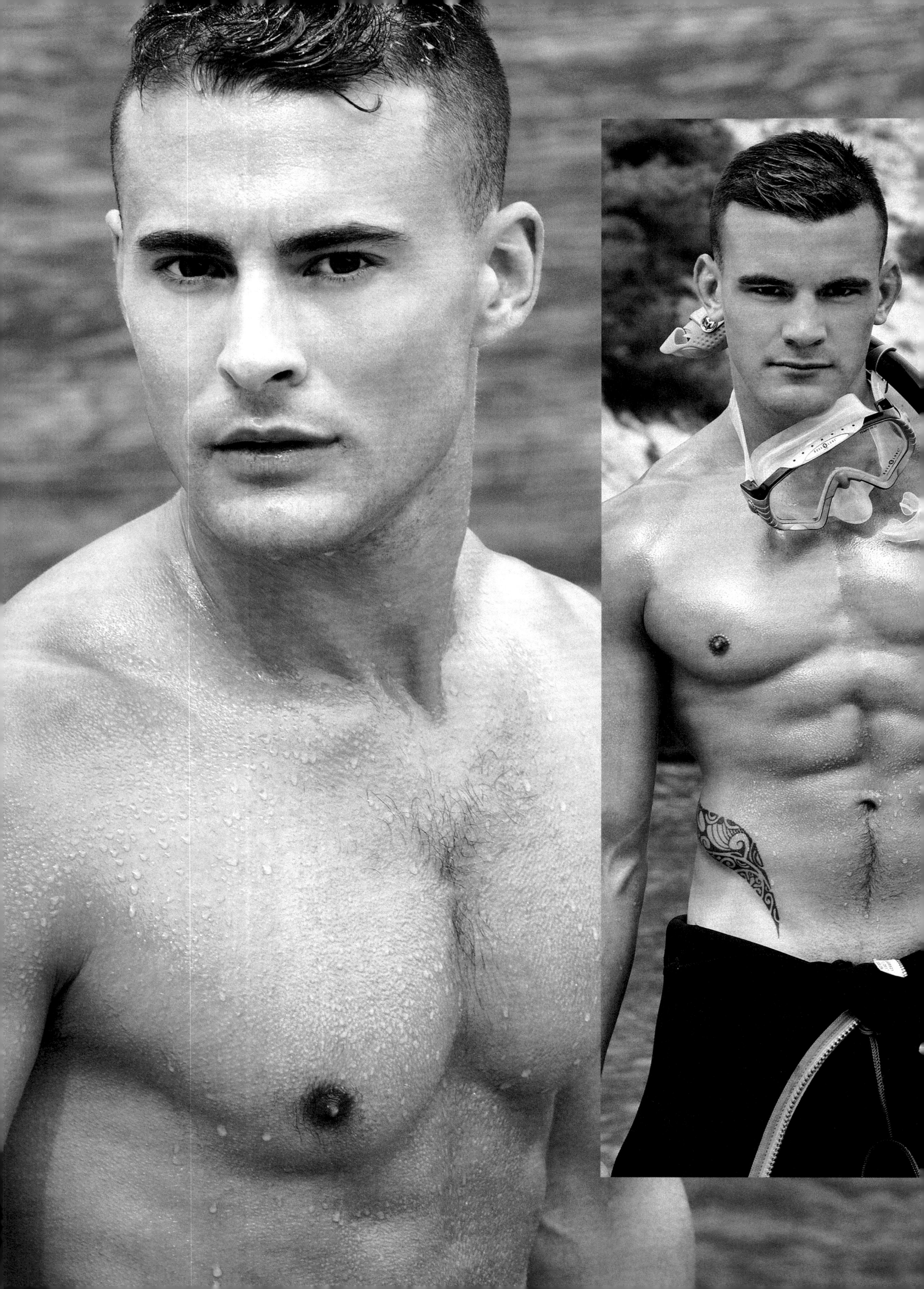

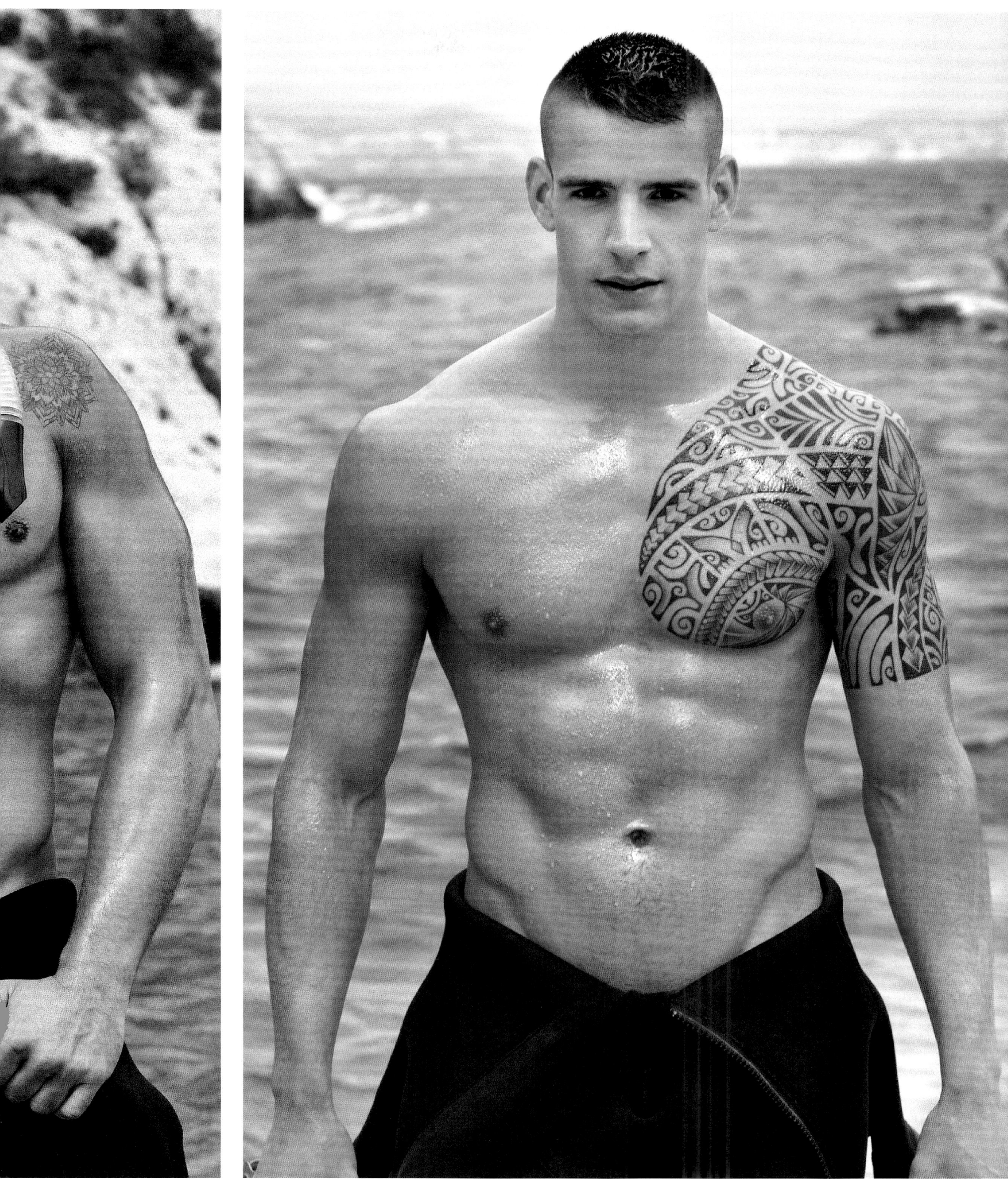

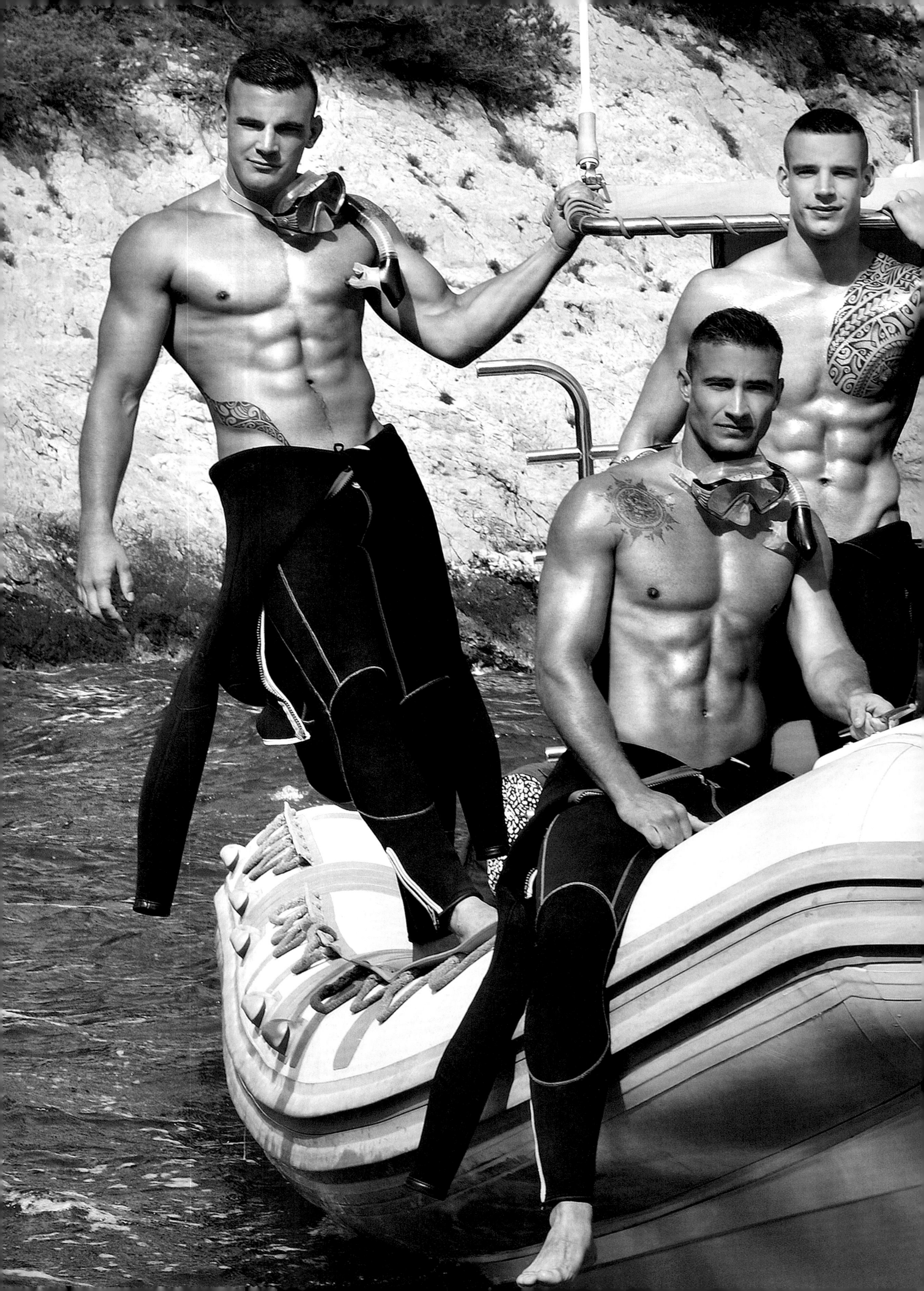

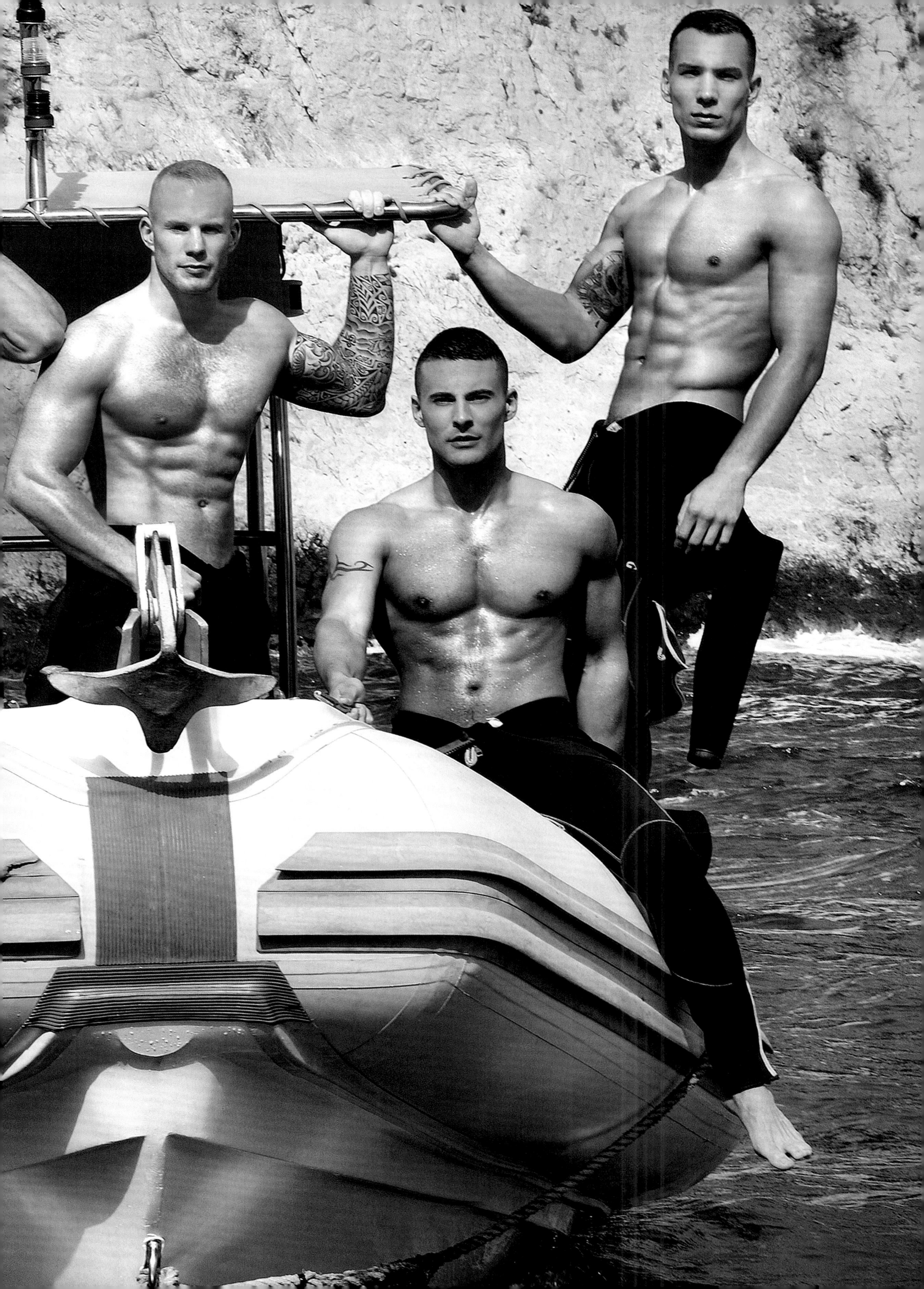

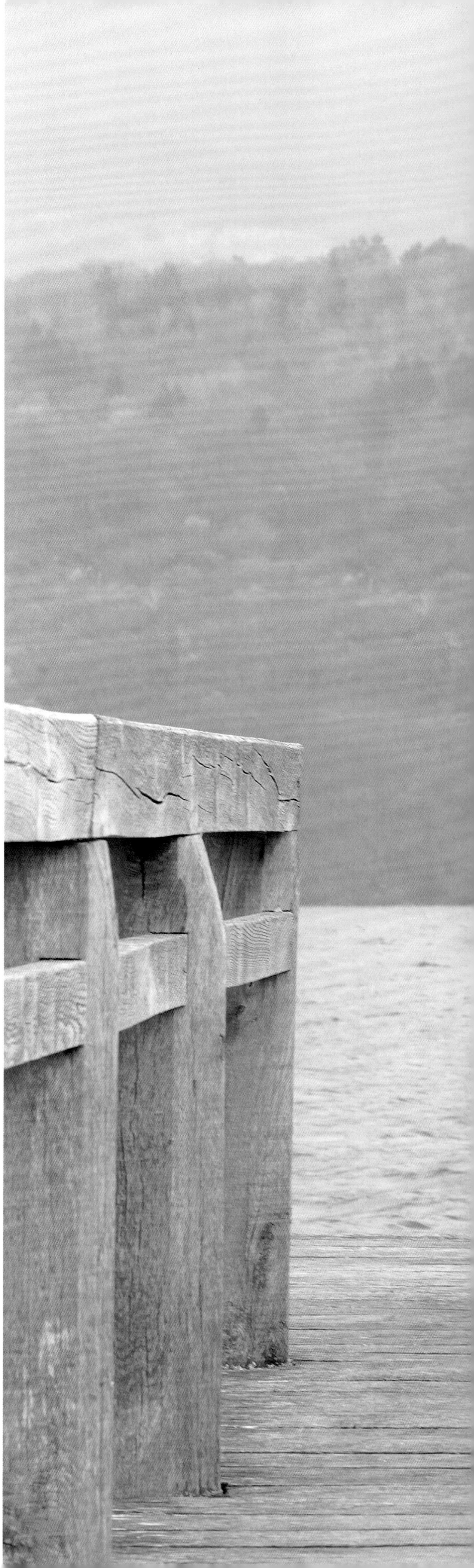

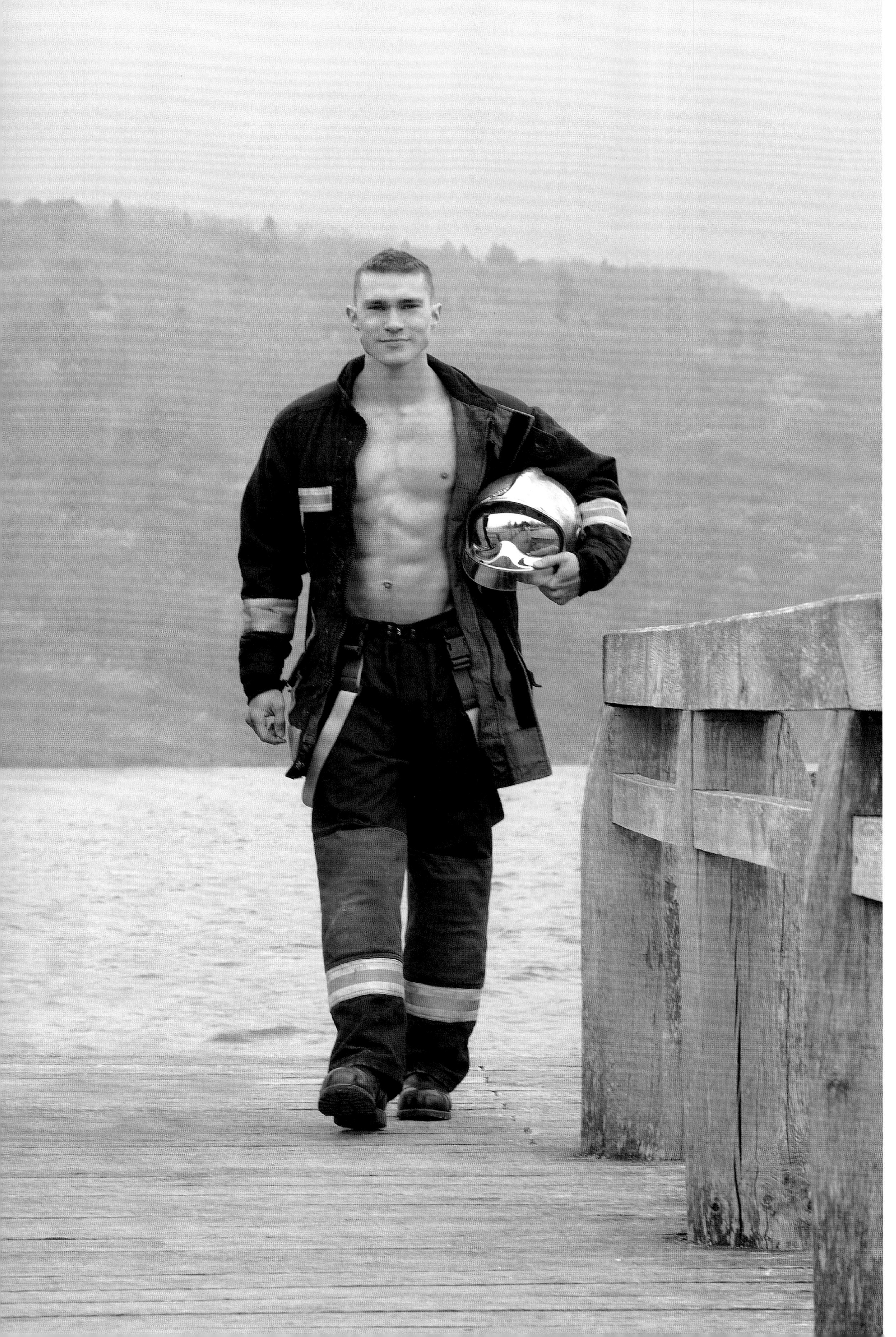

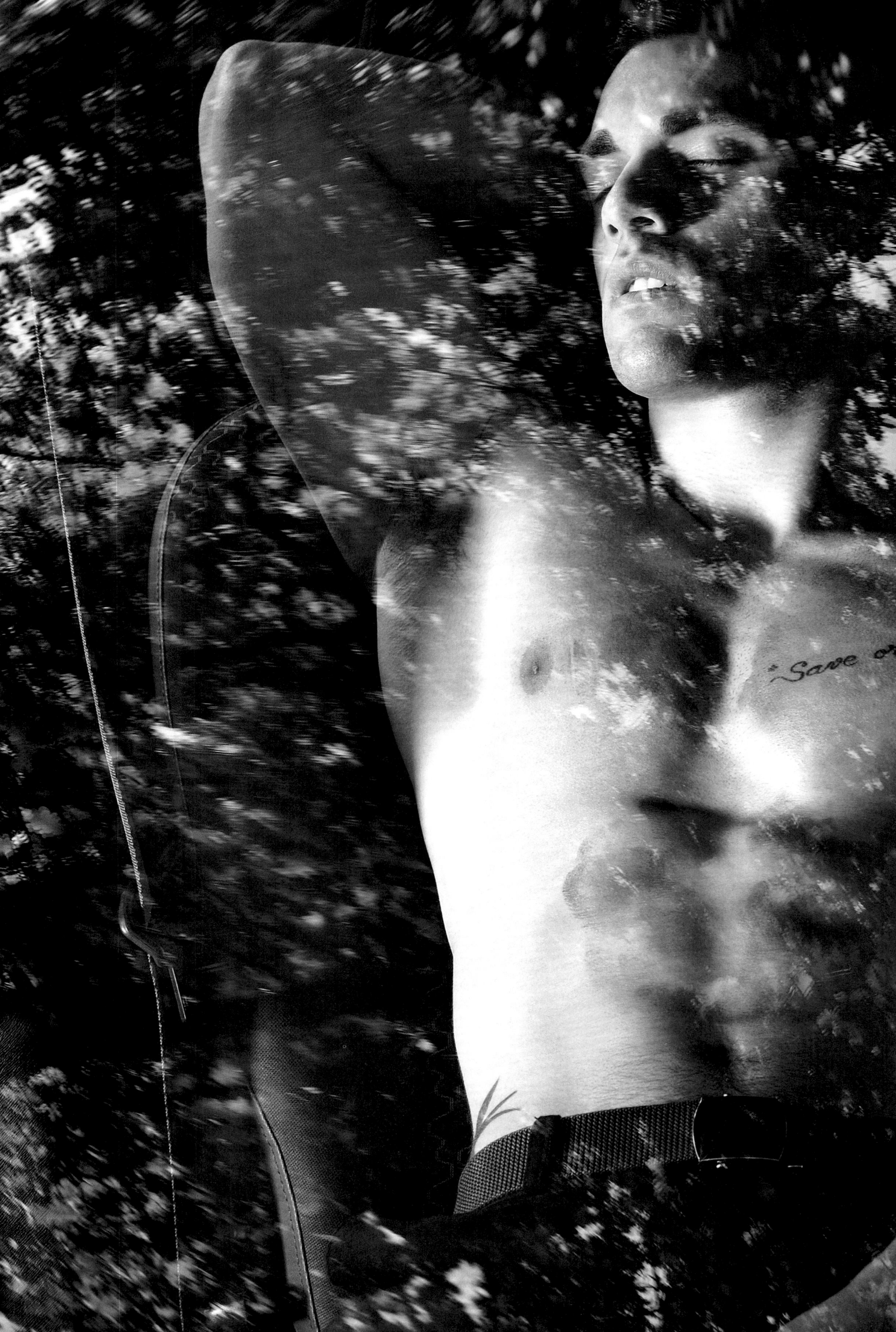
Save or

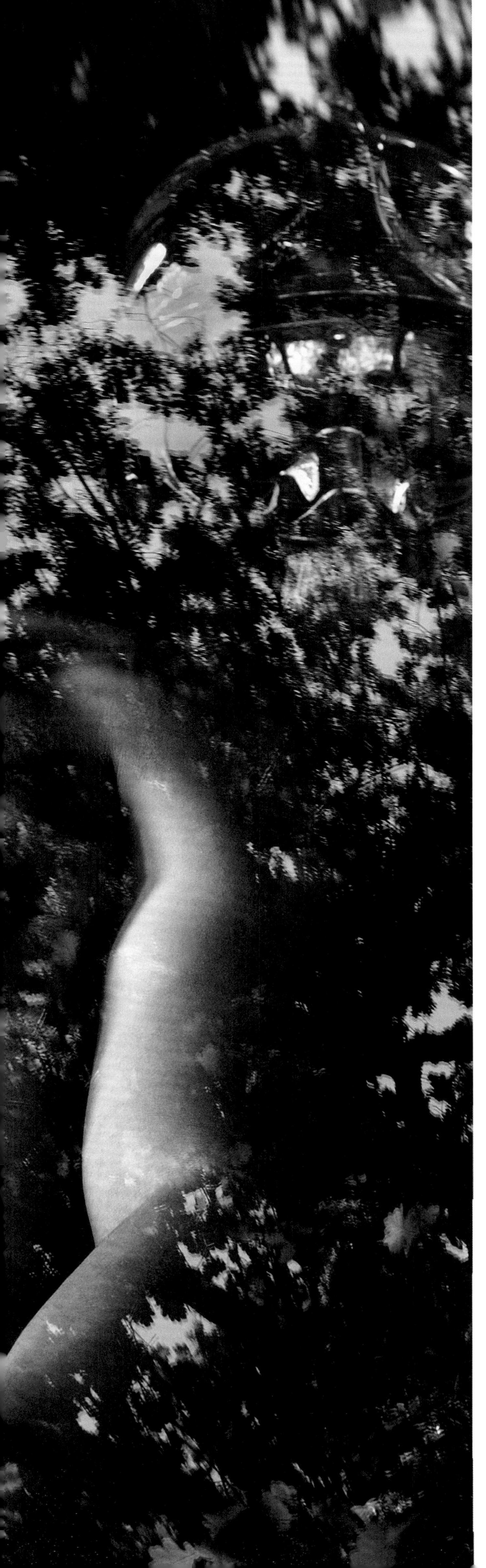

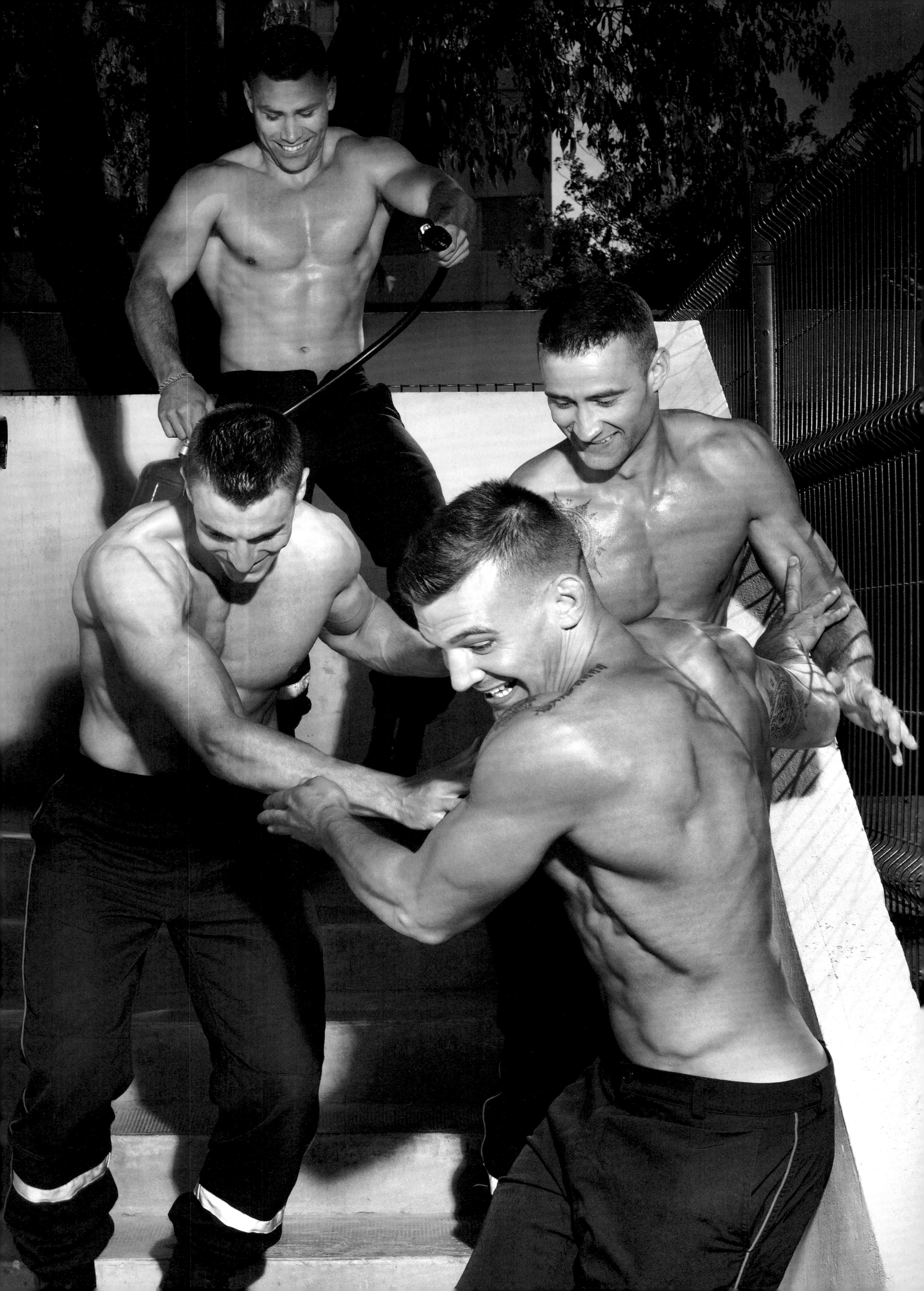

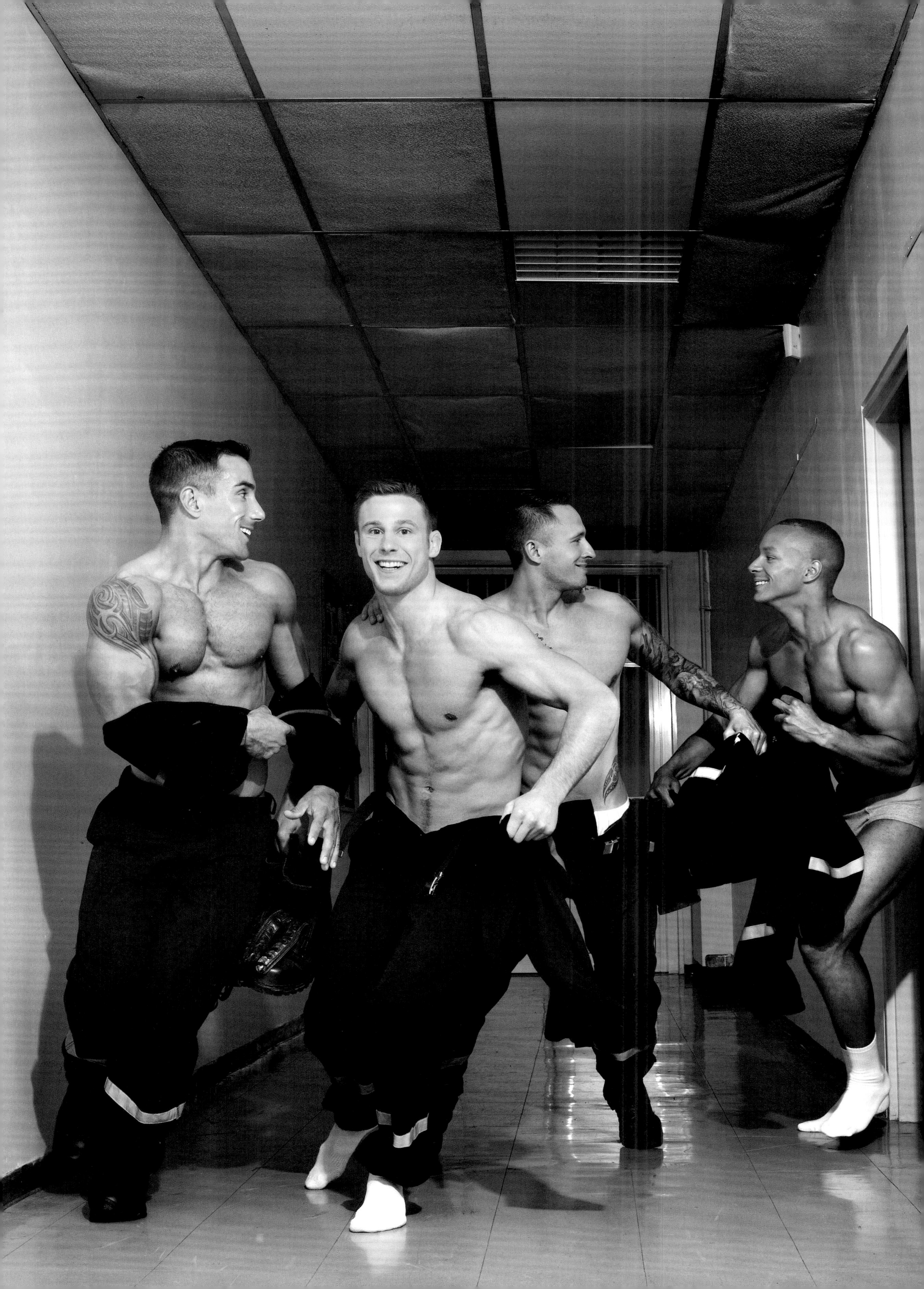

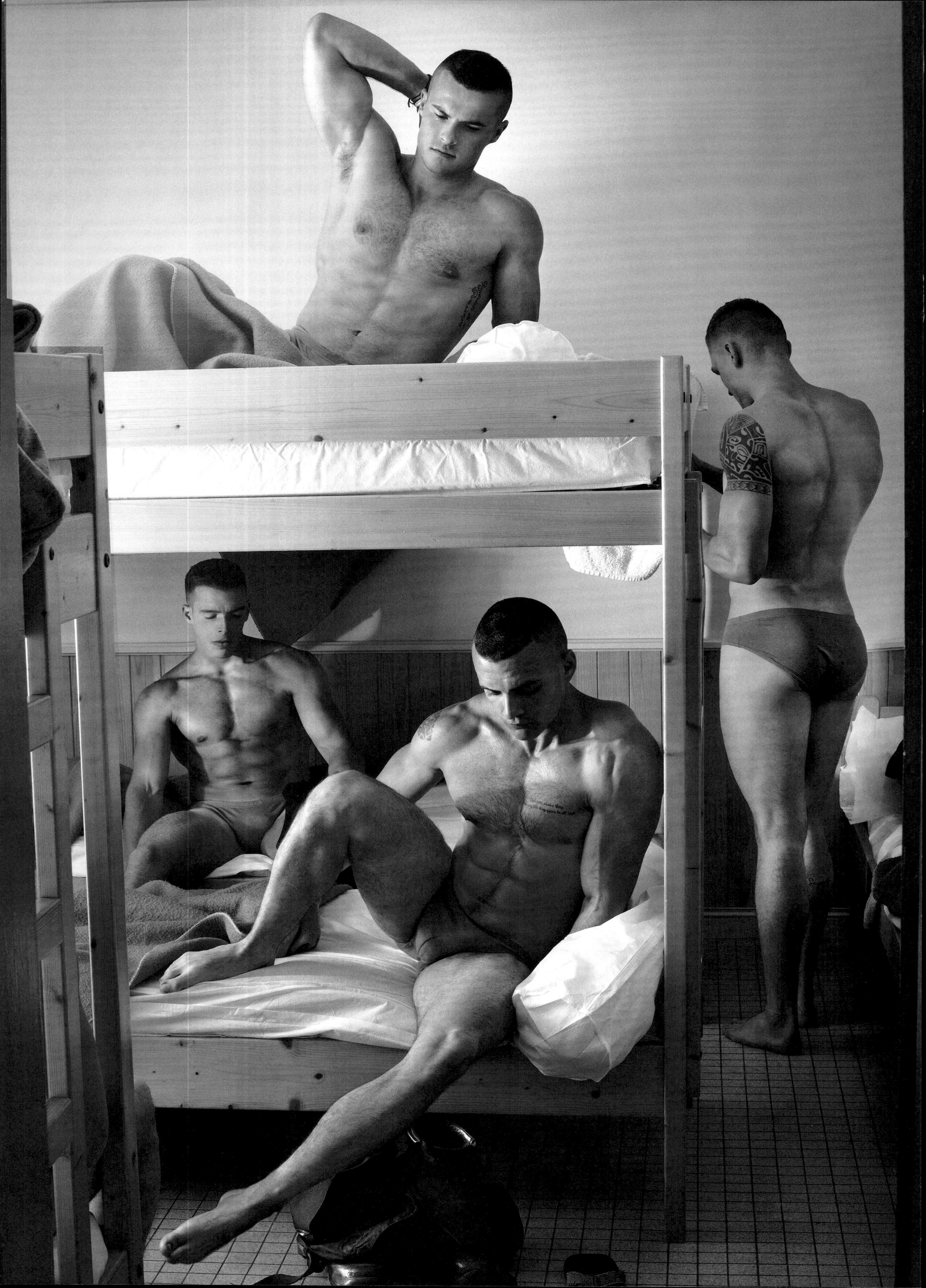

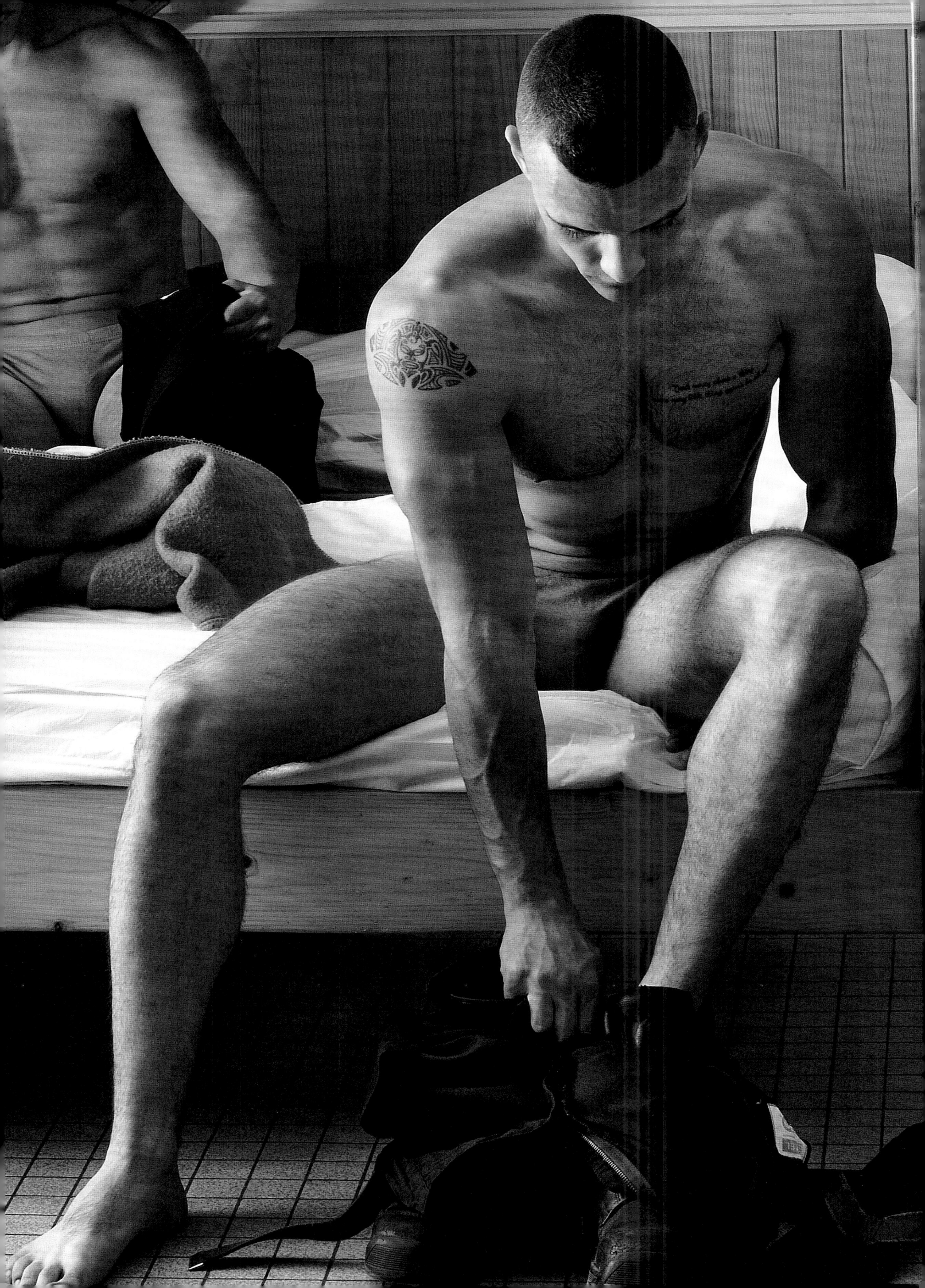

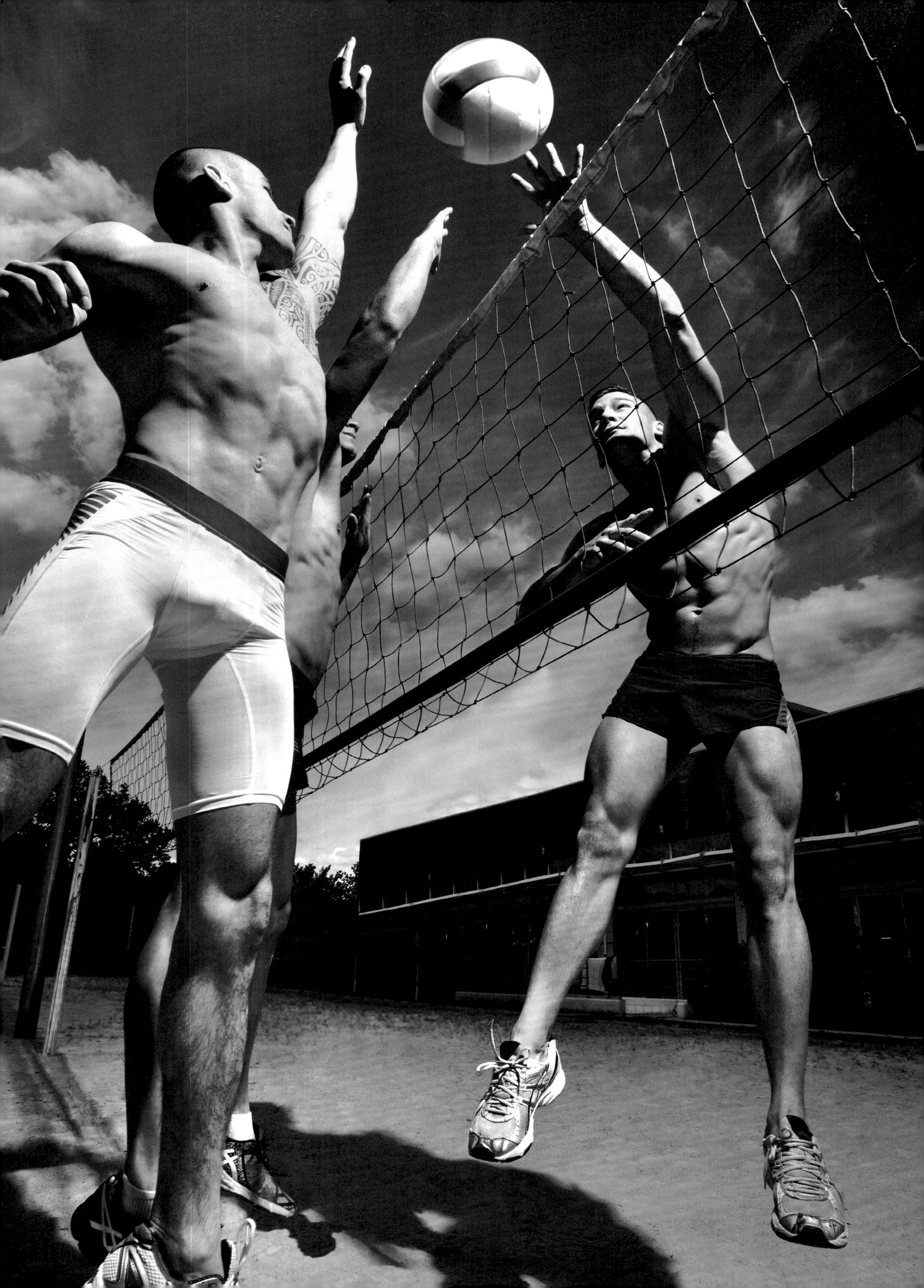

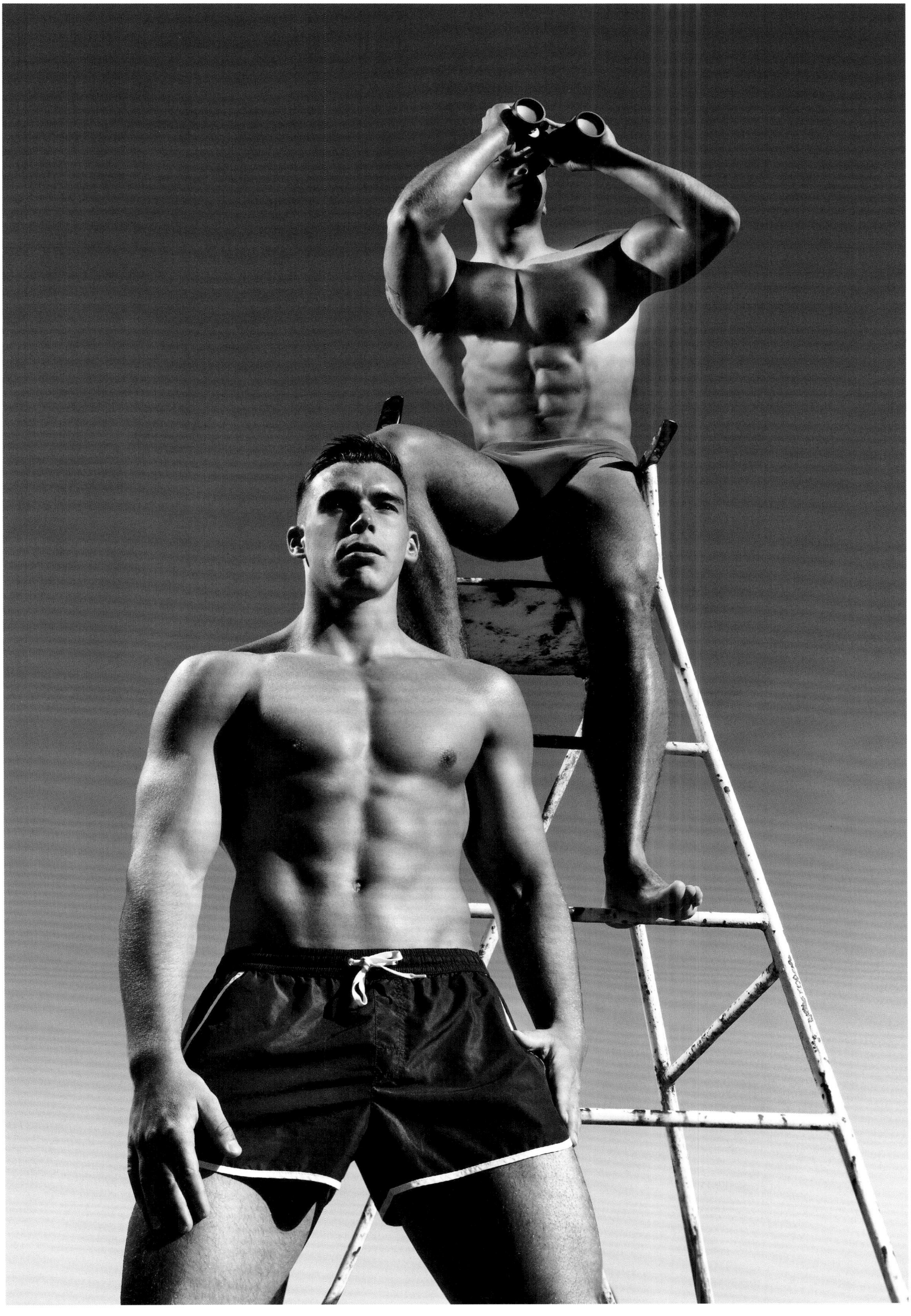

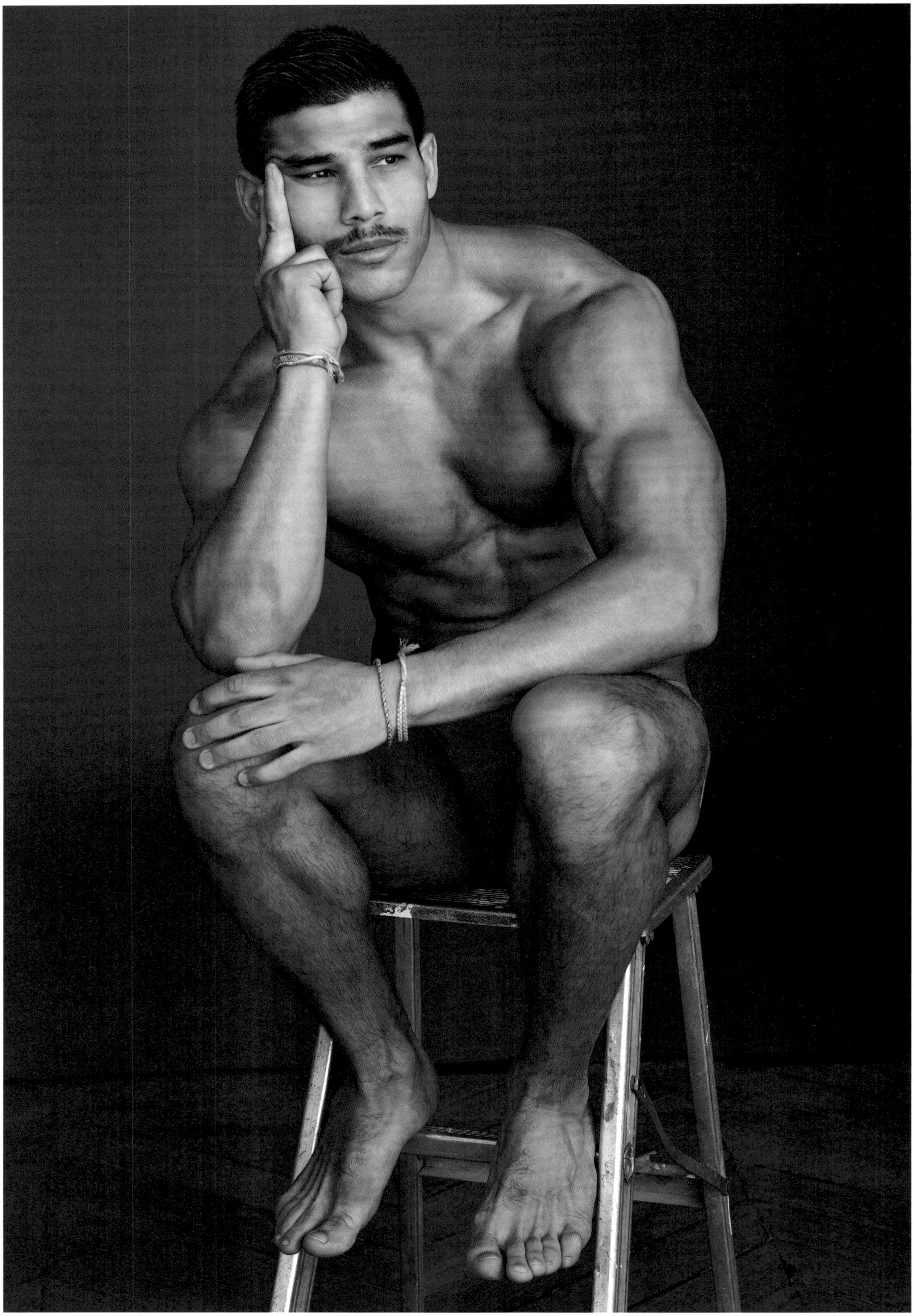

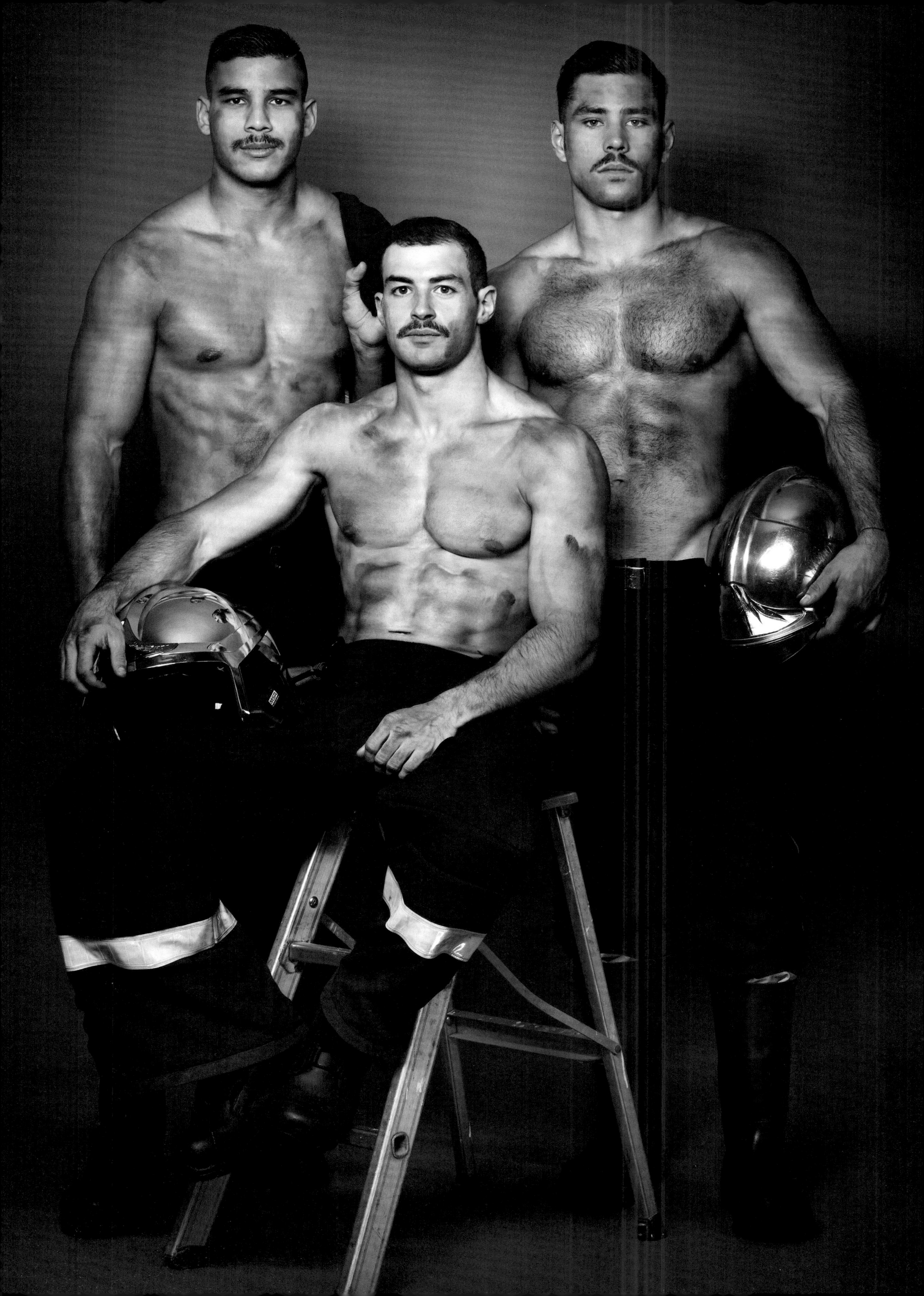

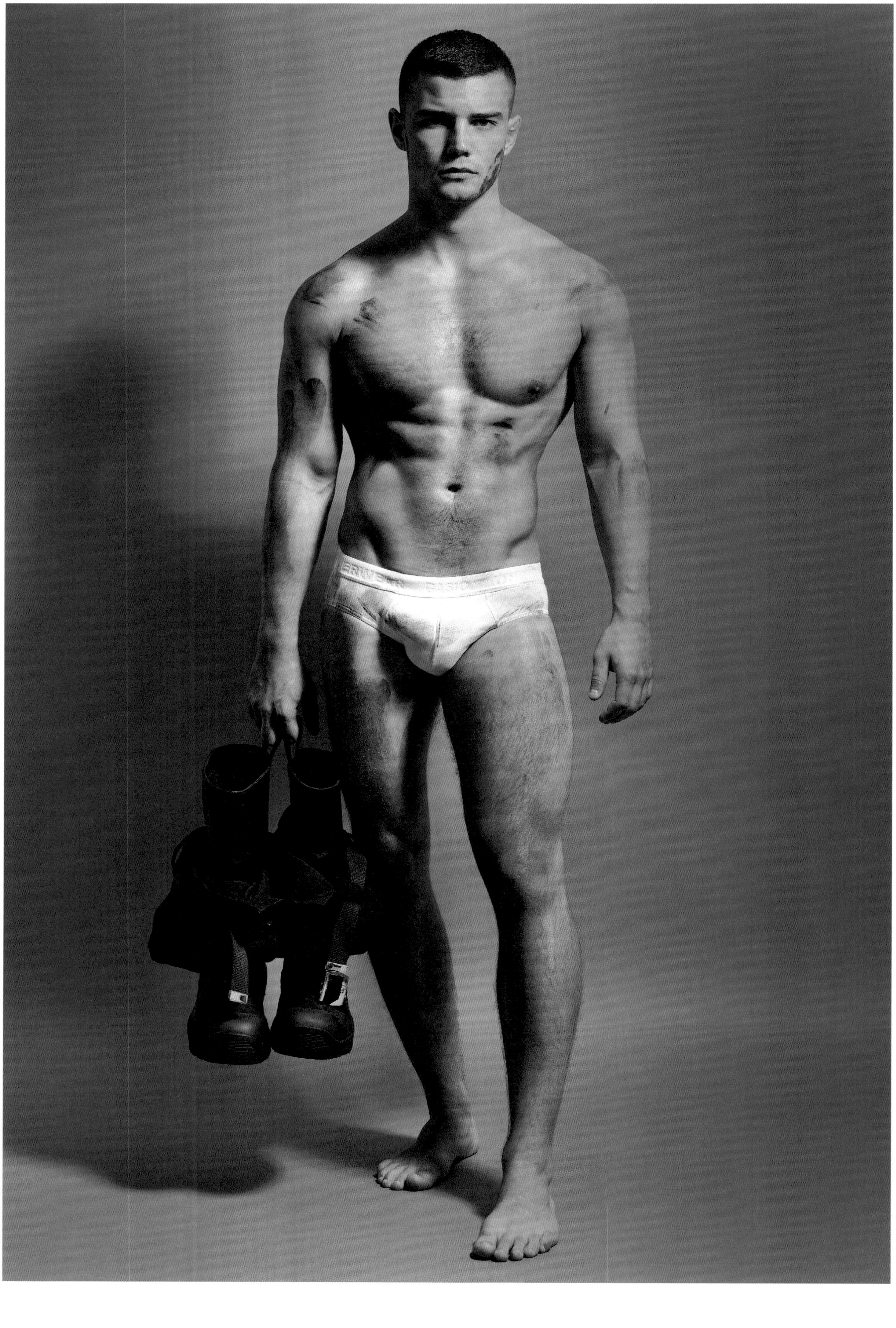

84

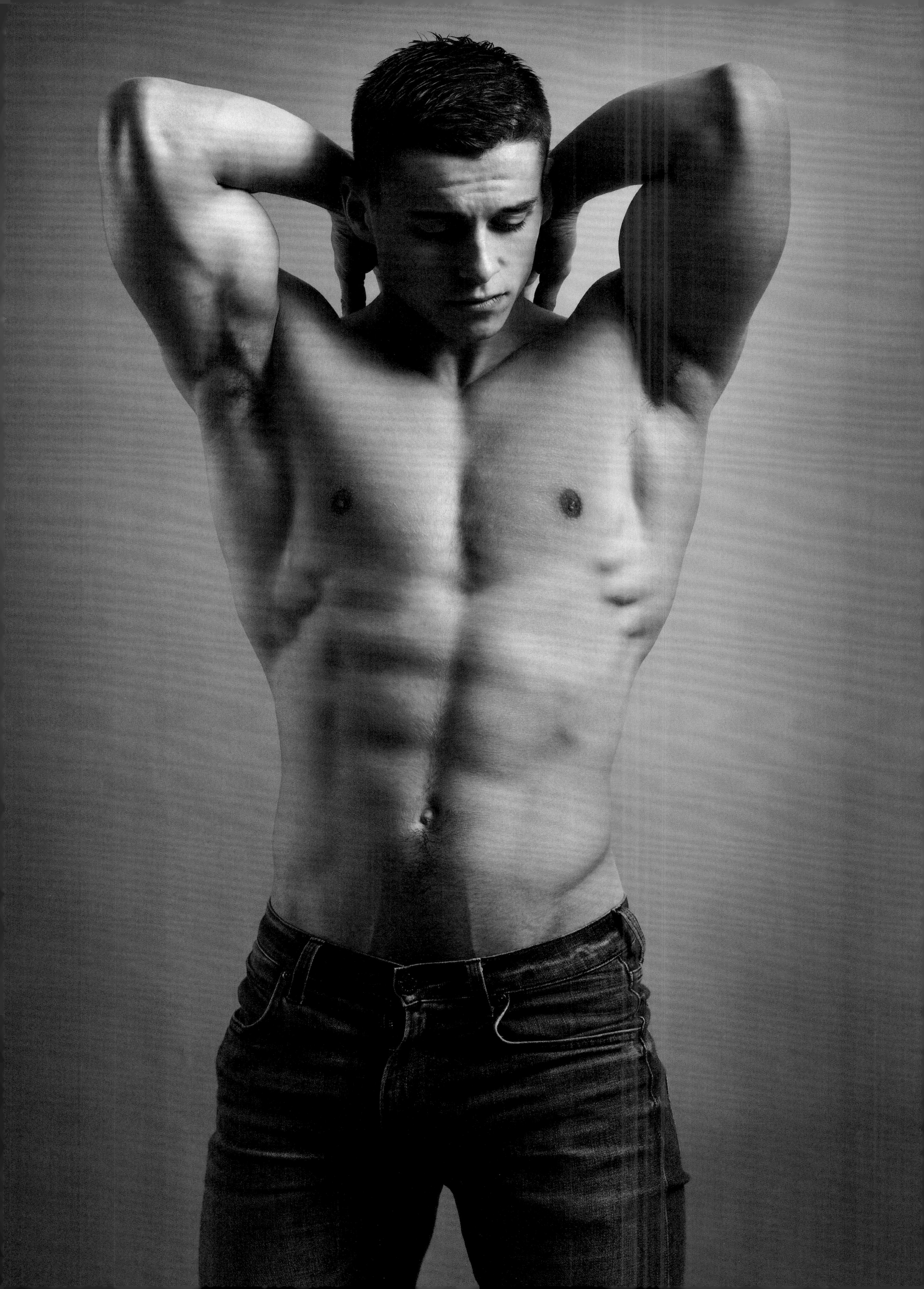

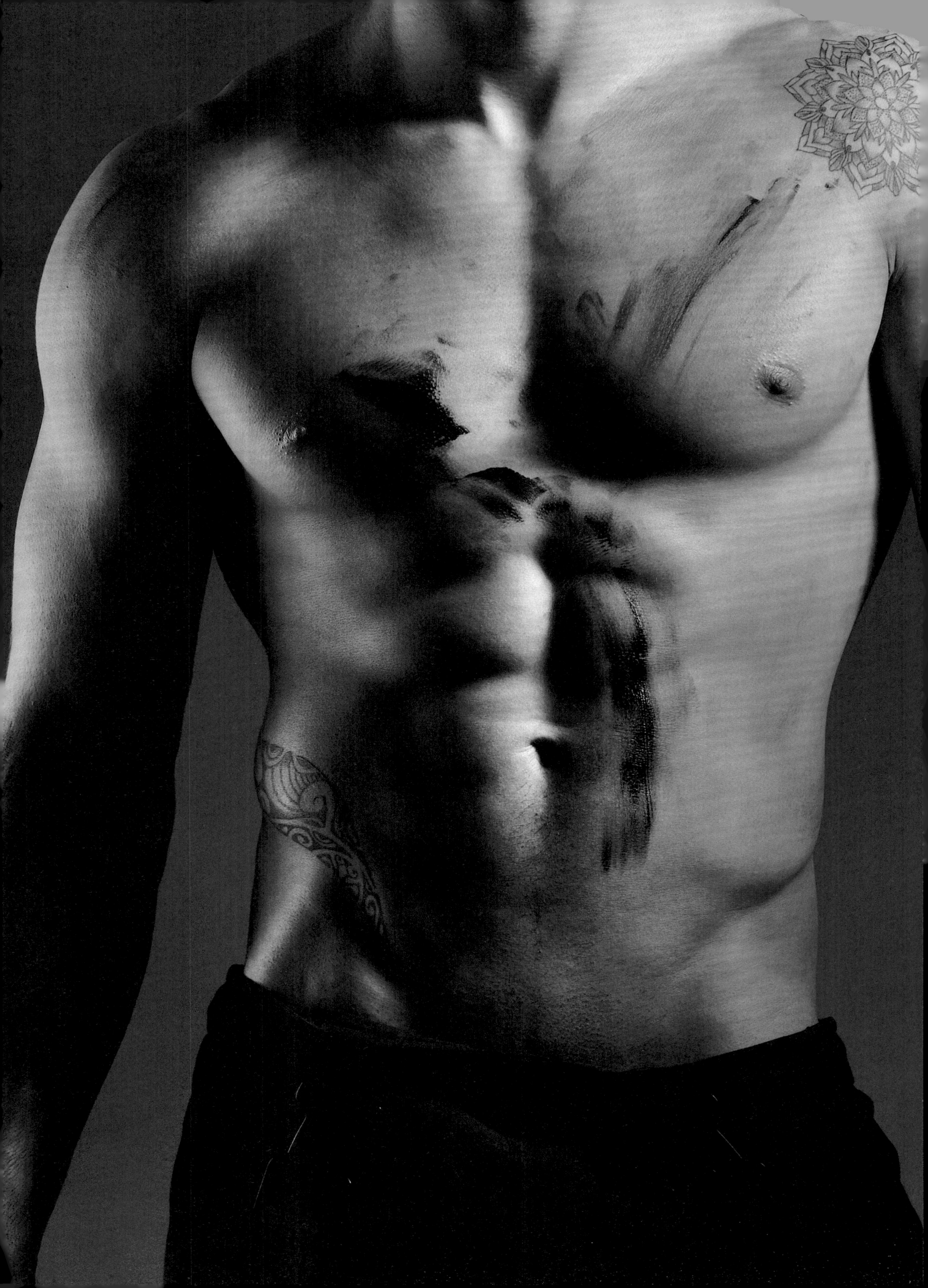

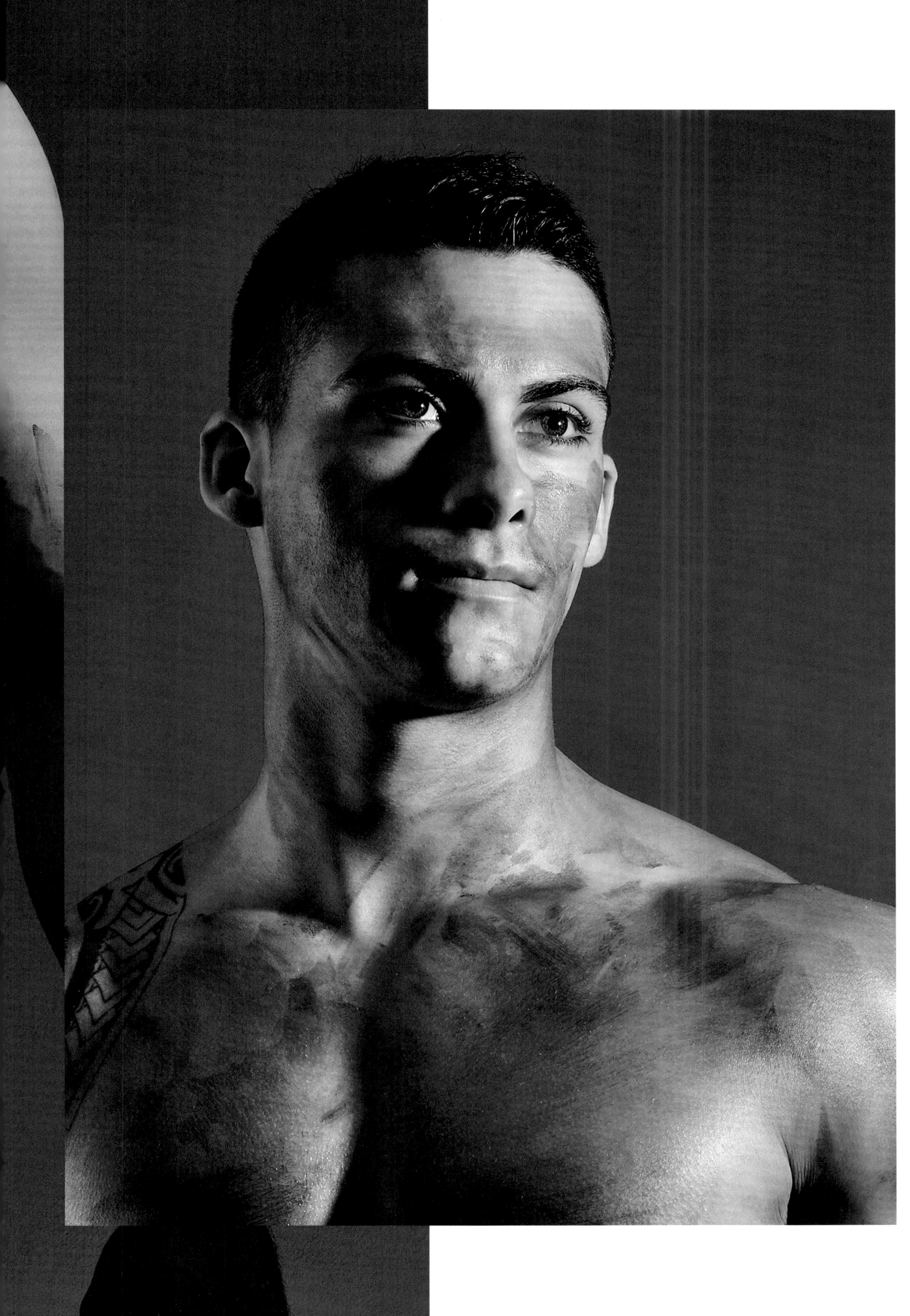

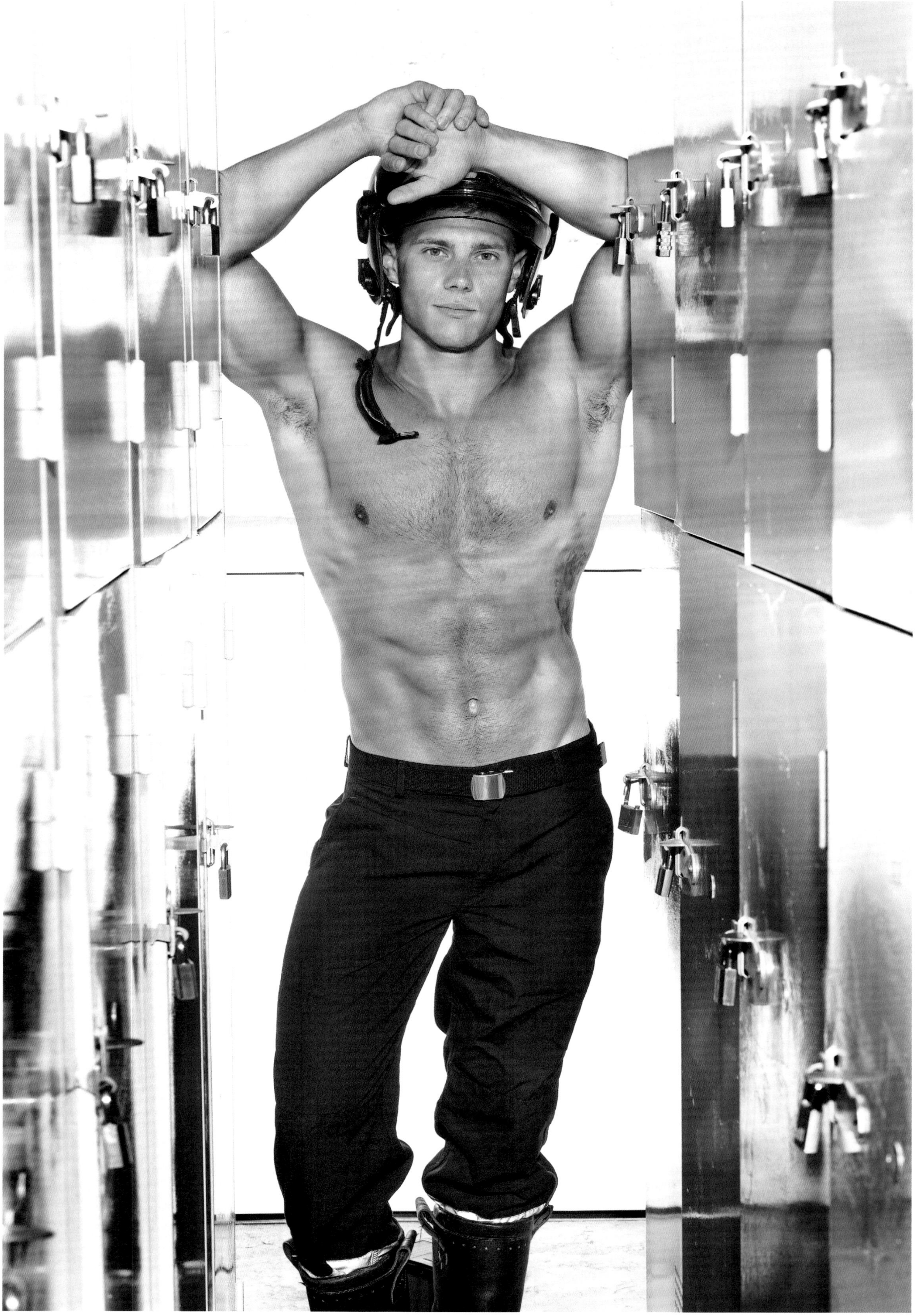

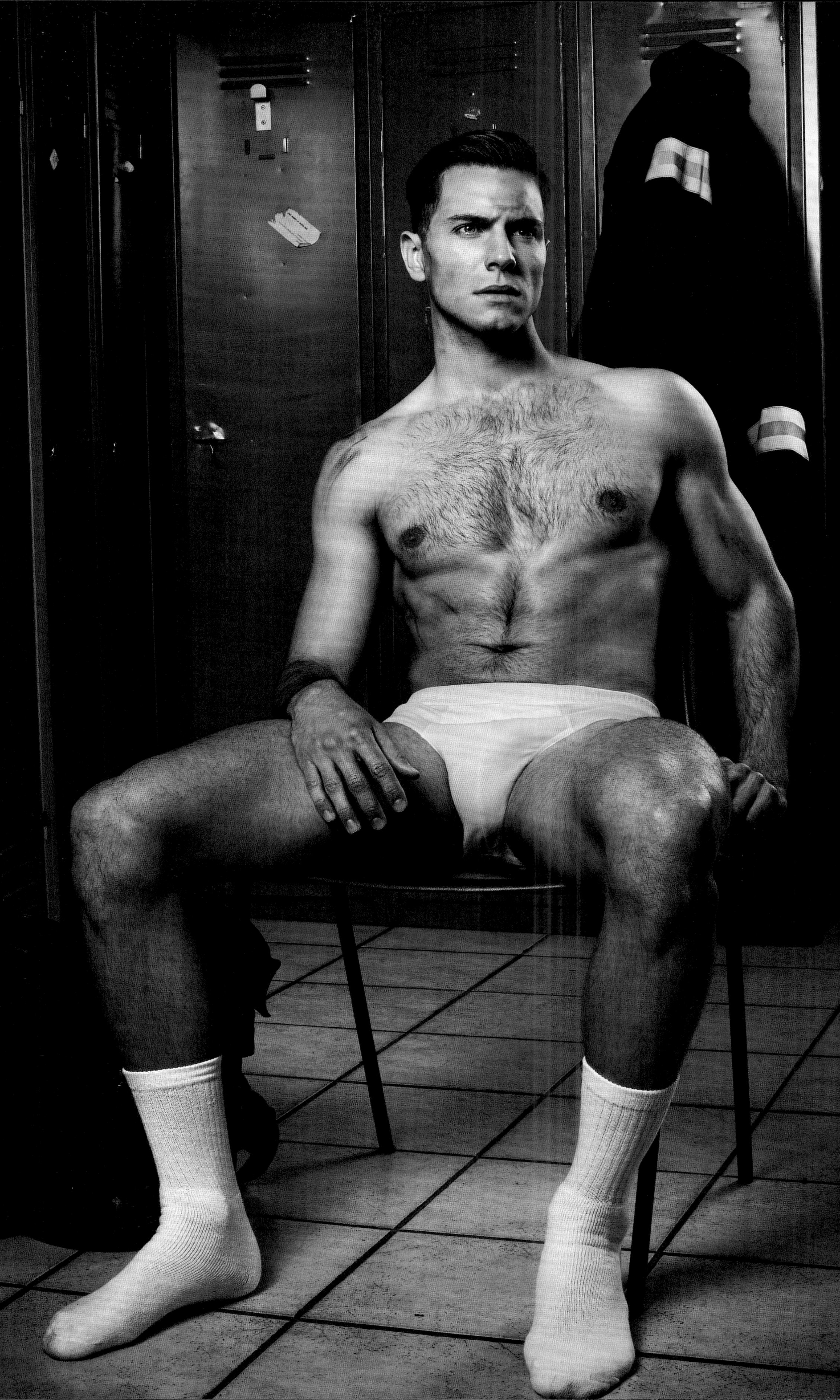

90

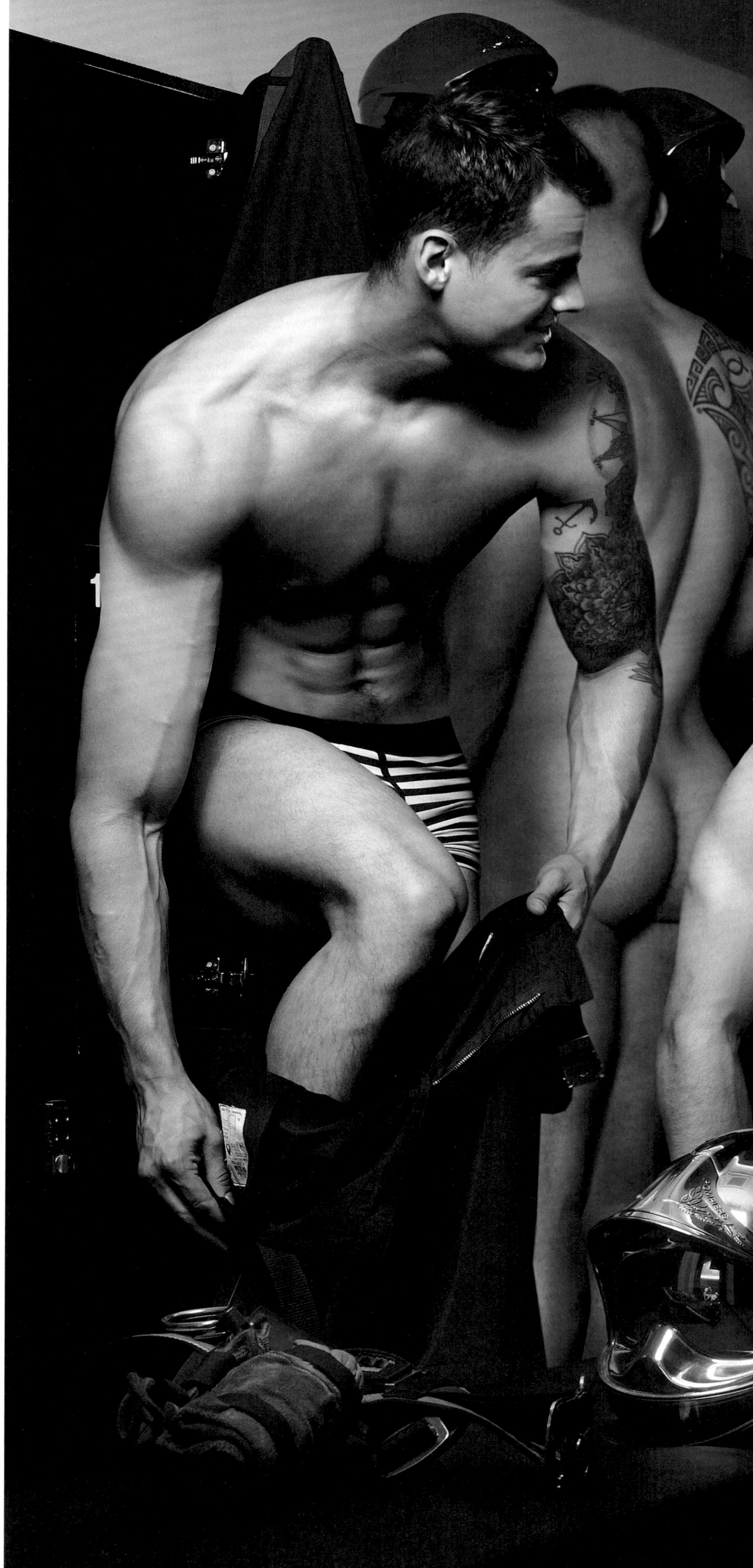

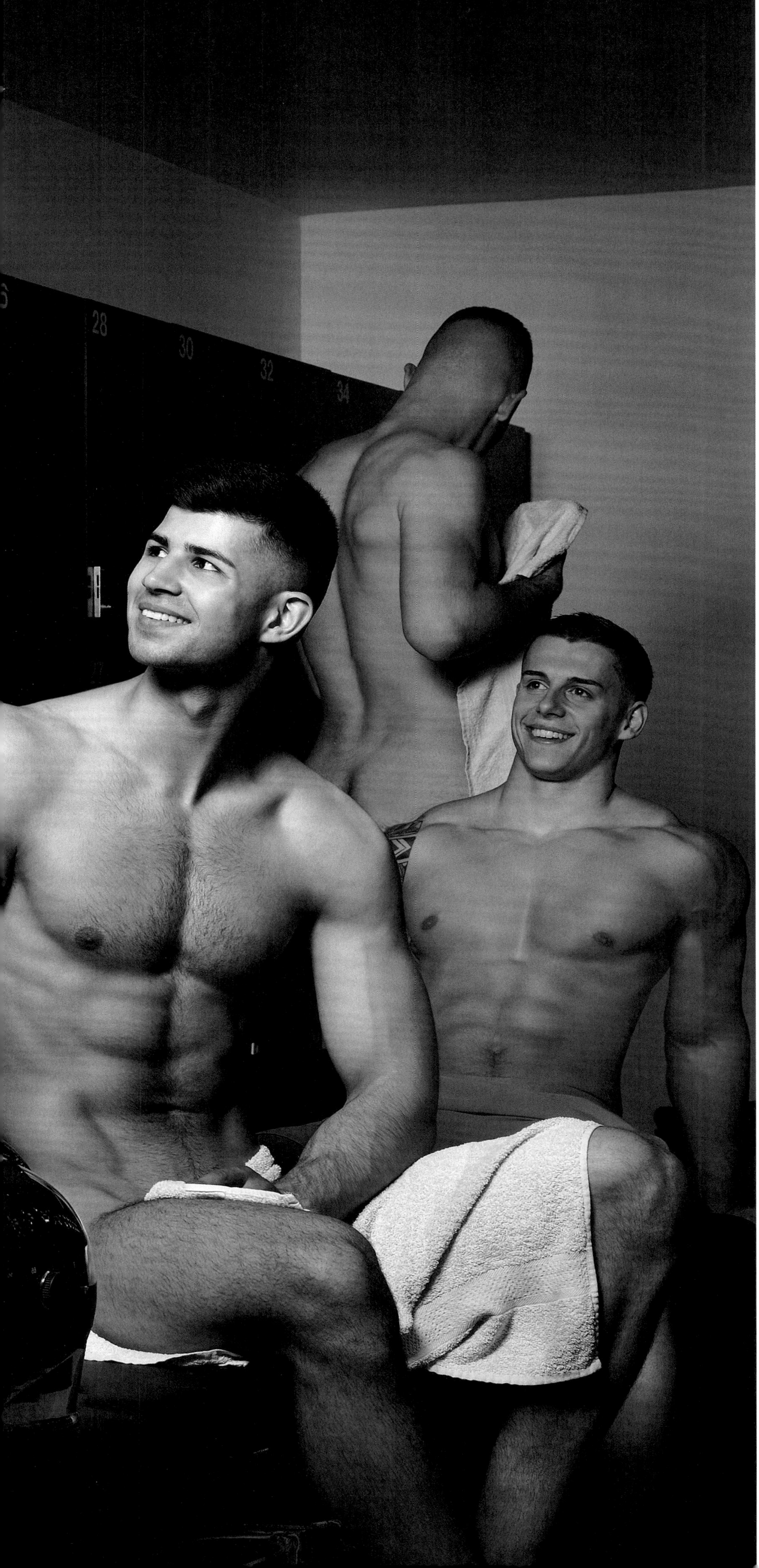

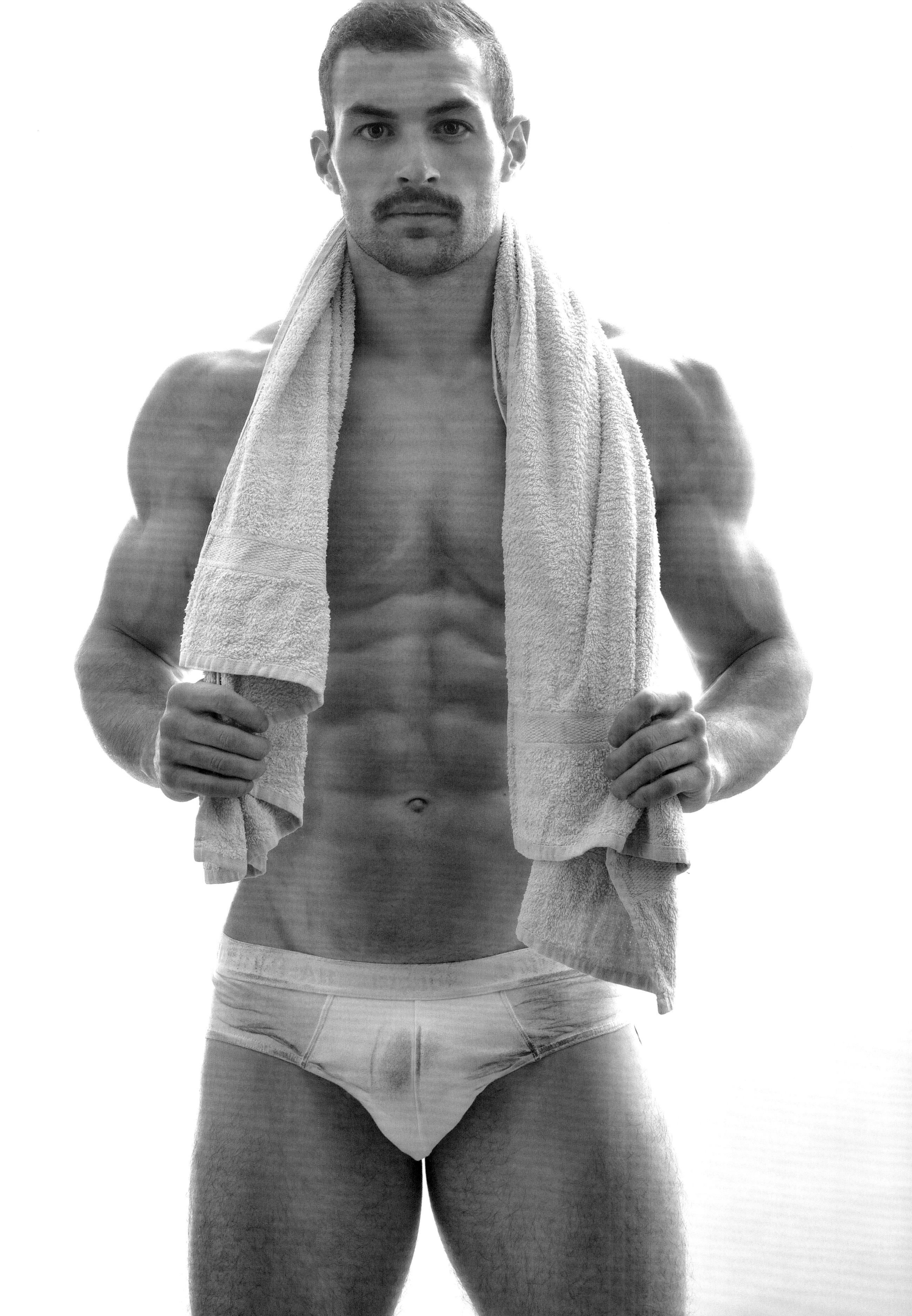

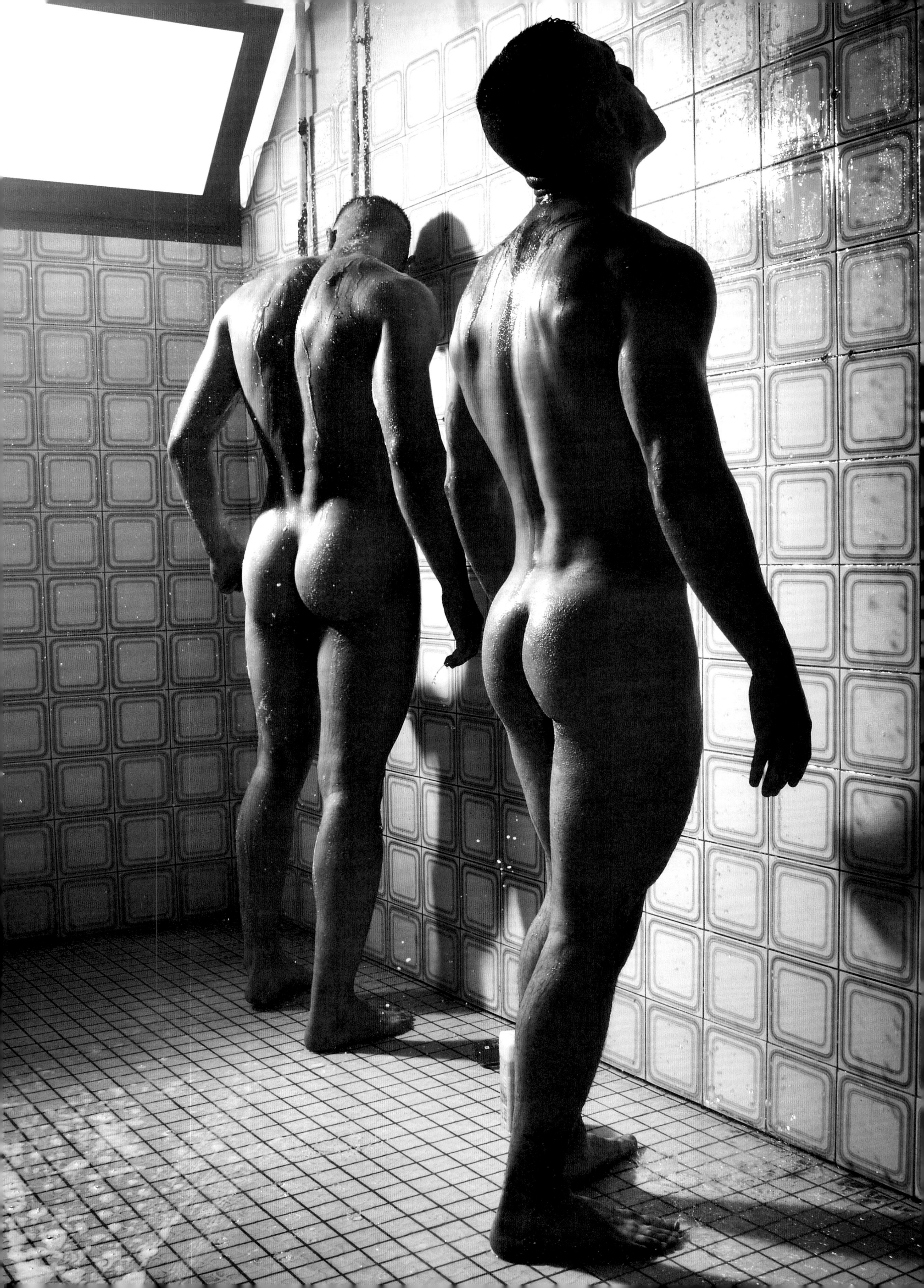

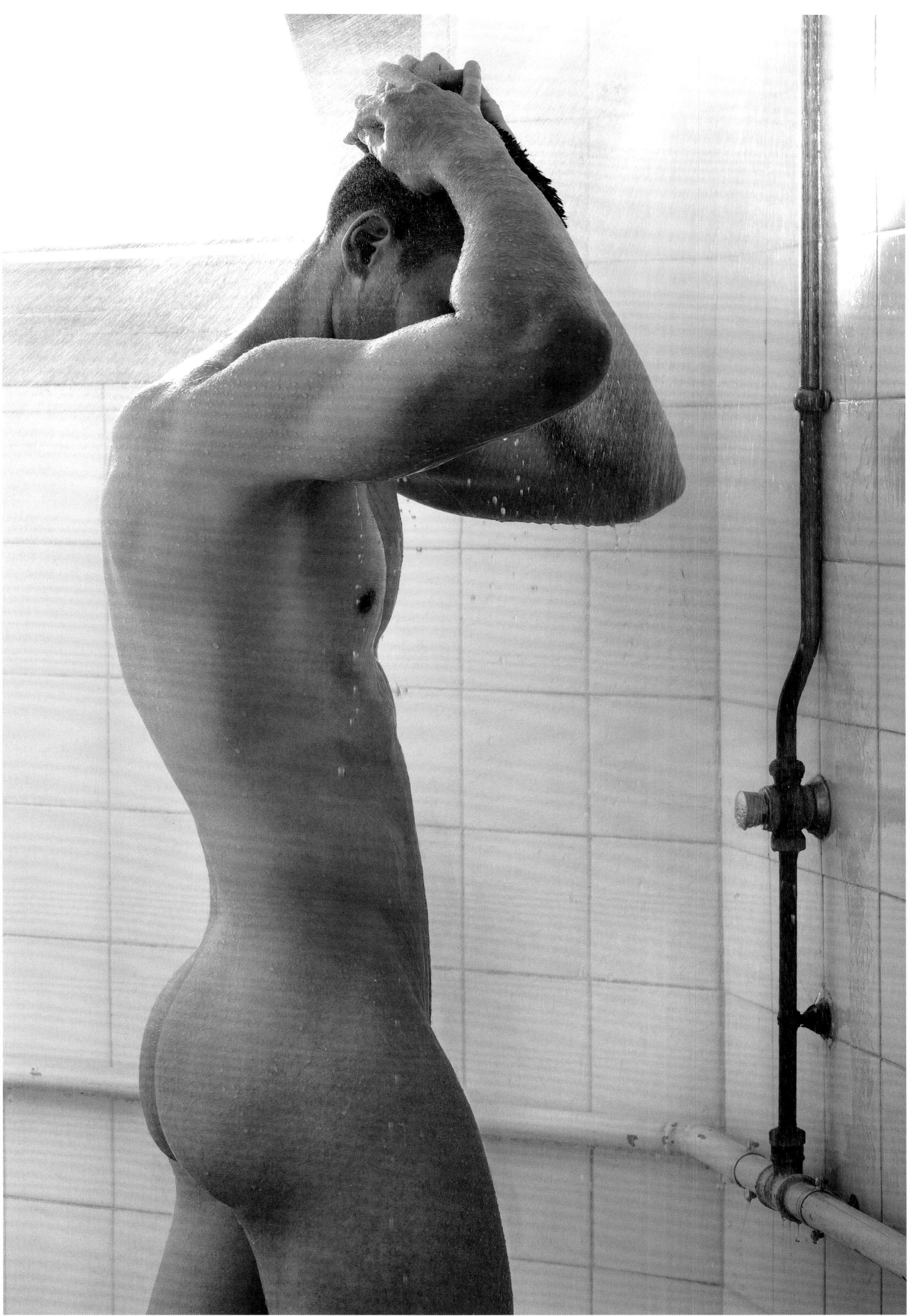

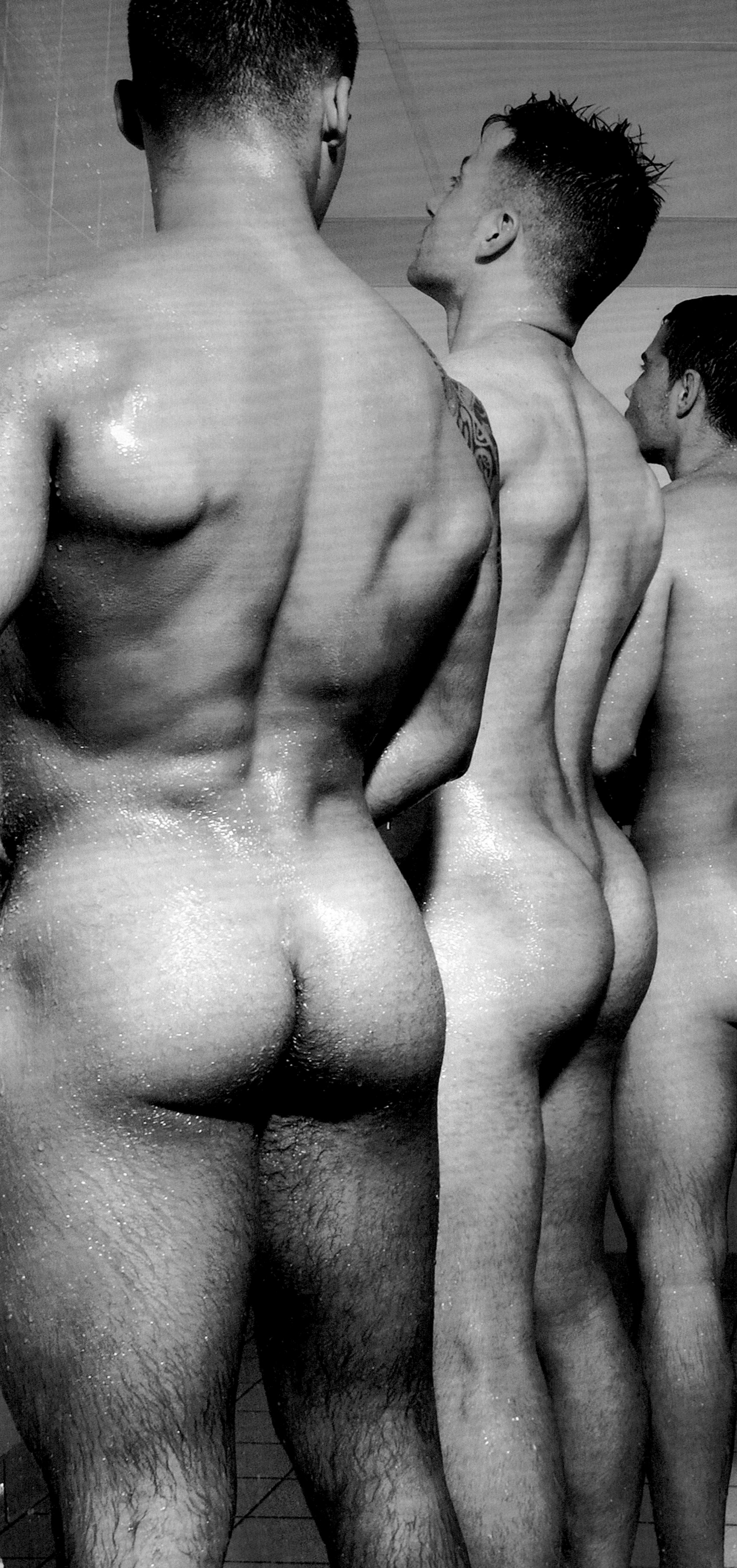

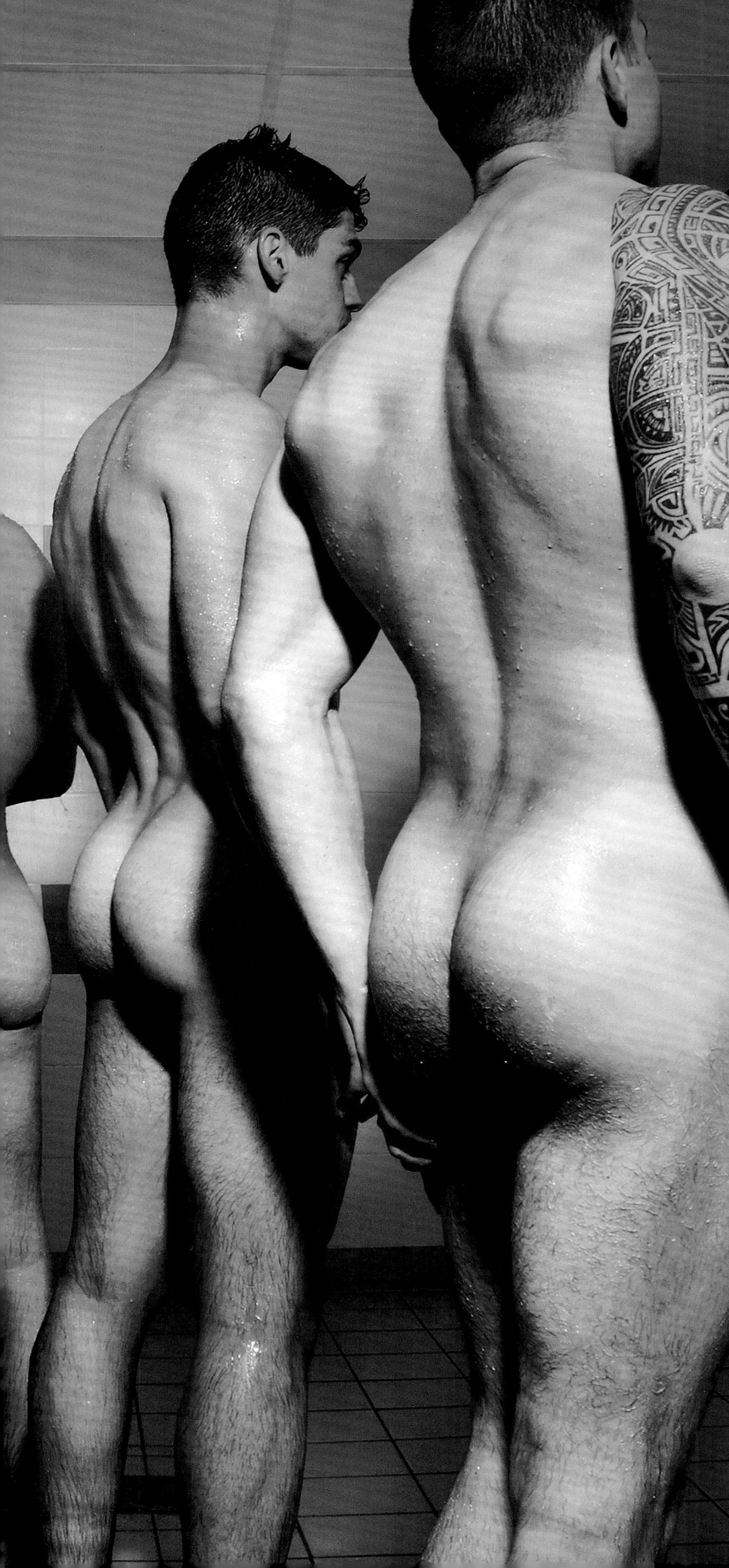

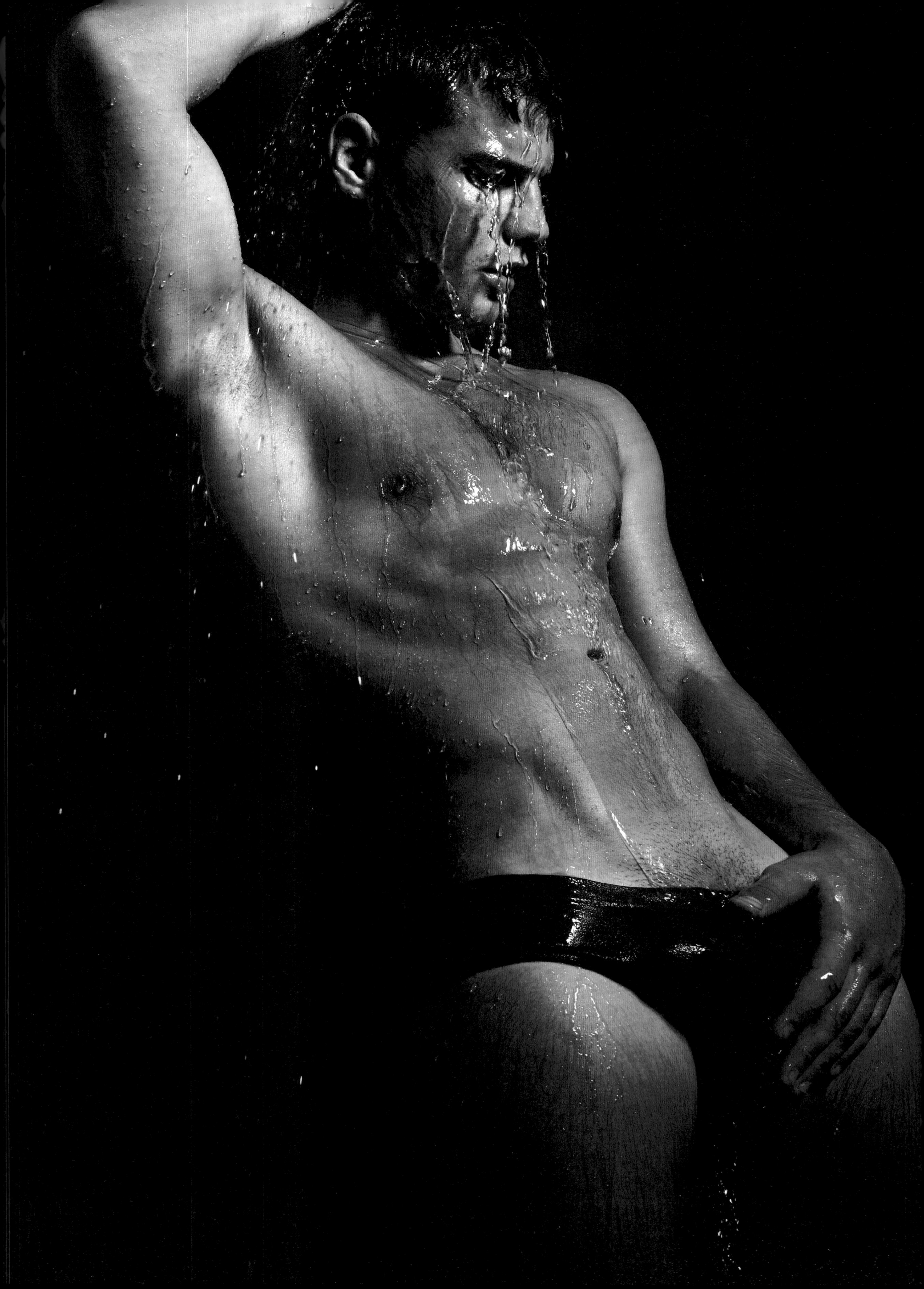

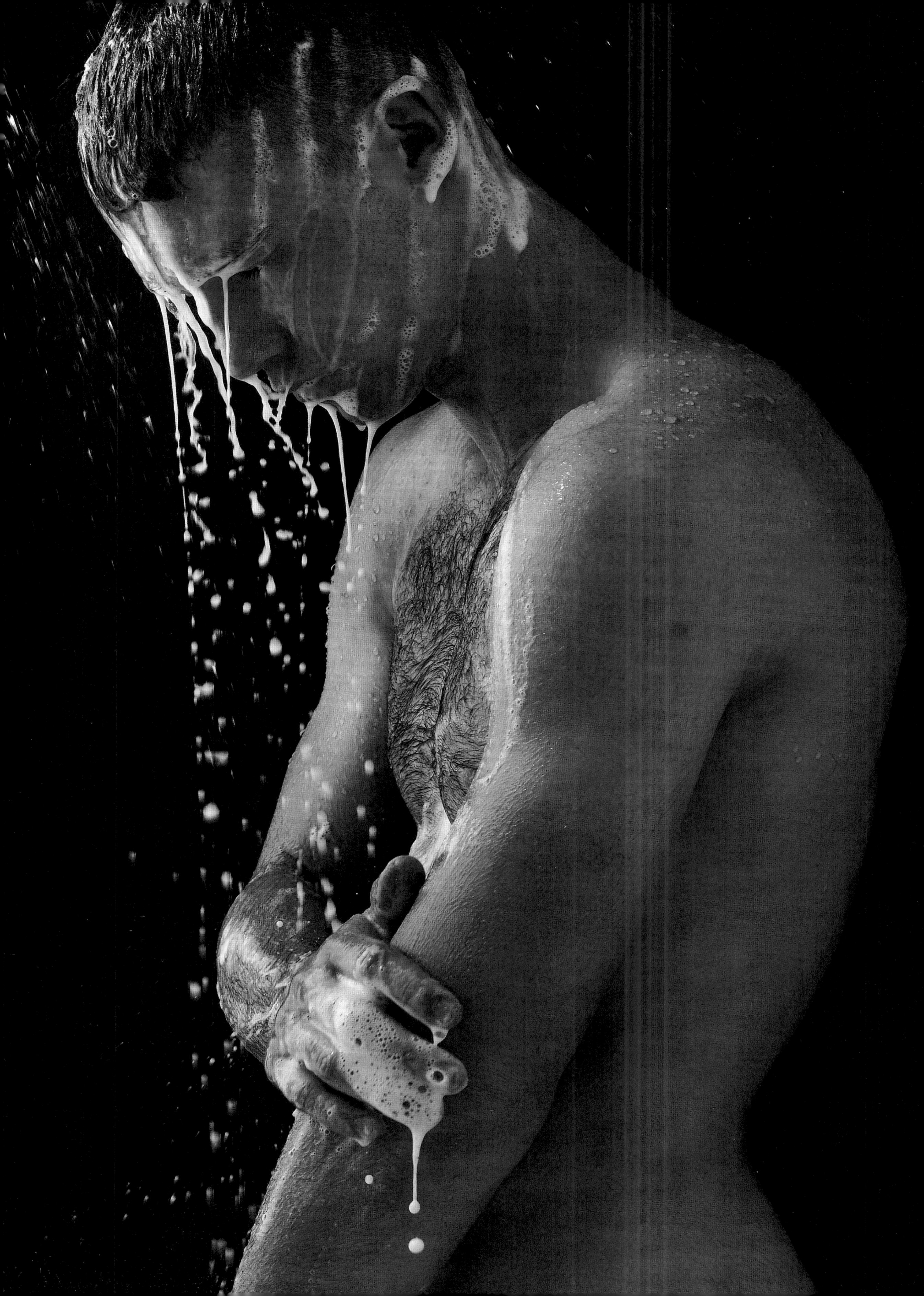

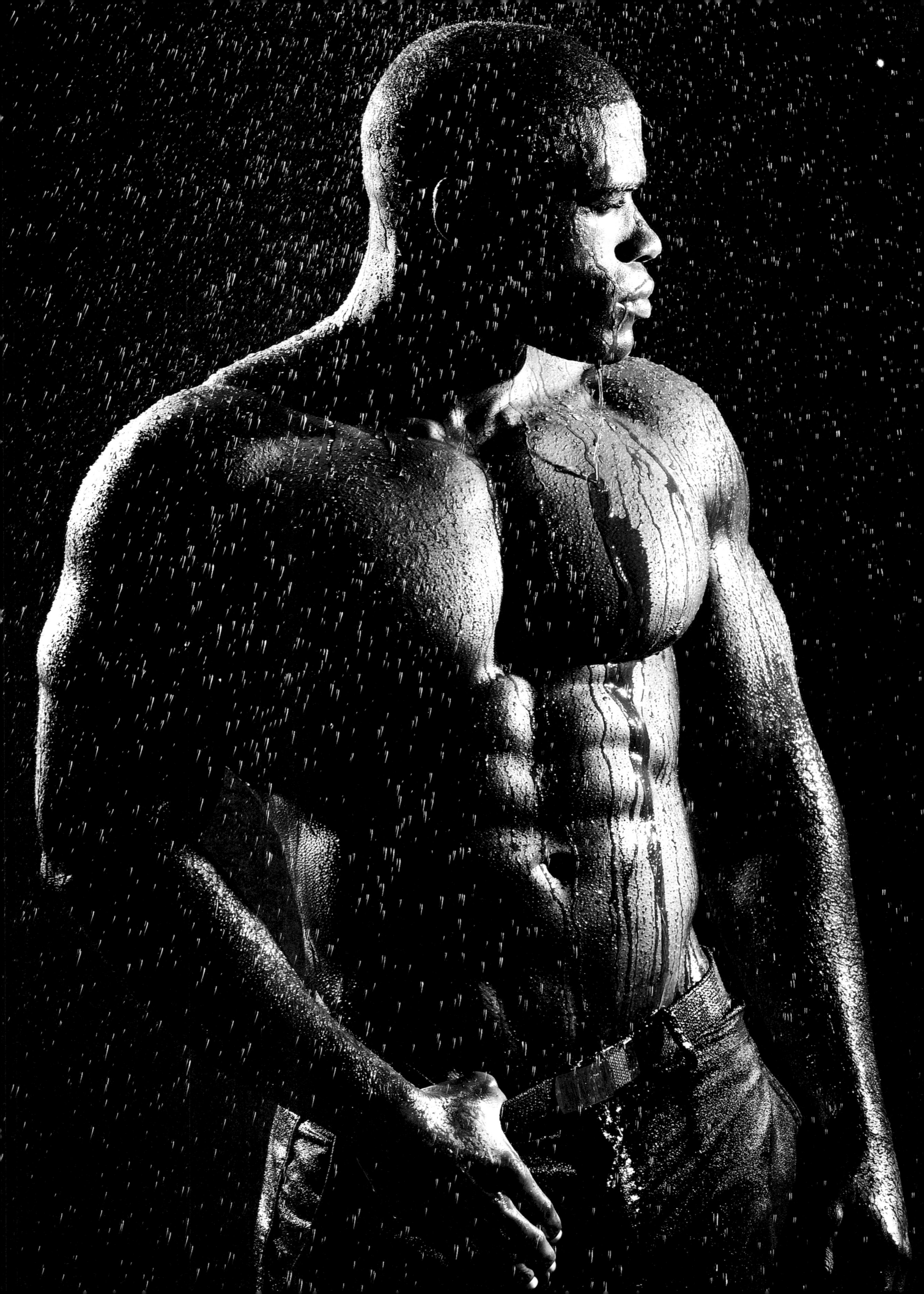

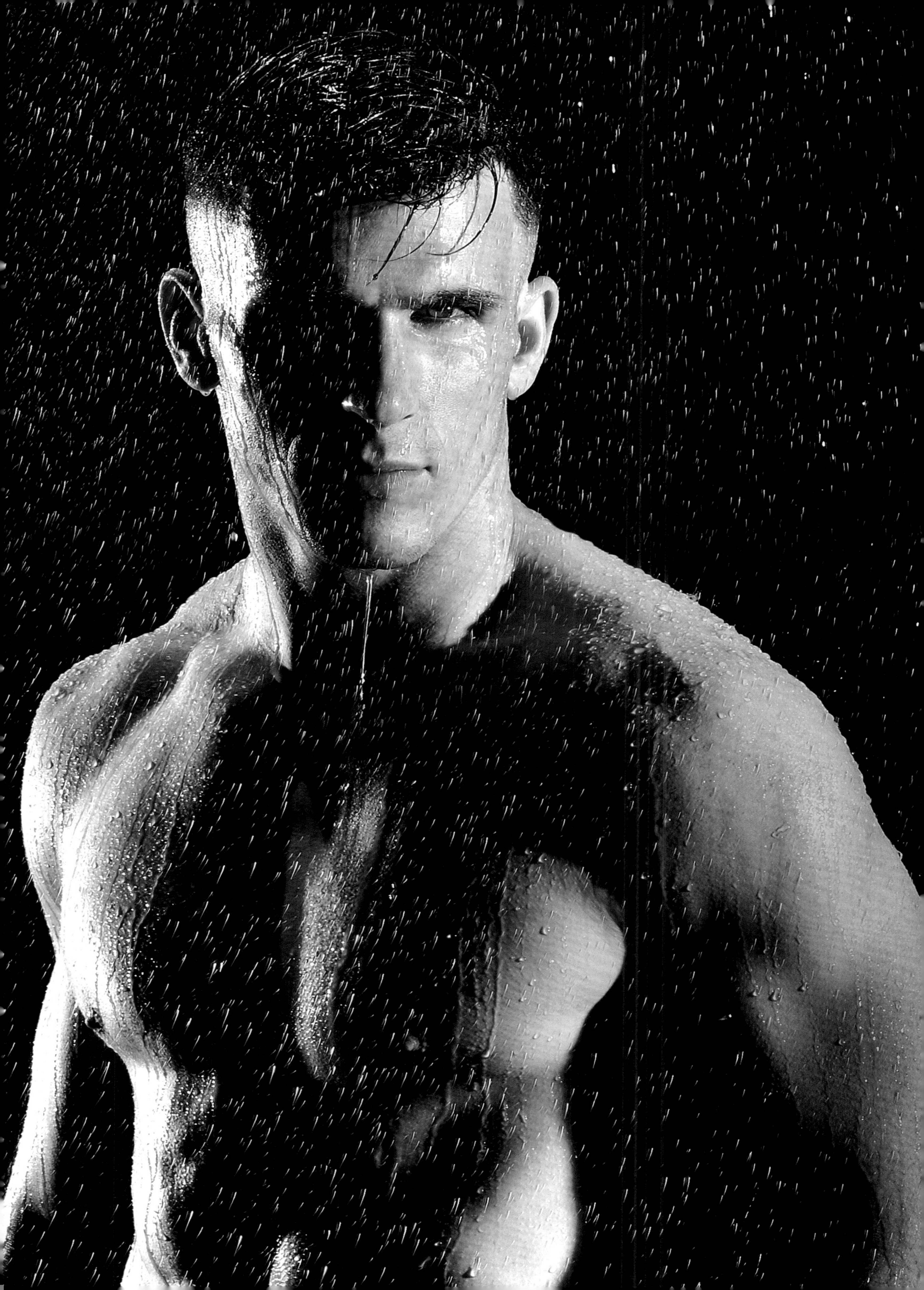

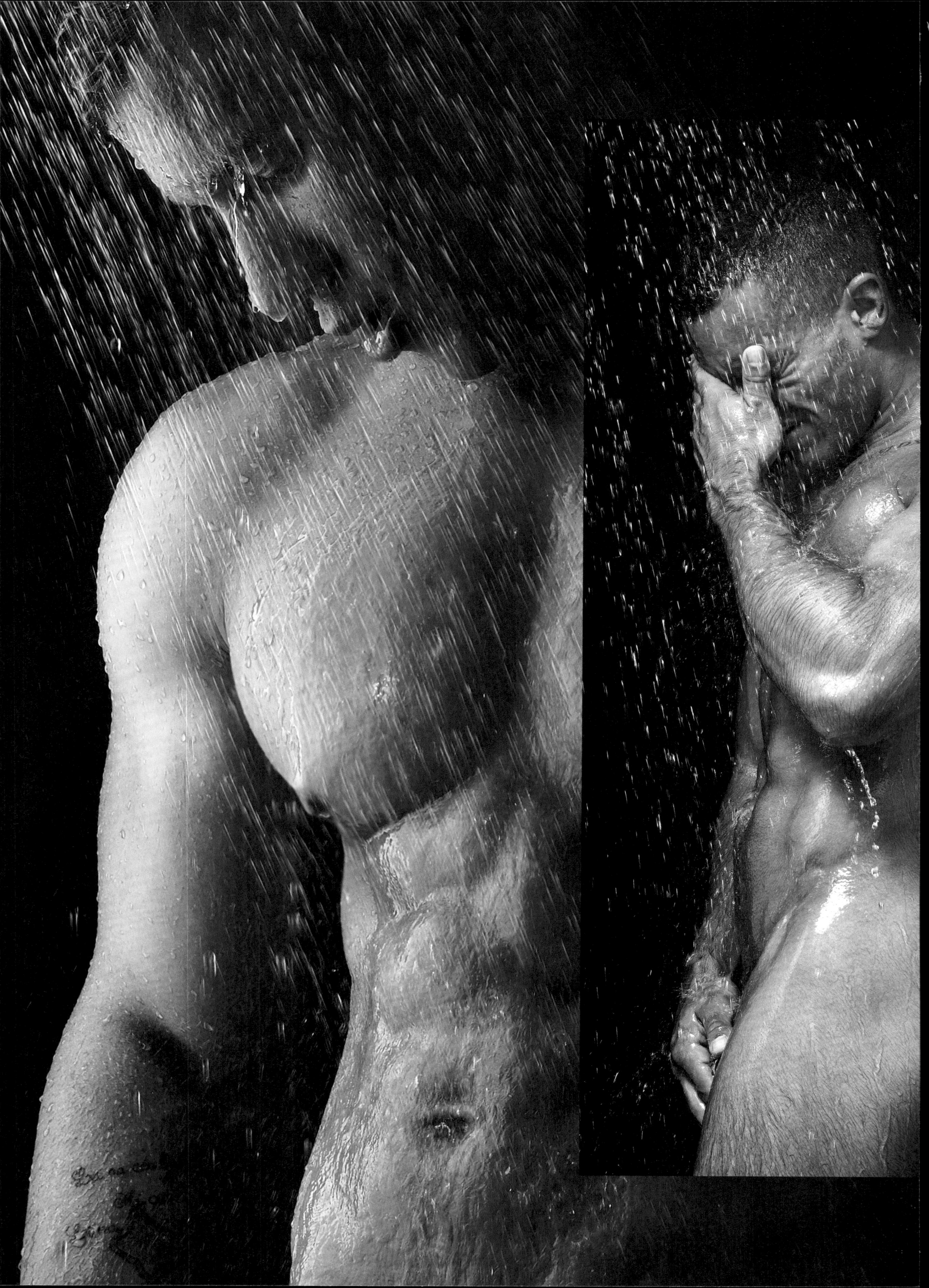

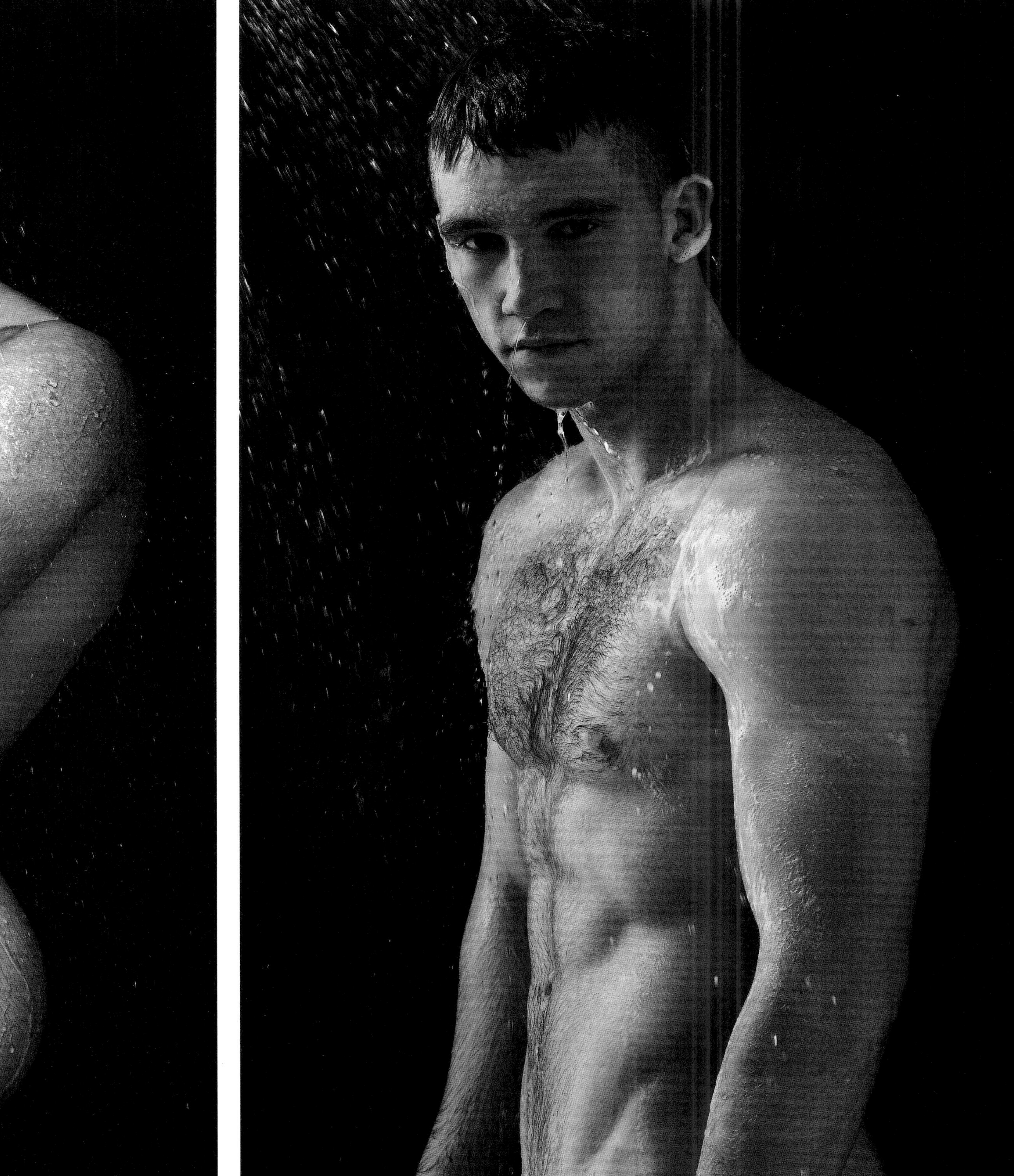

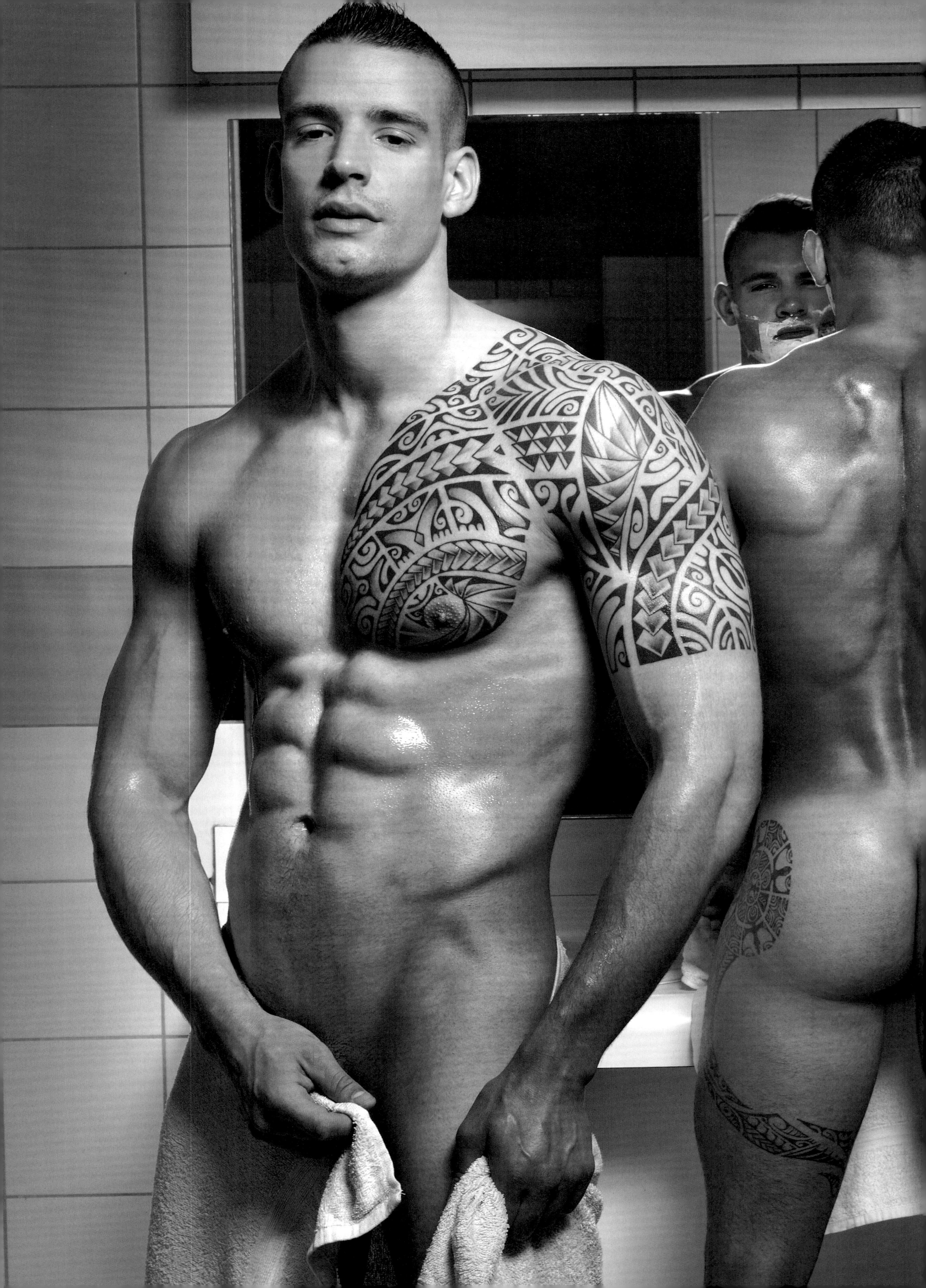

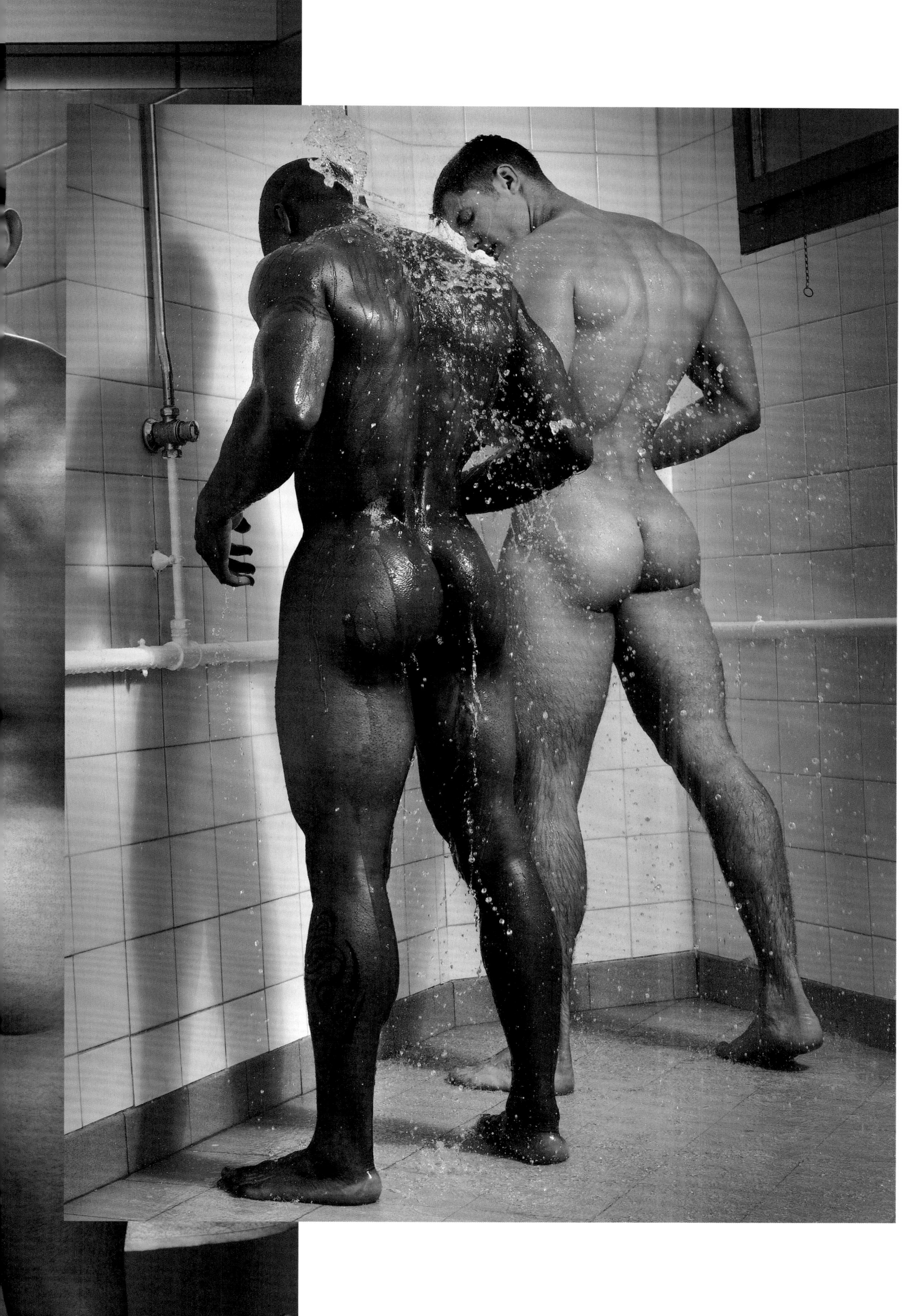

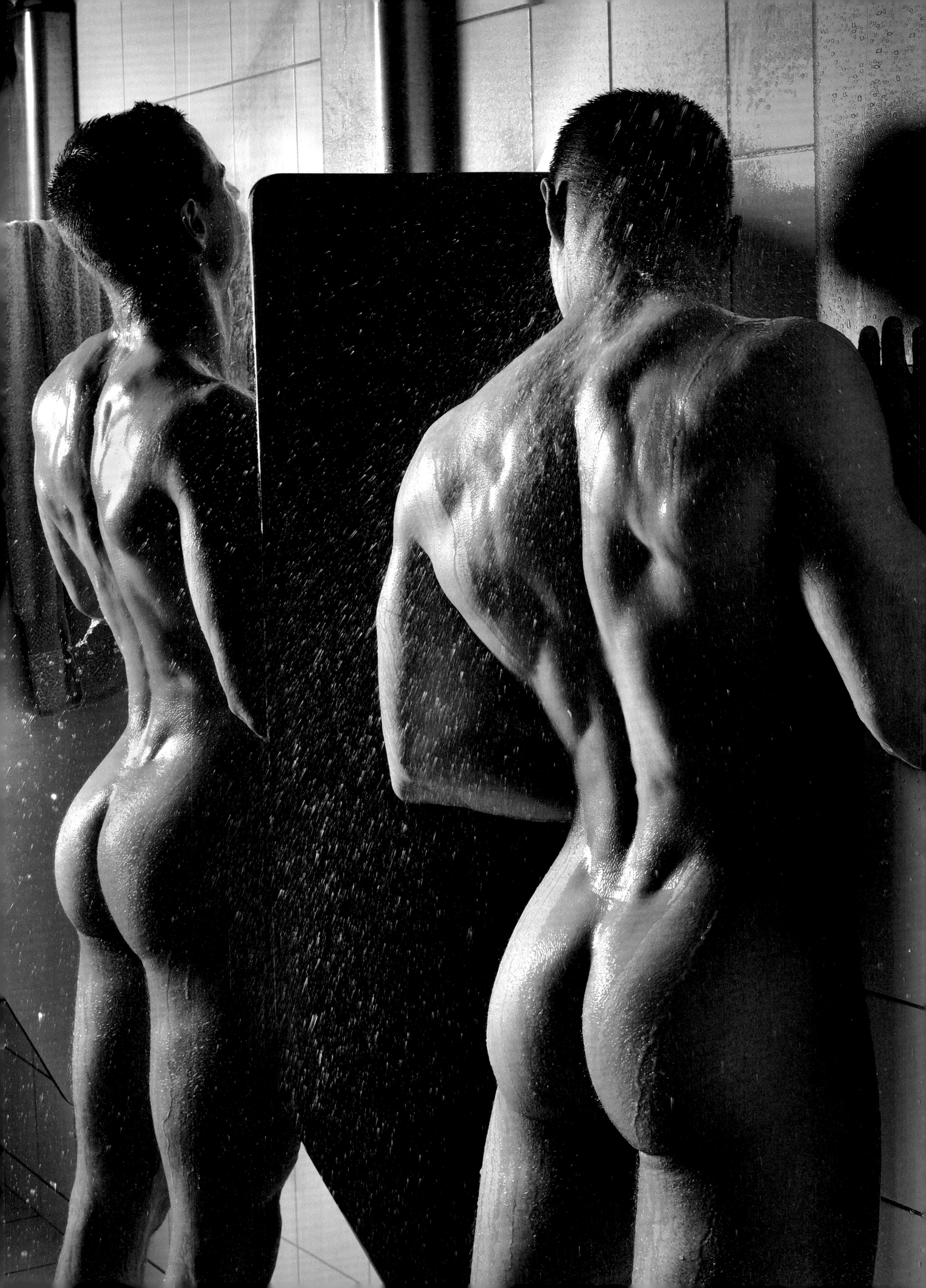

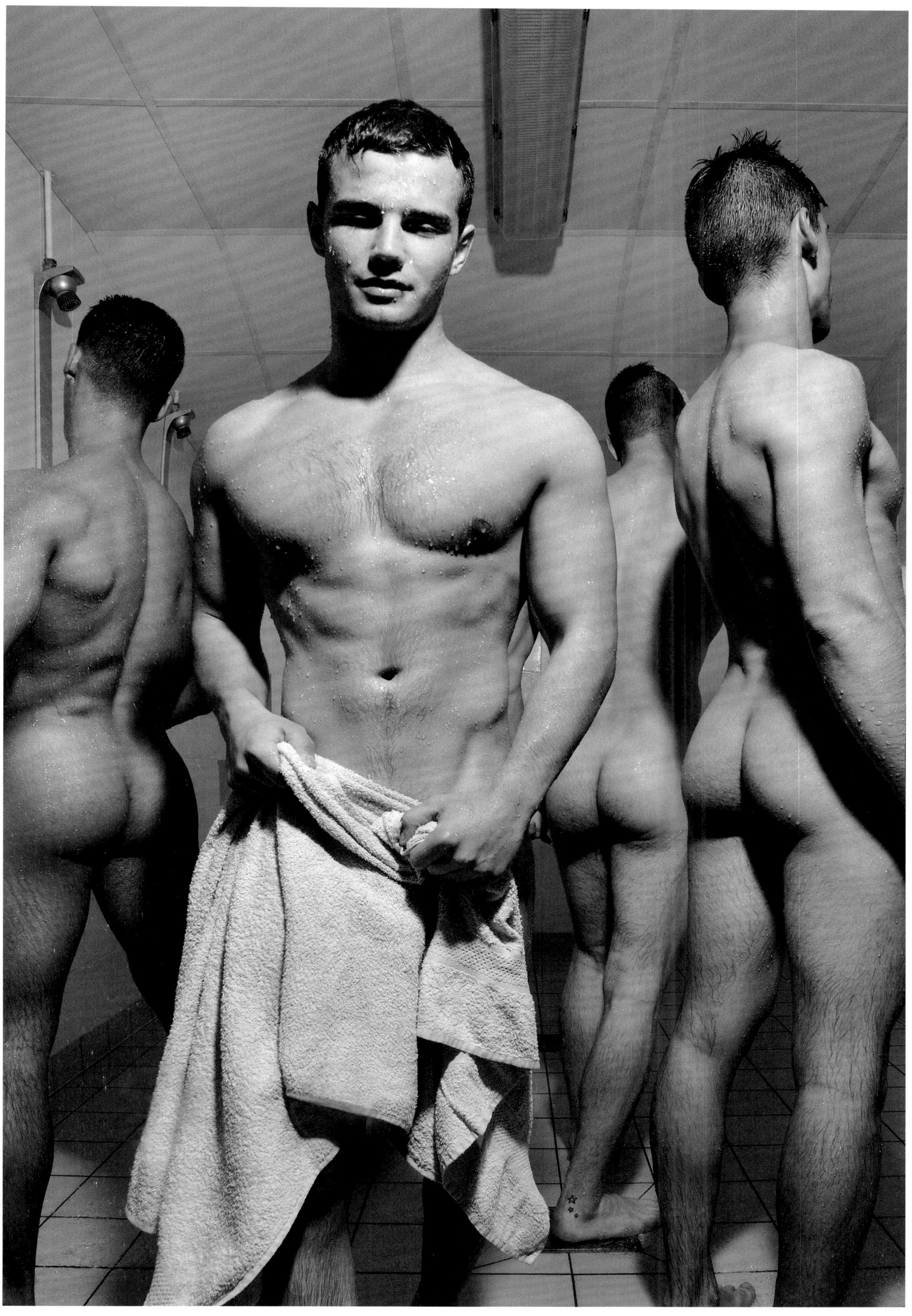

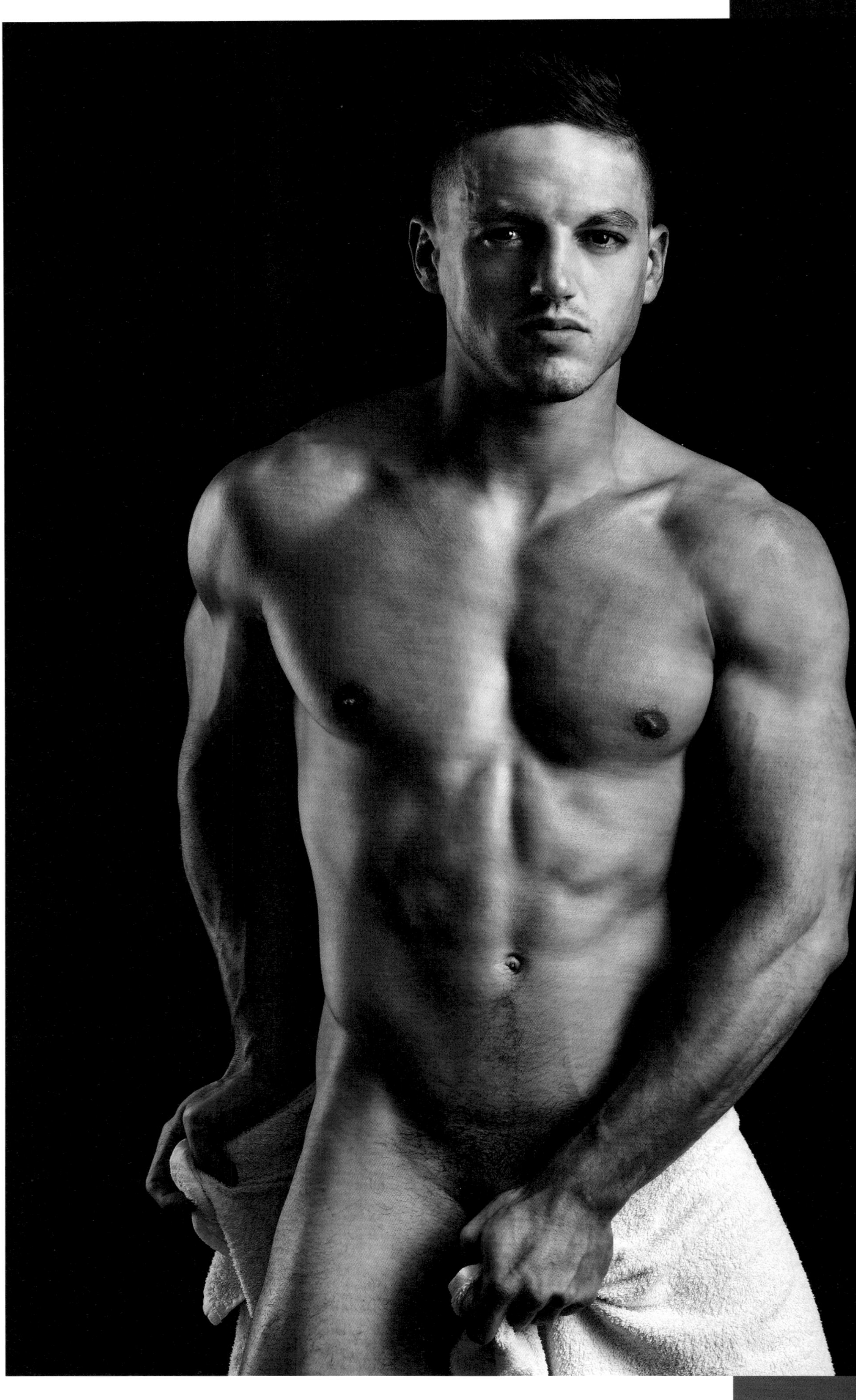

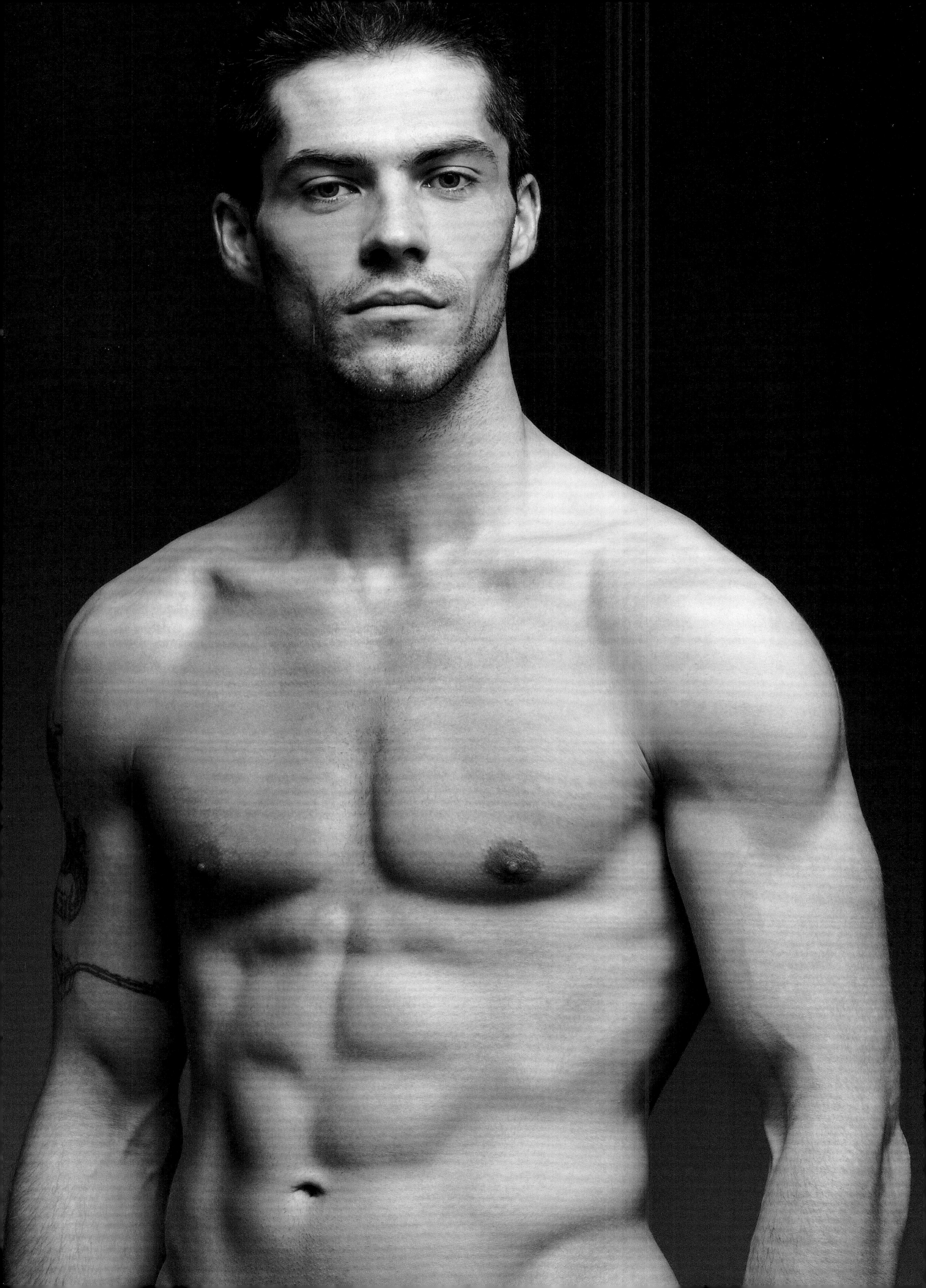

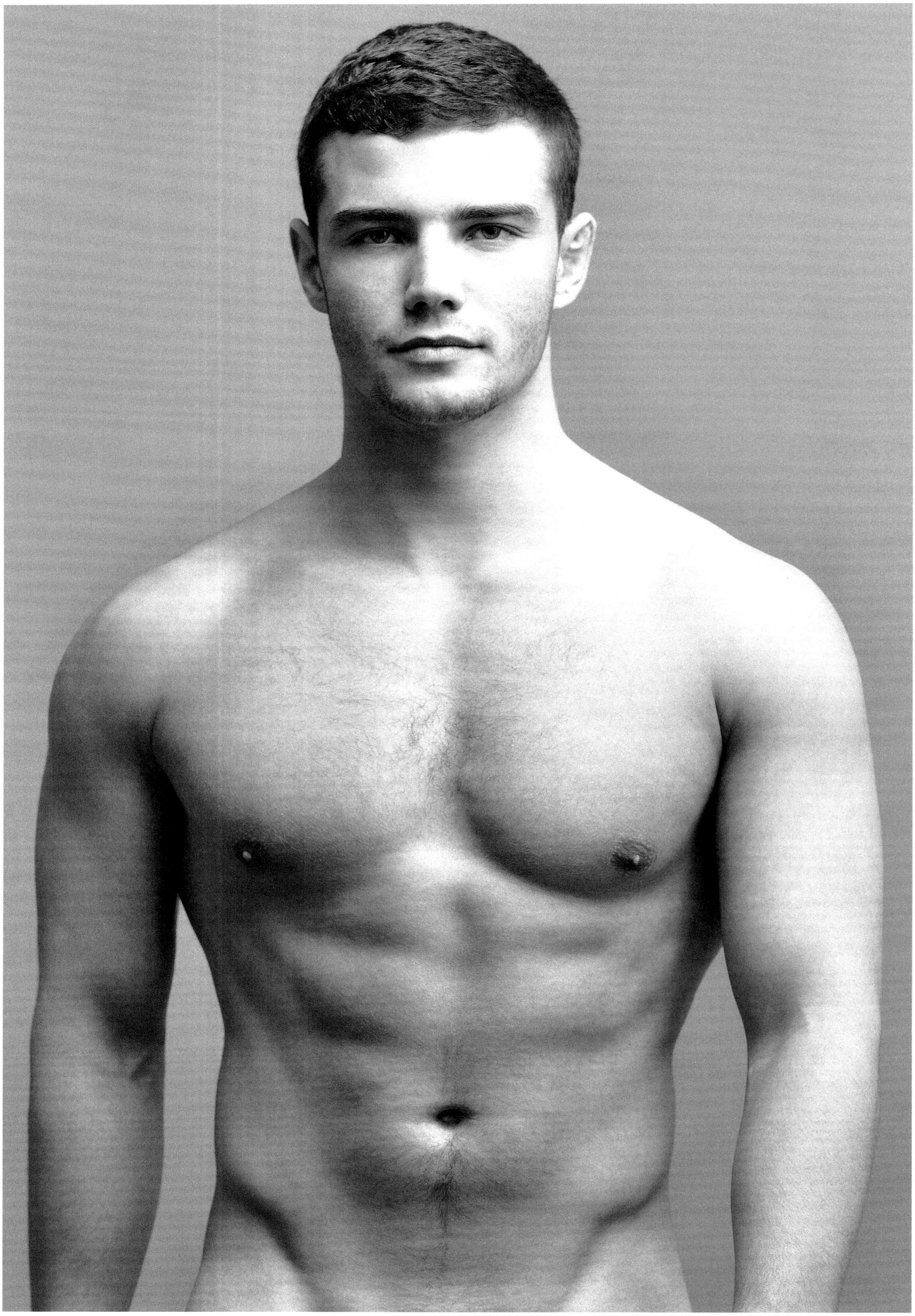

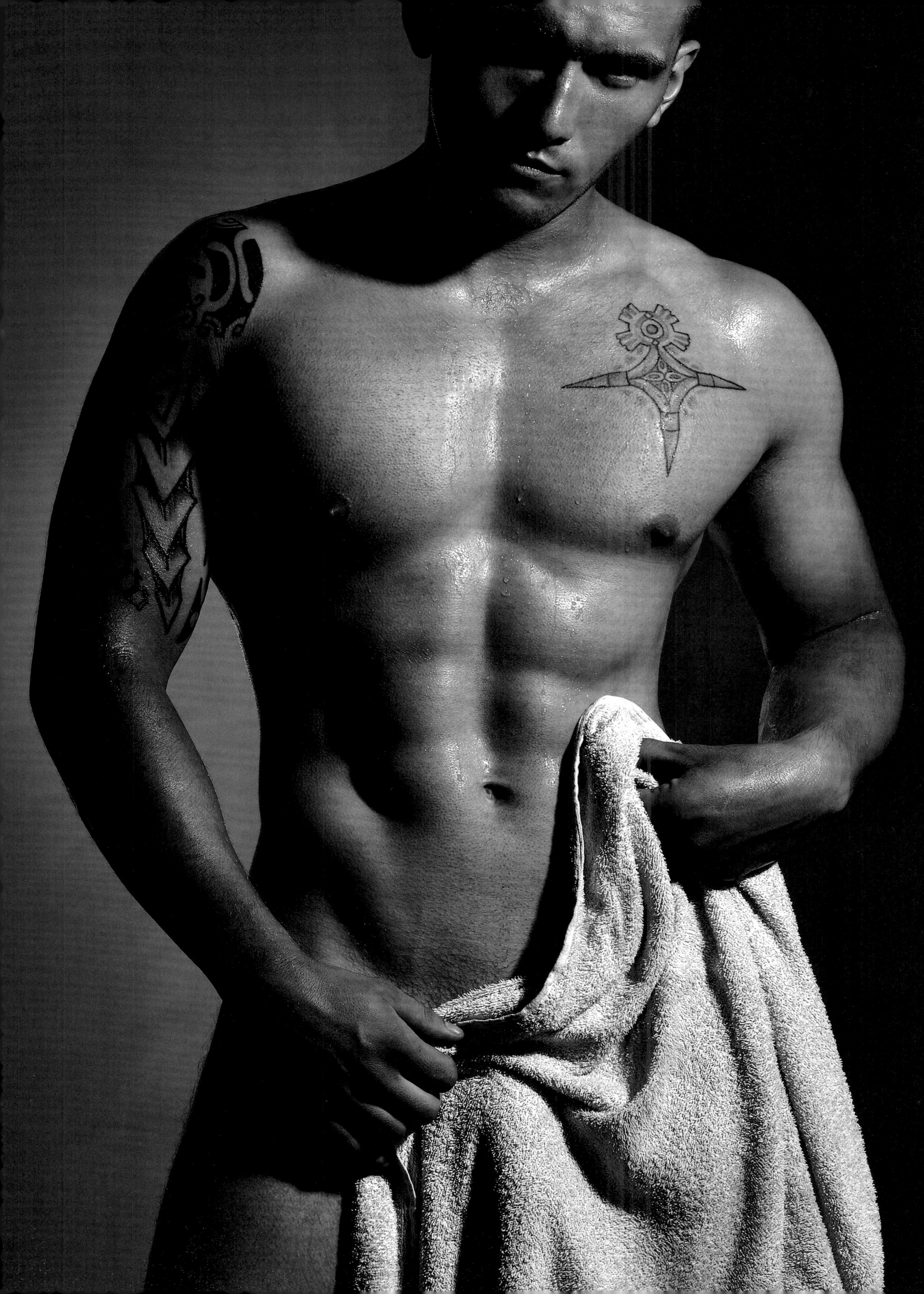

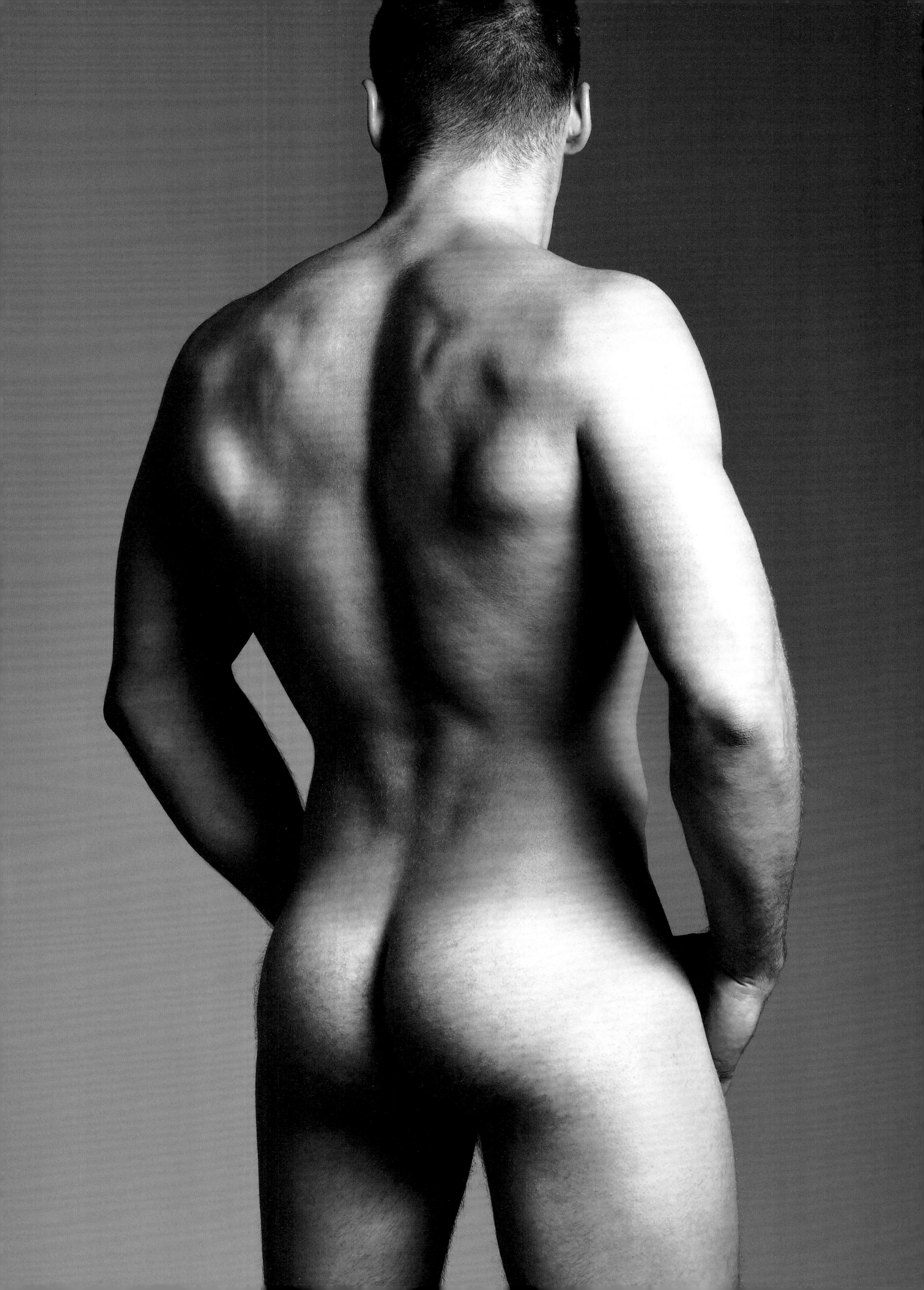

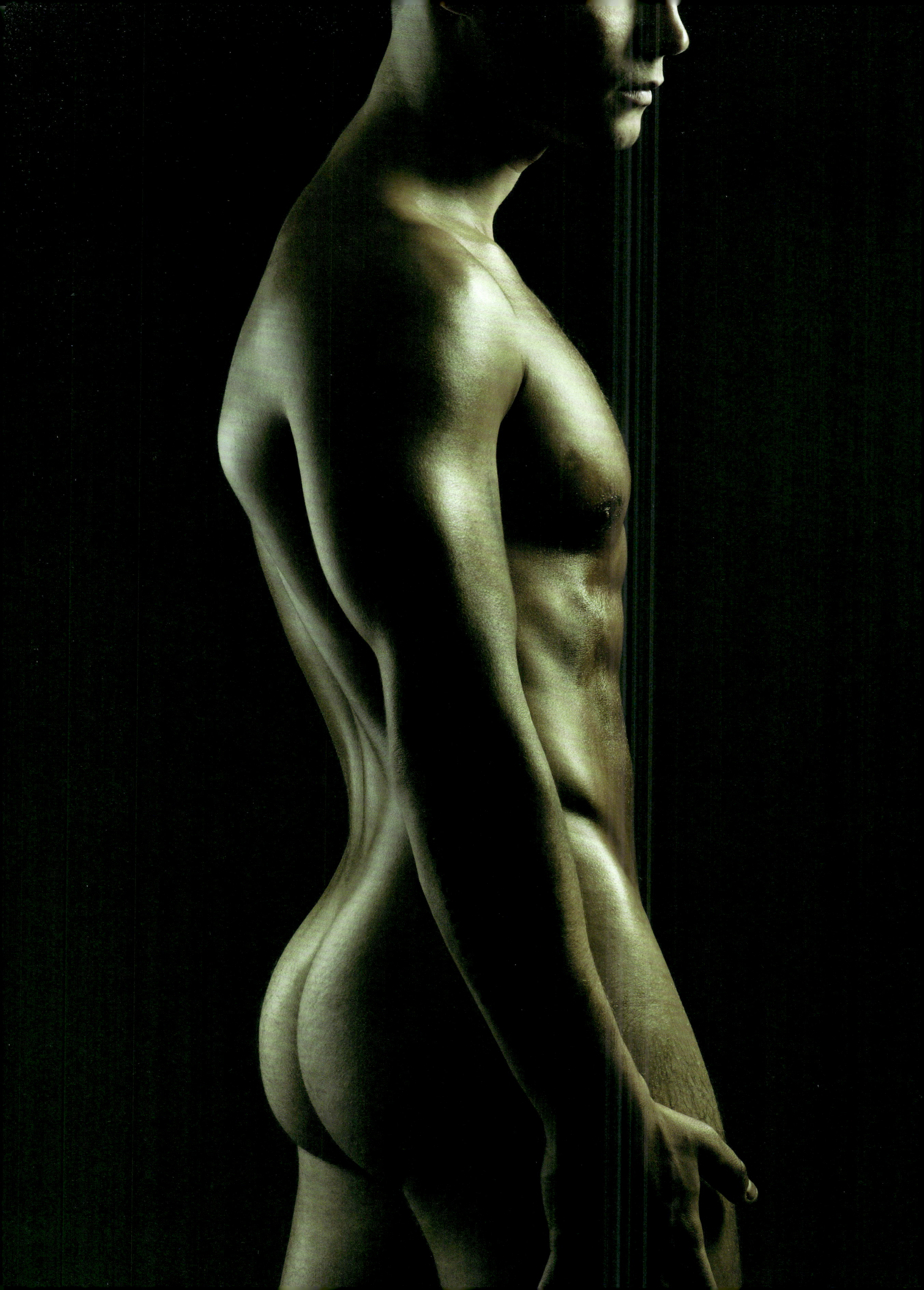

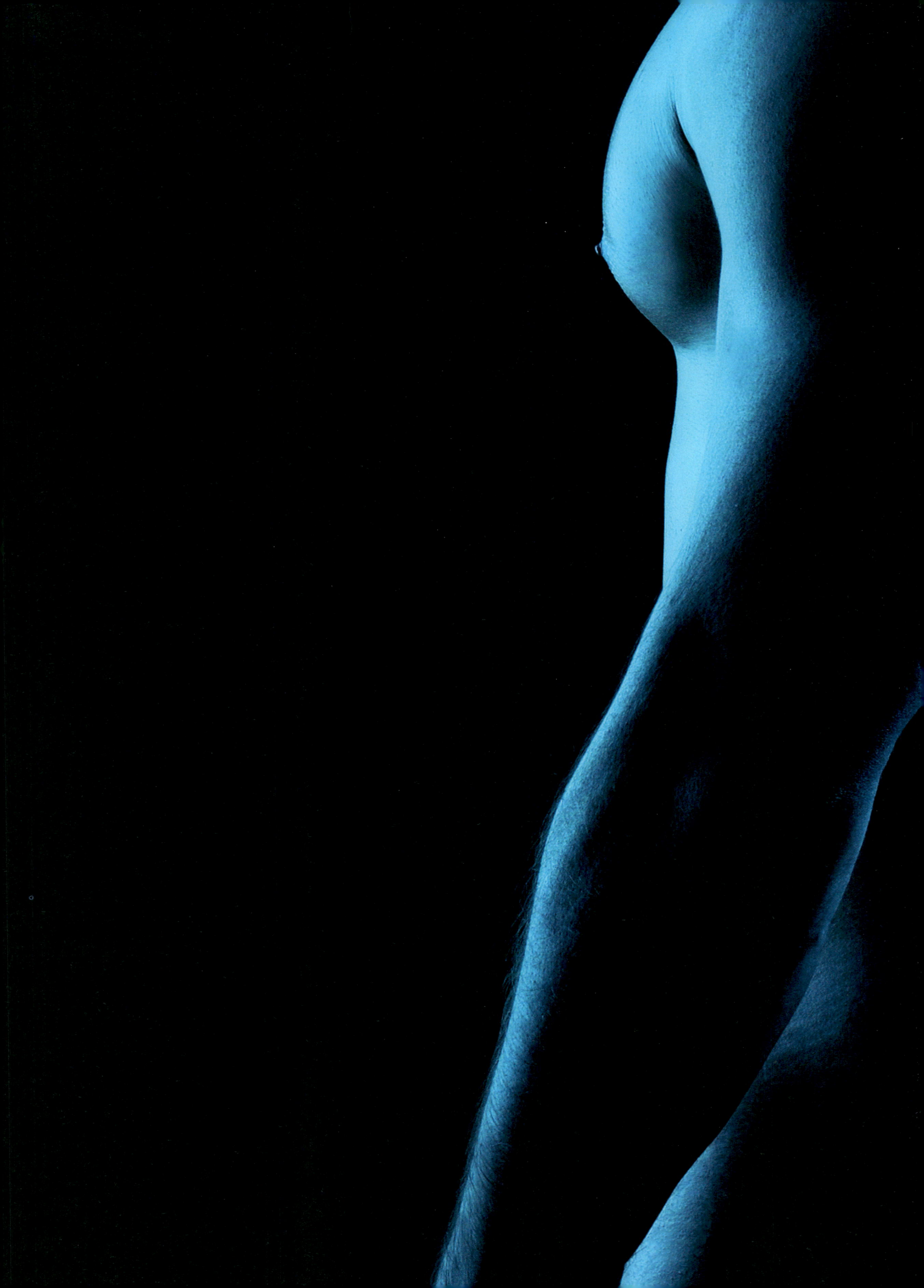

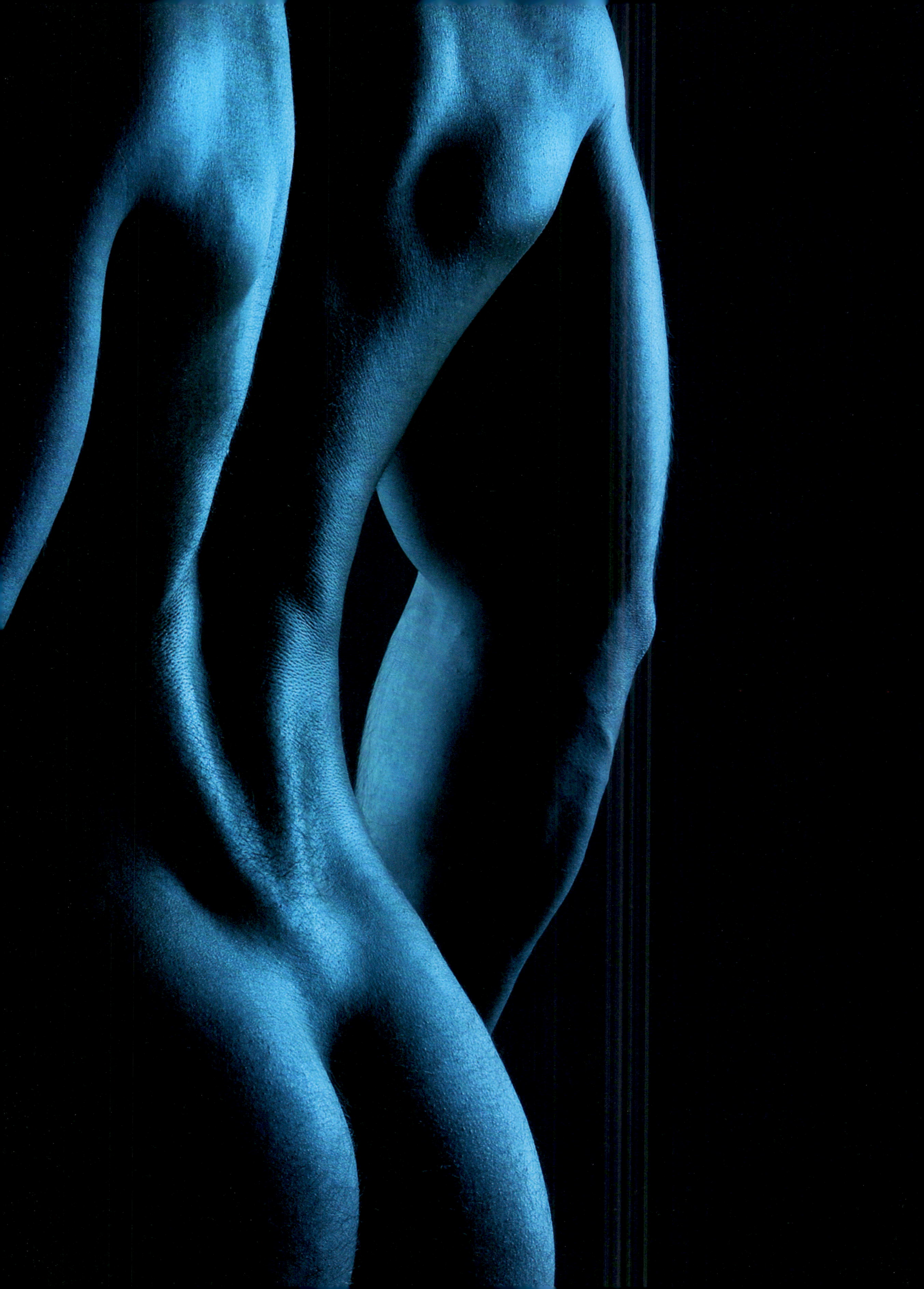

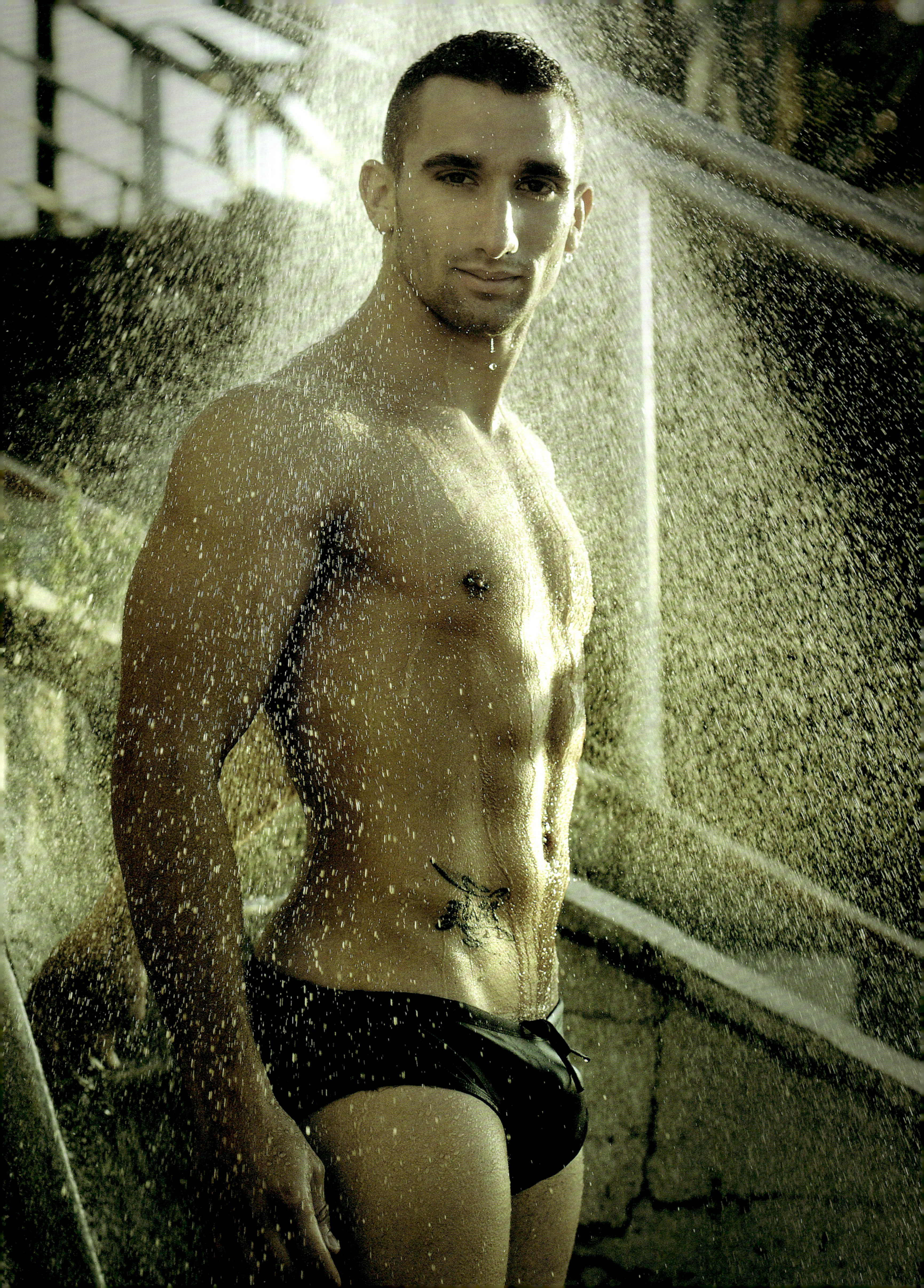

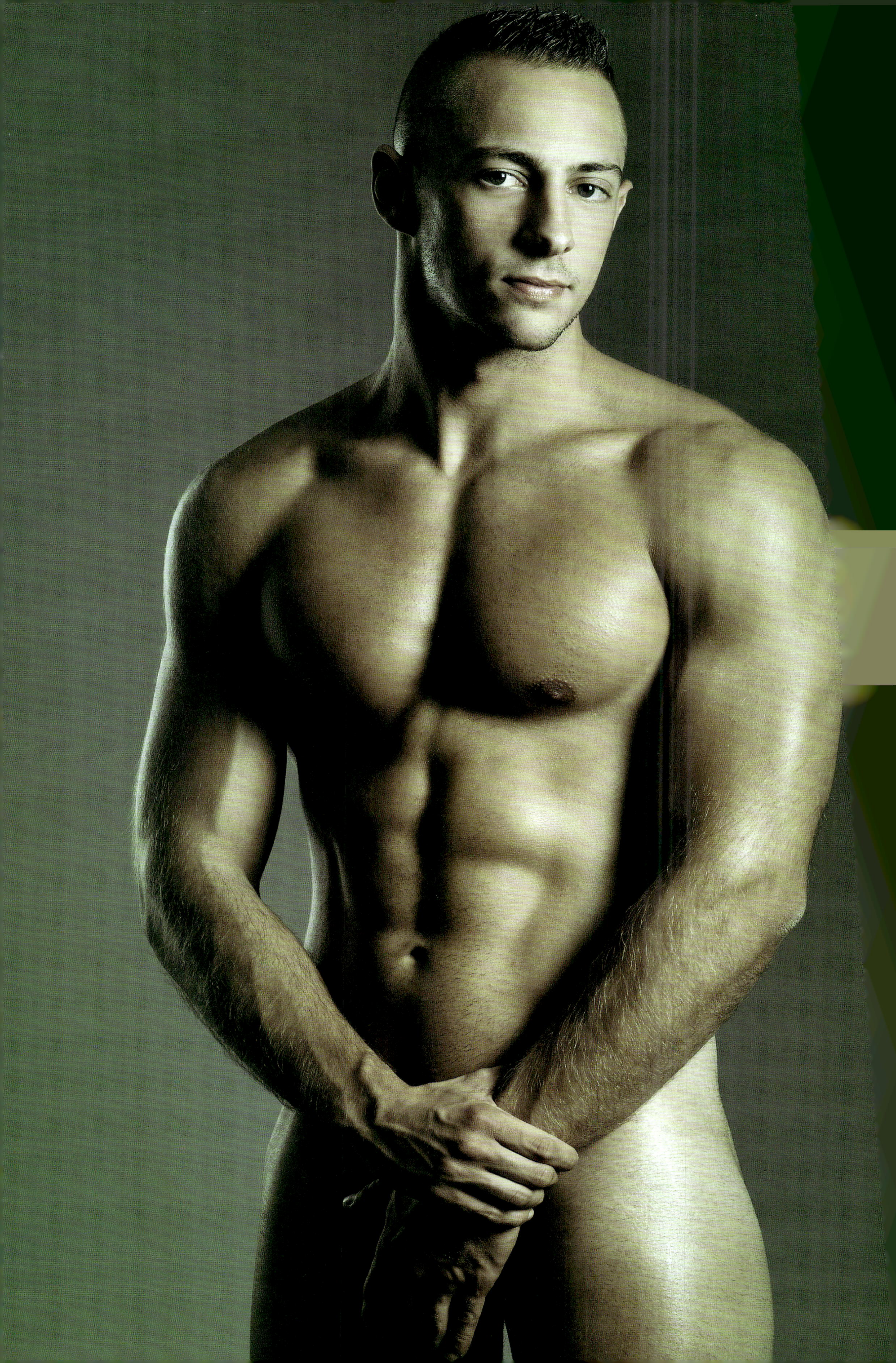

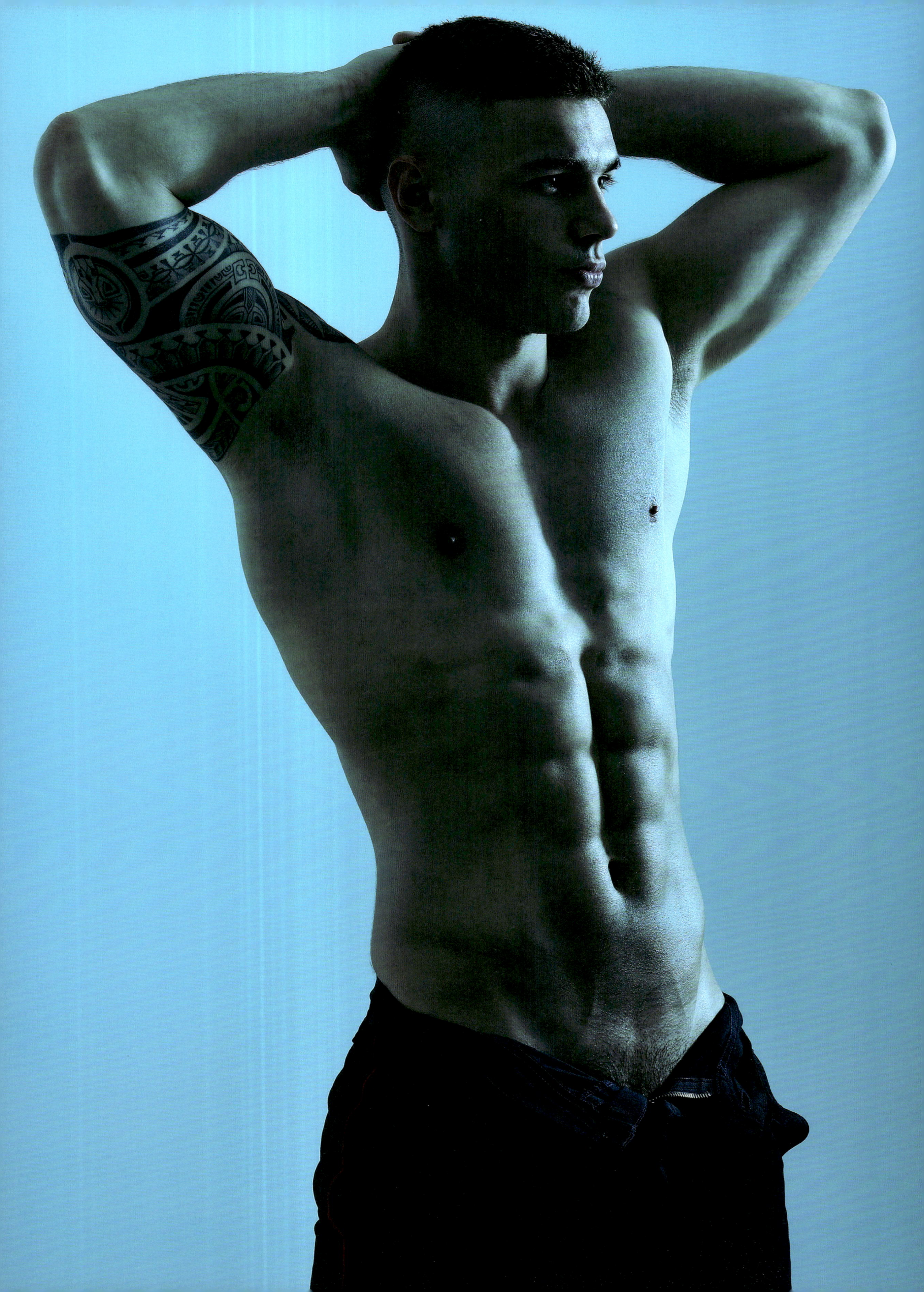

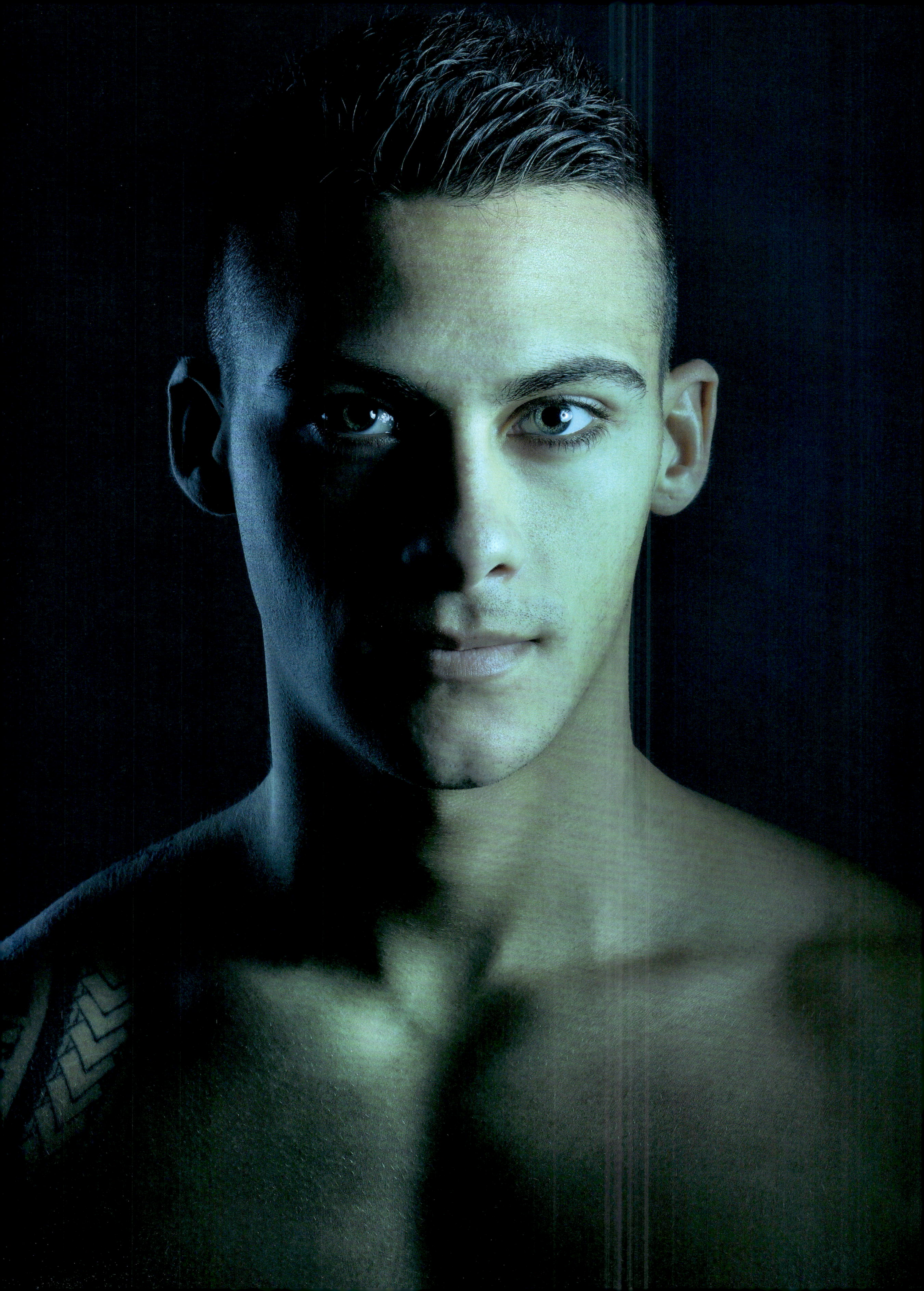

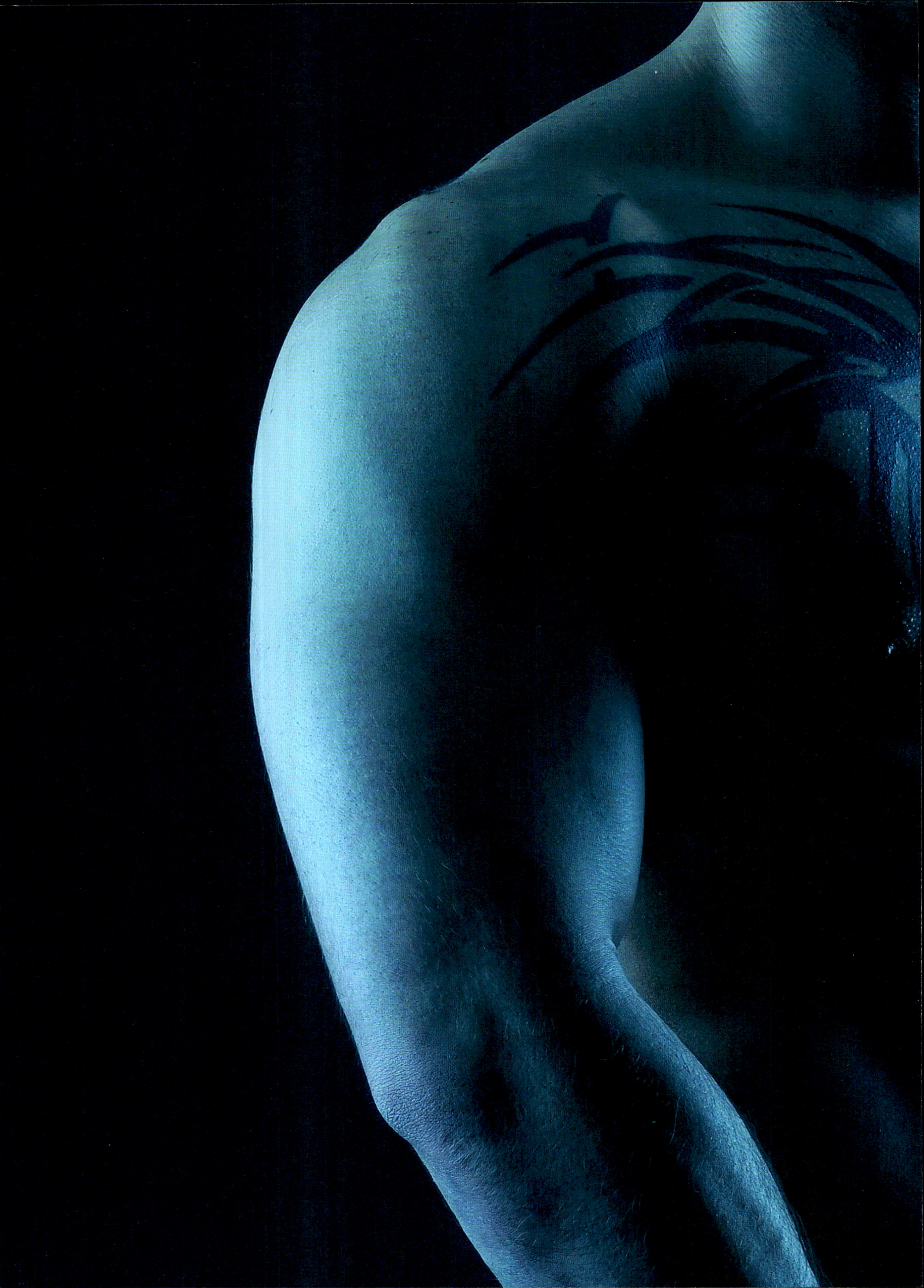

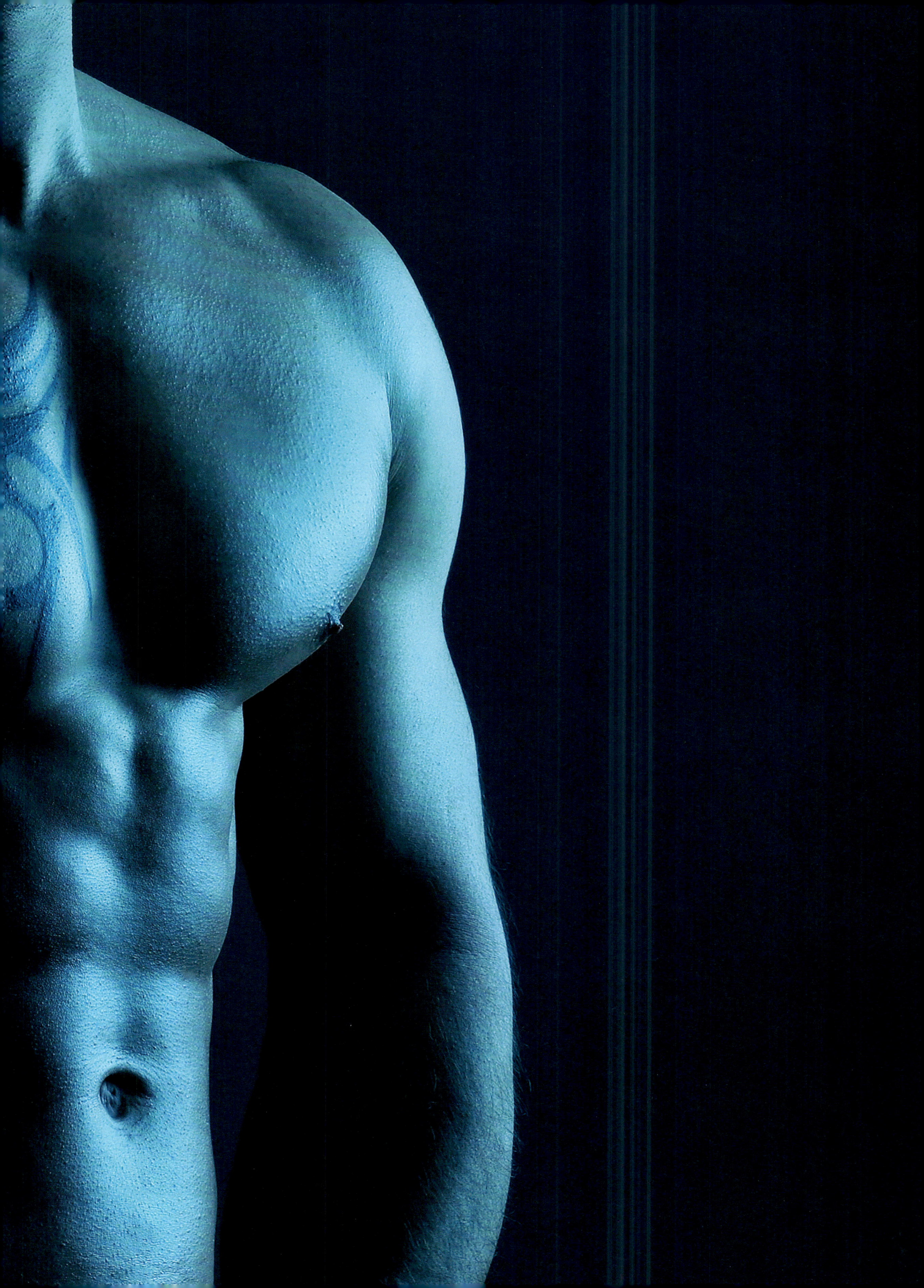

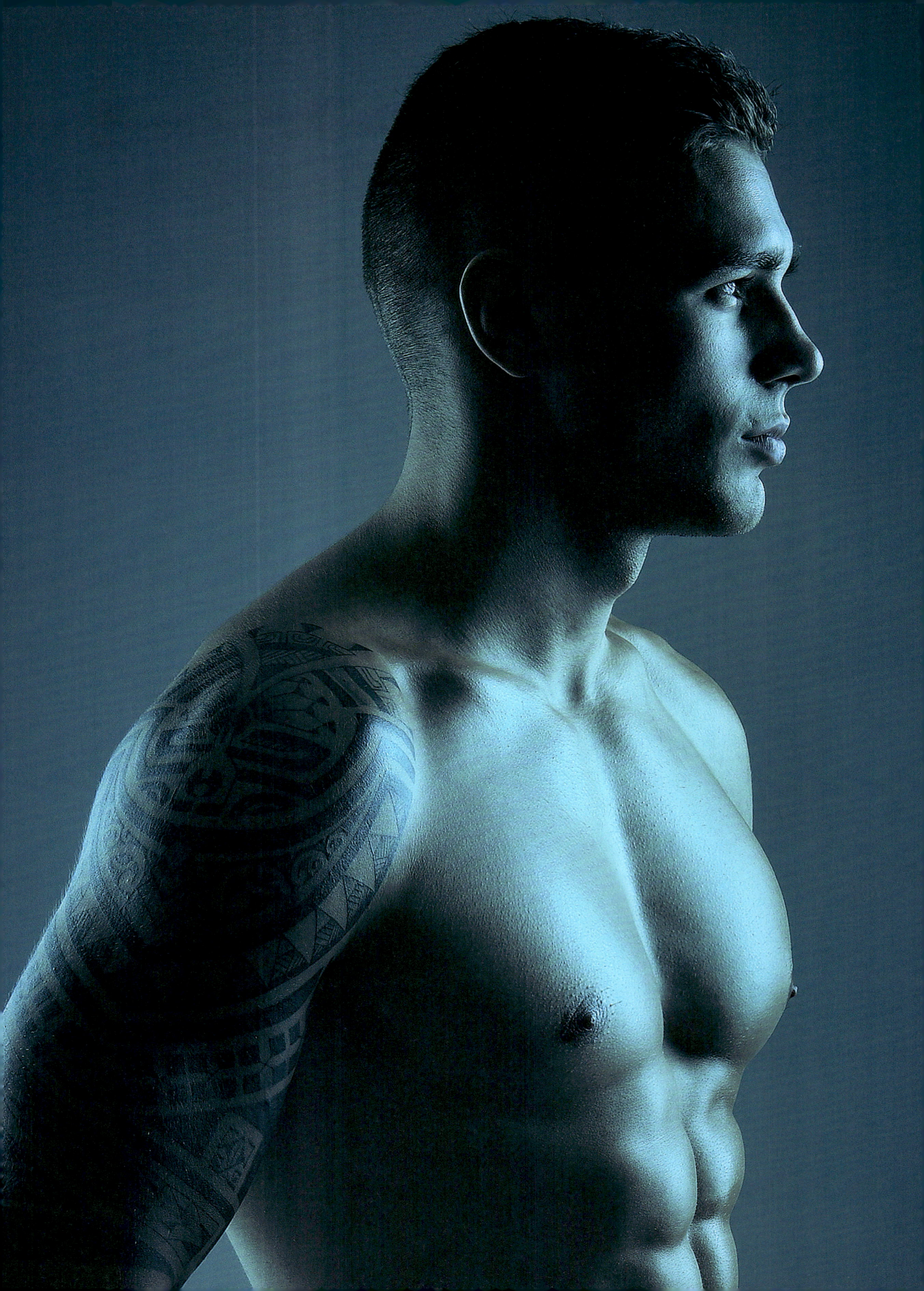

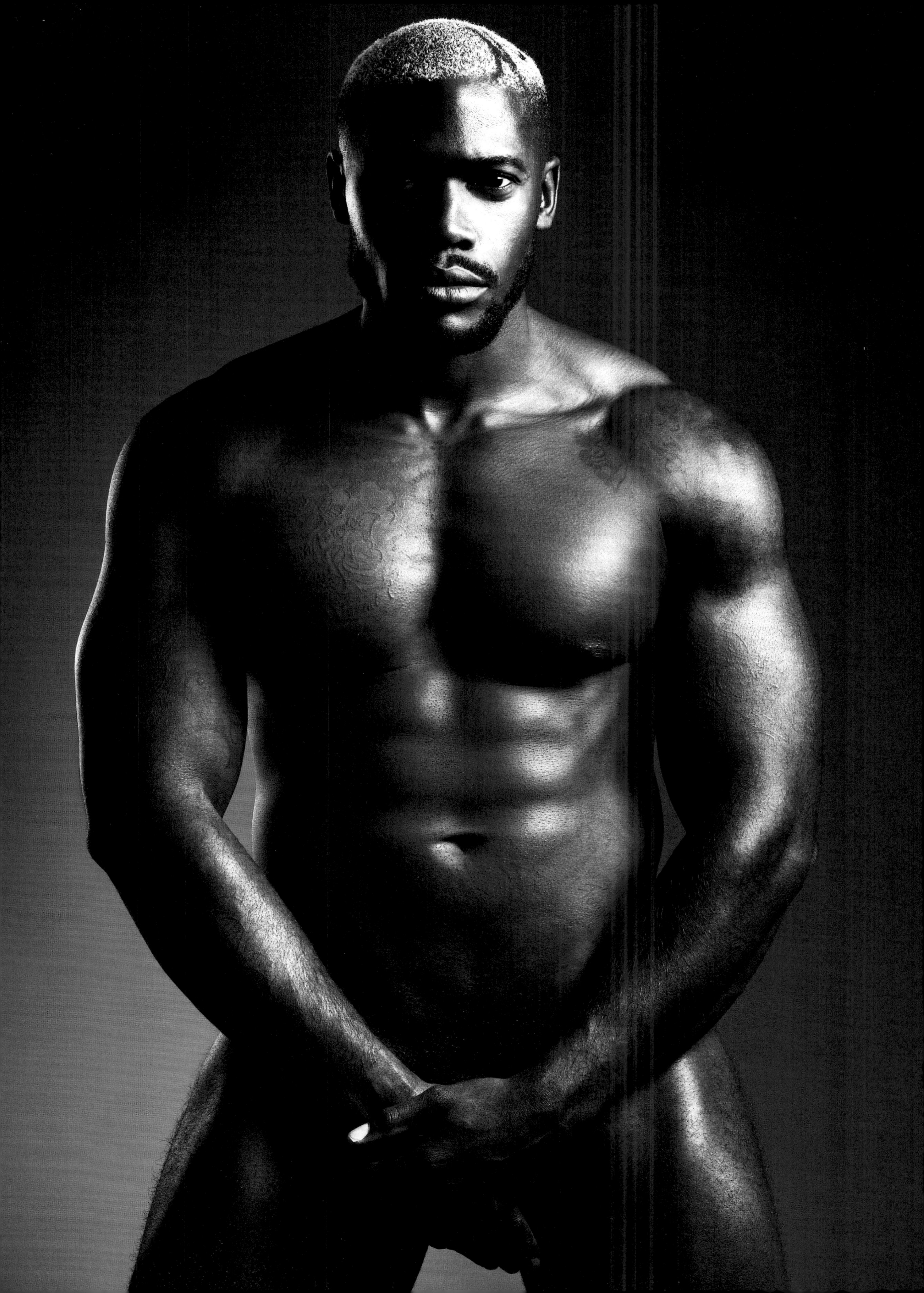

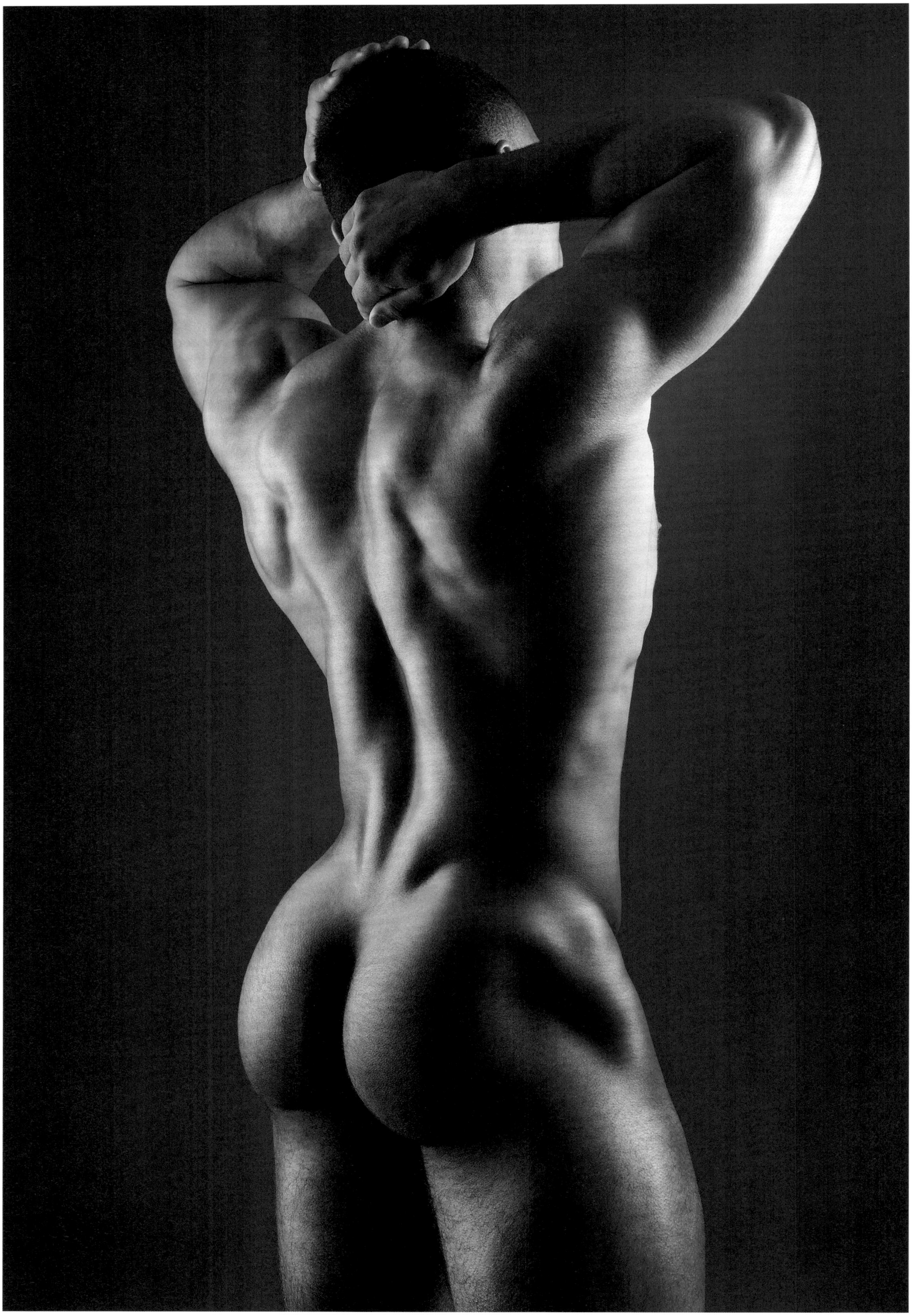

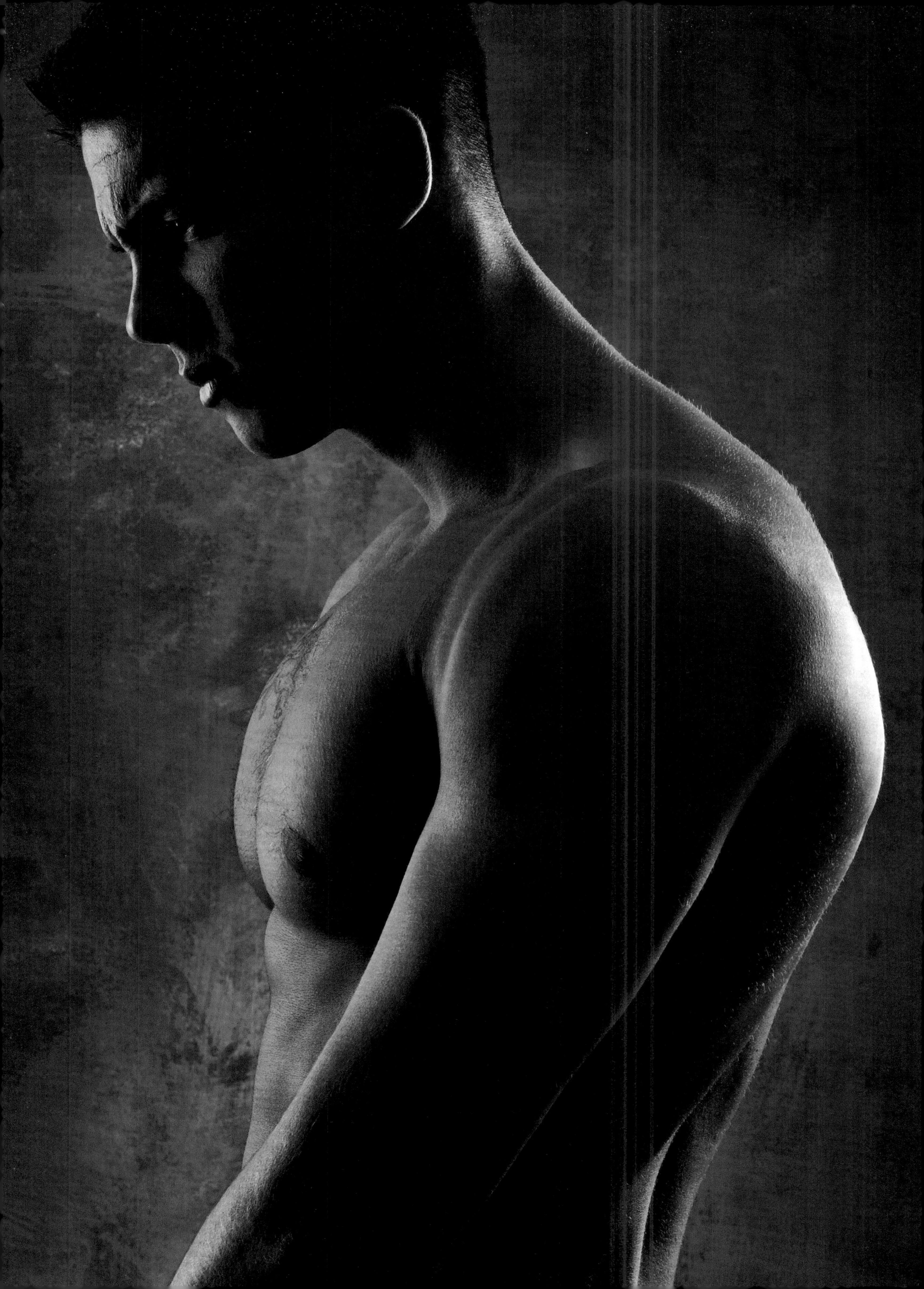

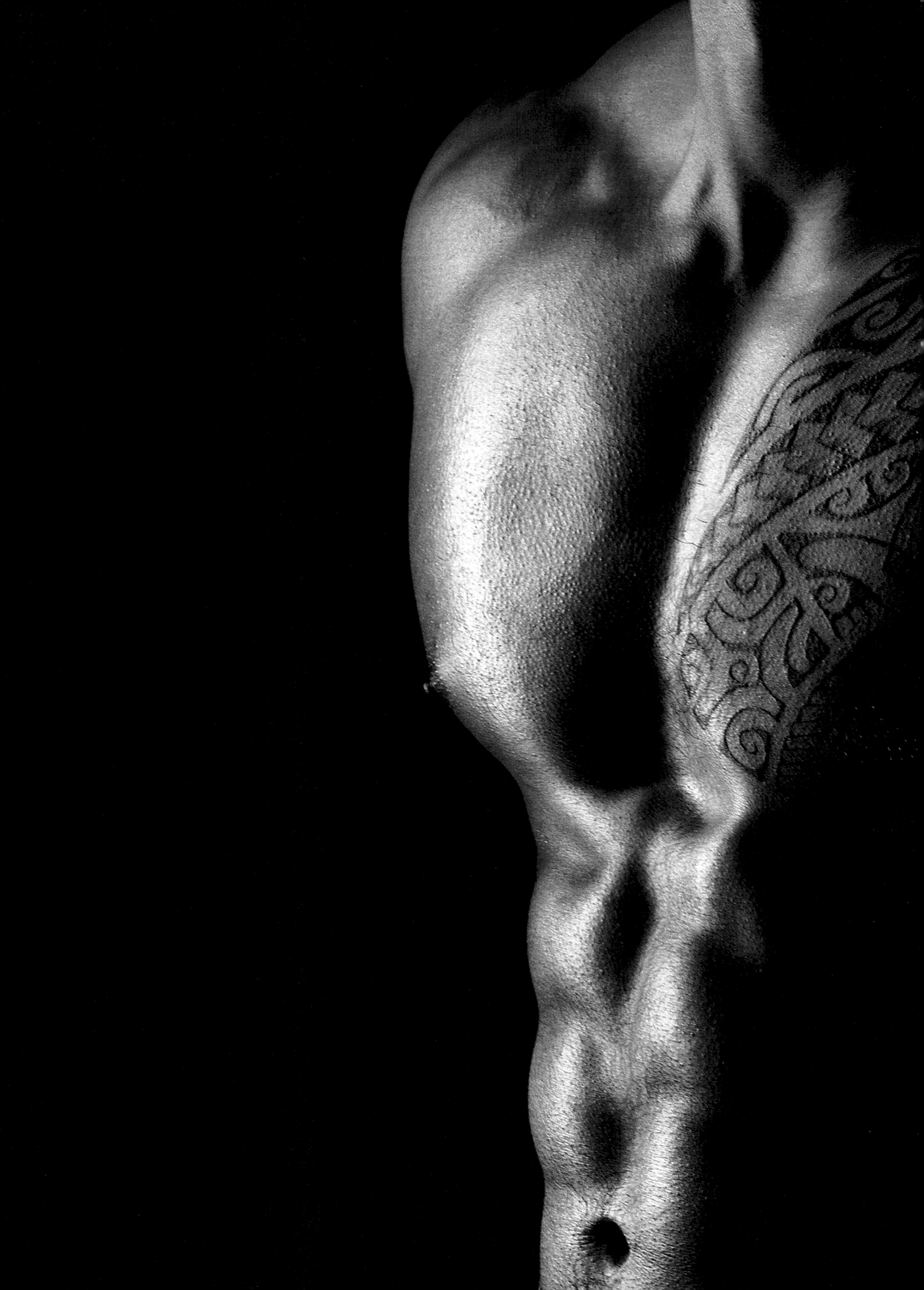

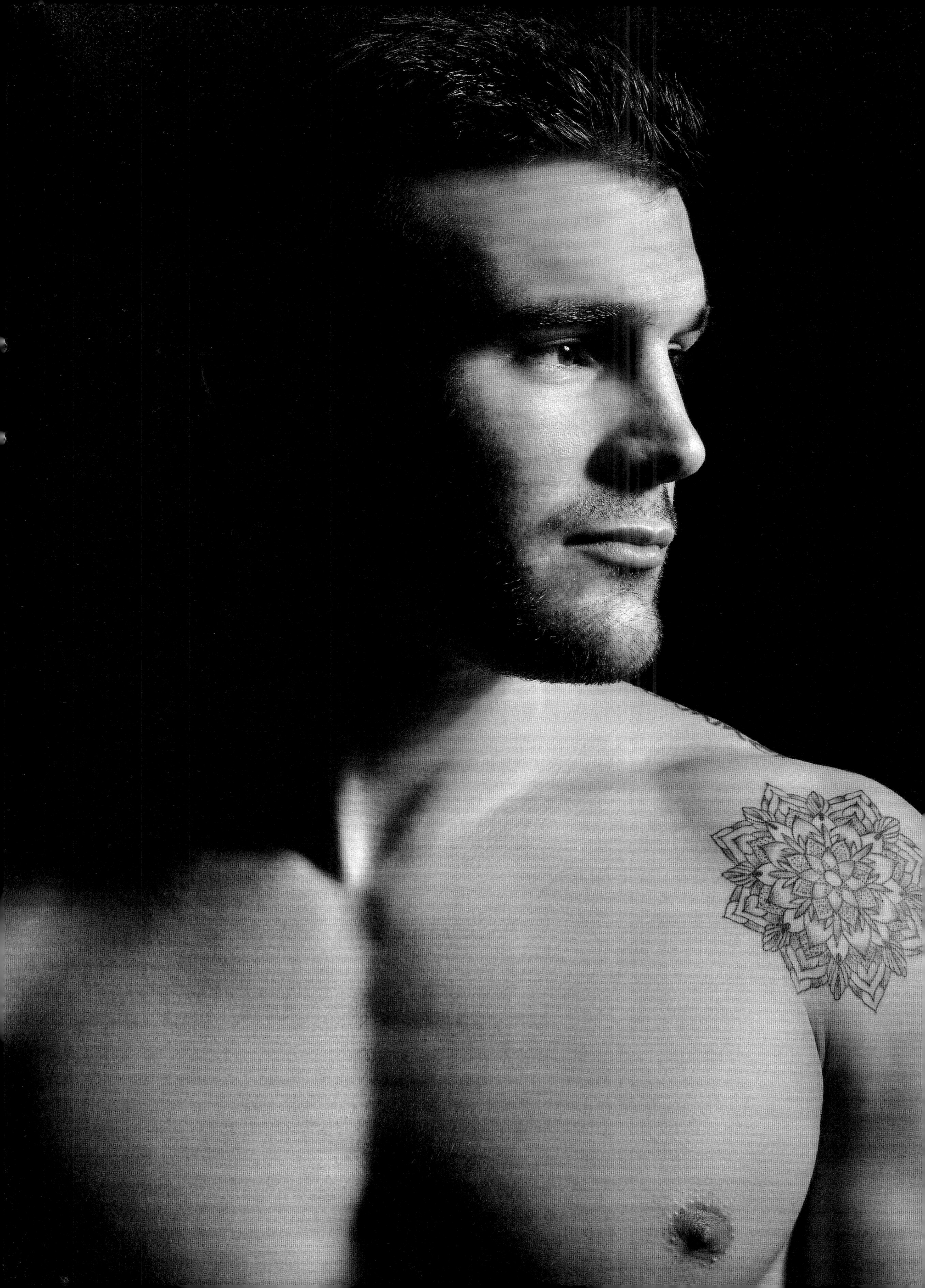

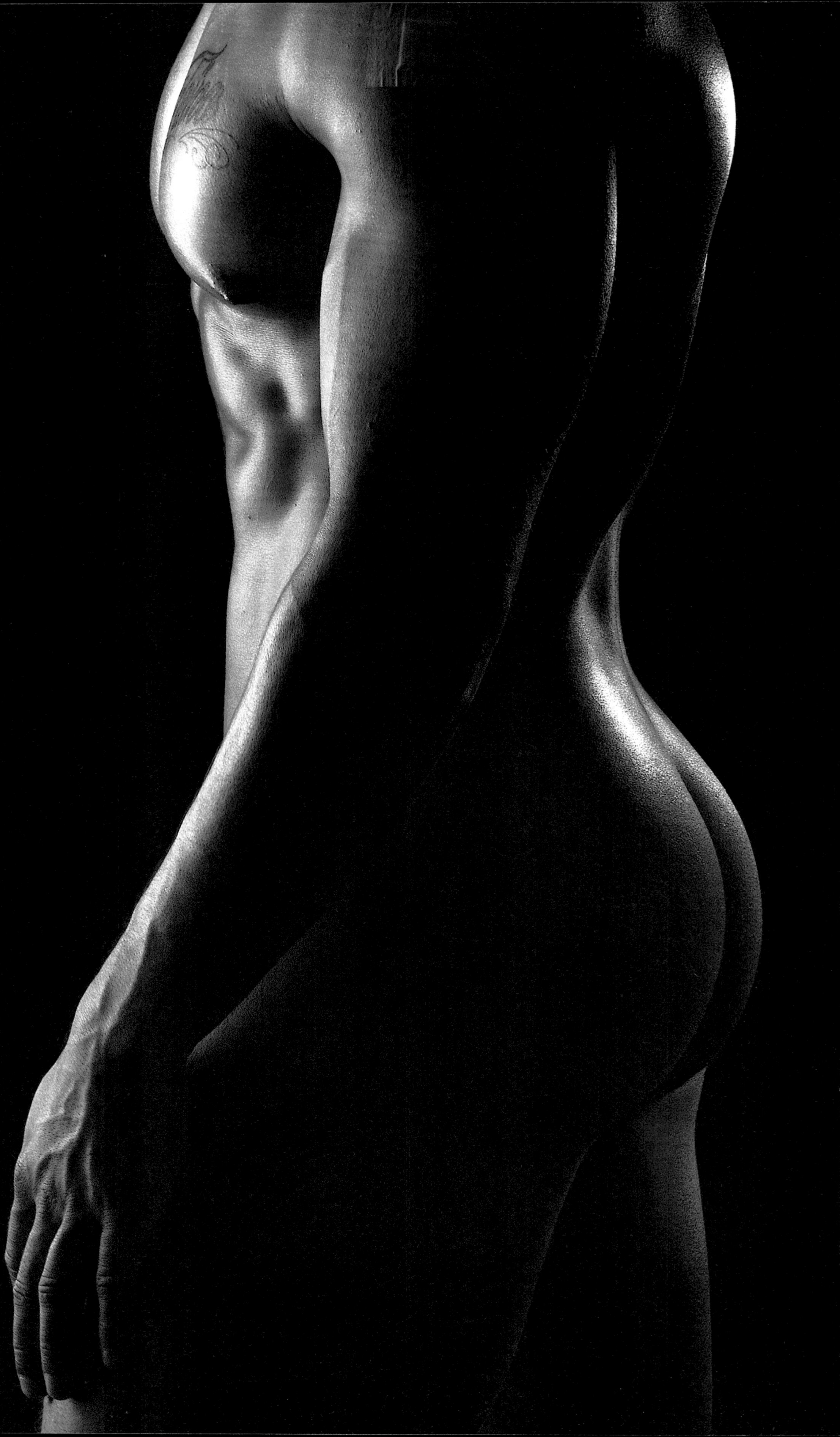

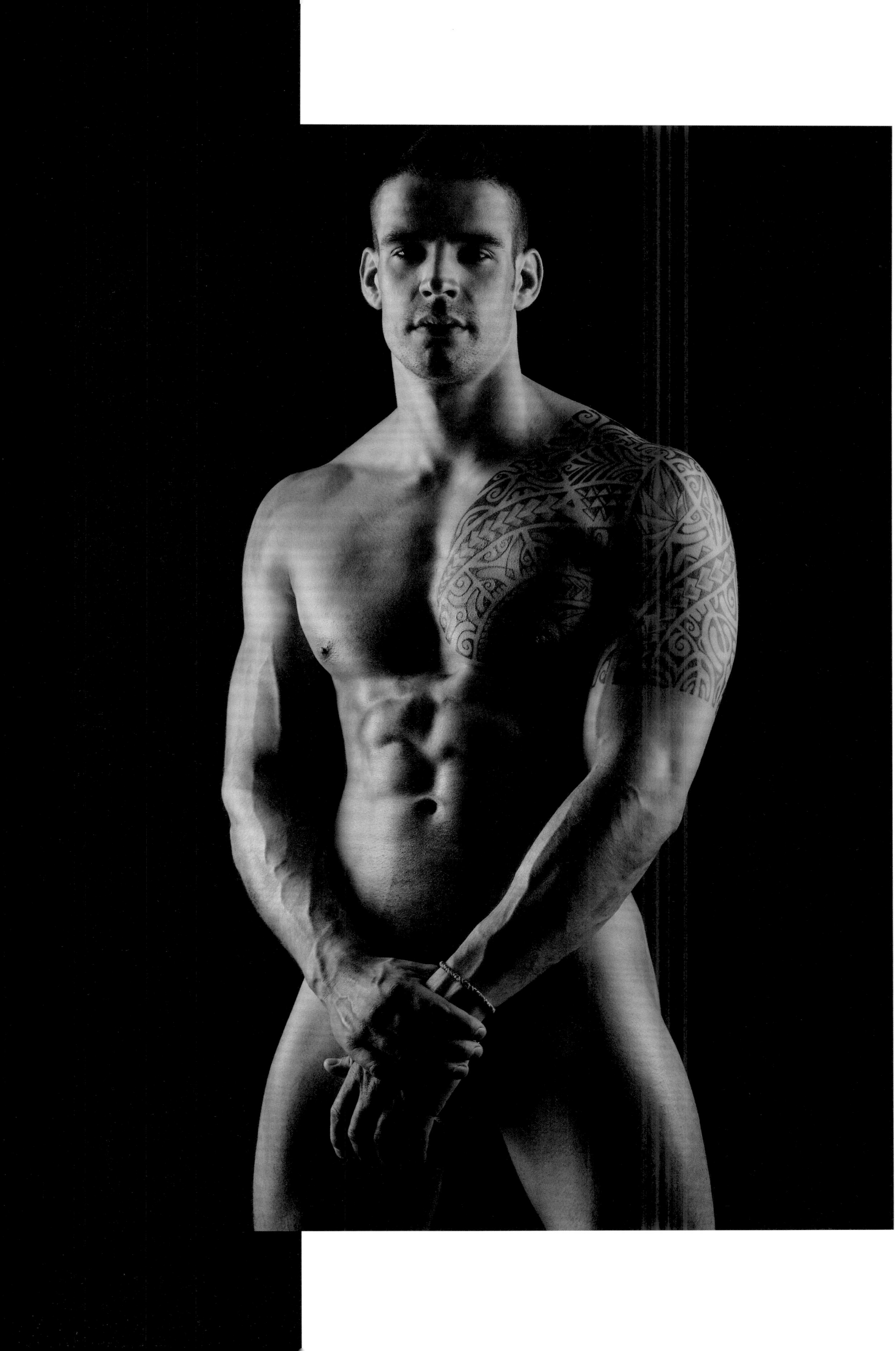

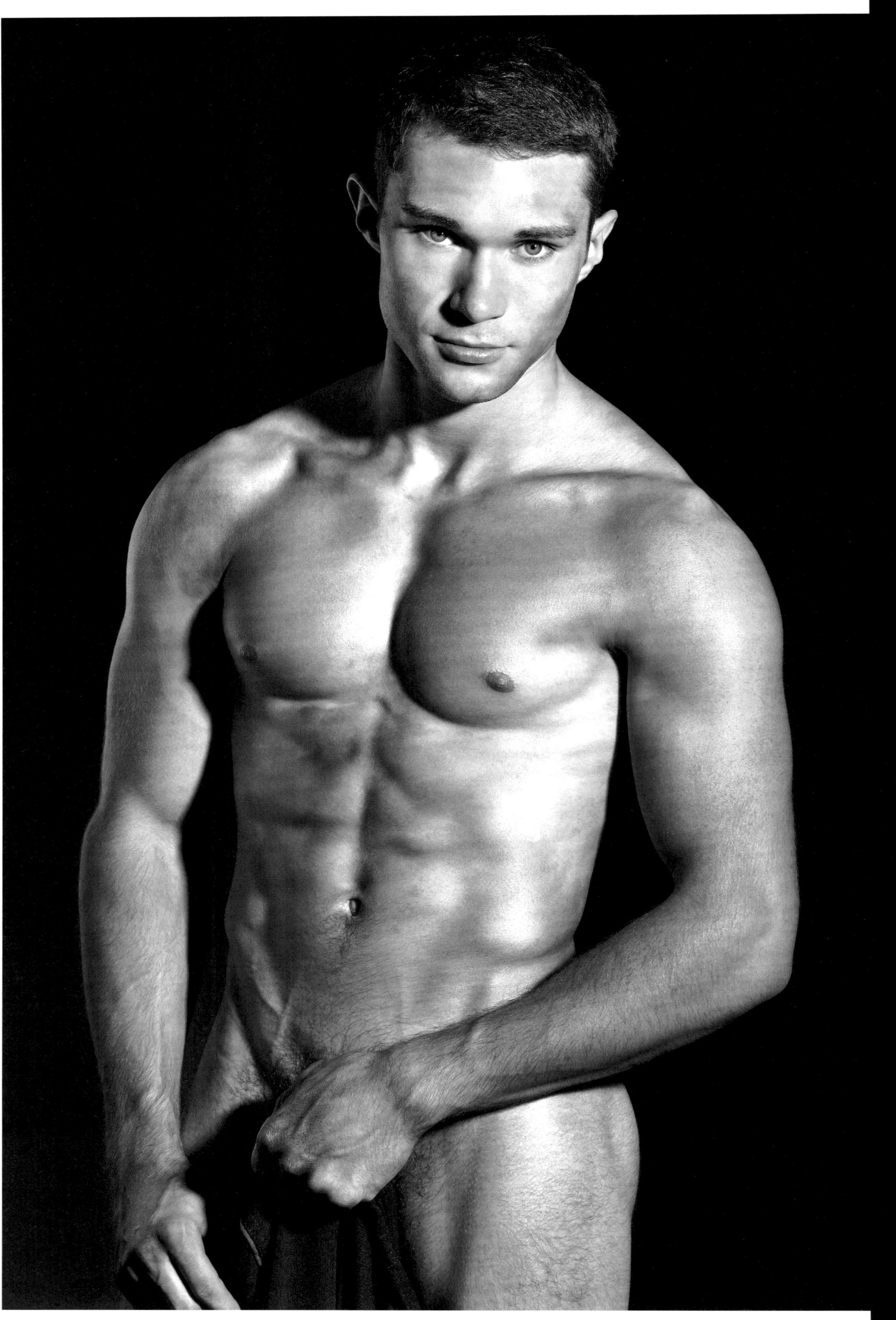

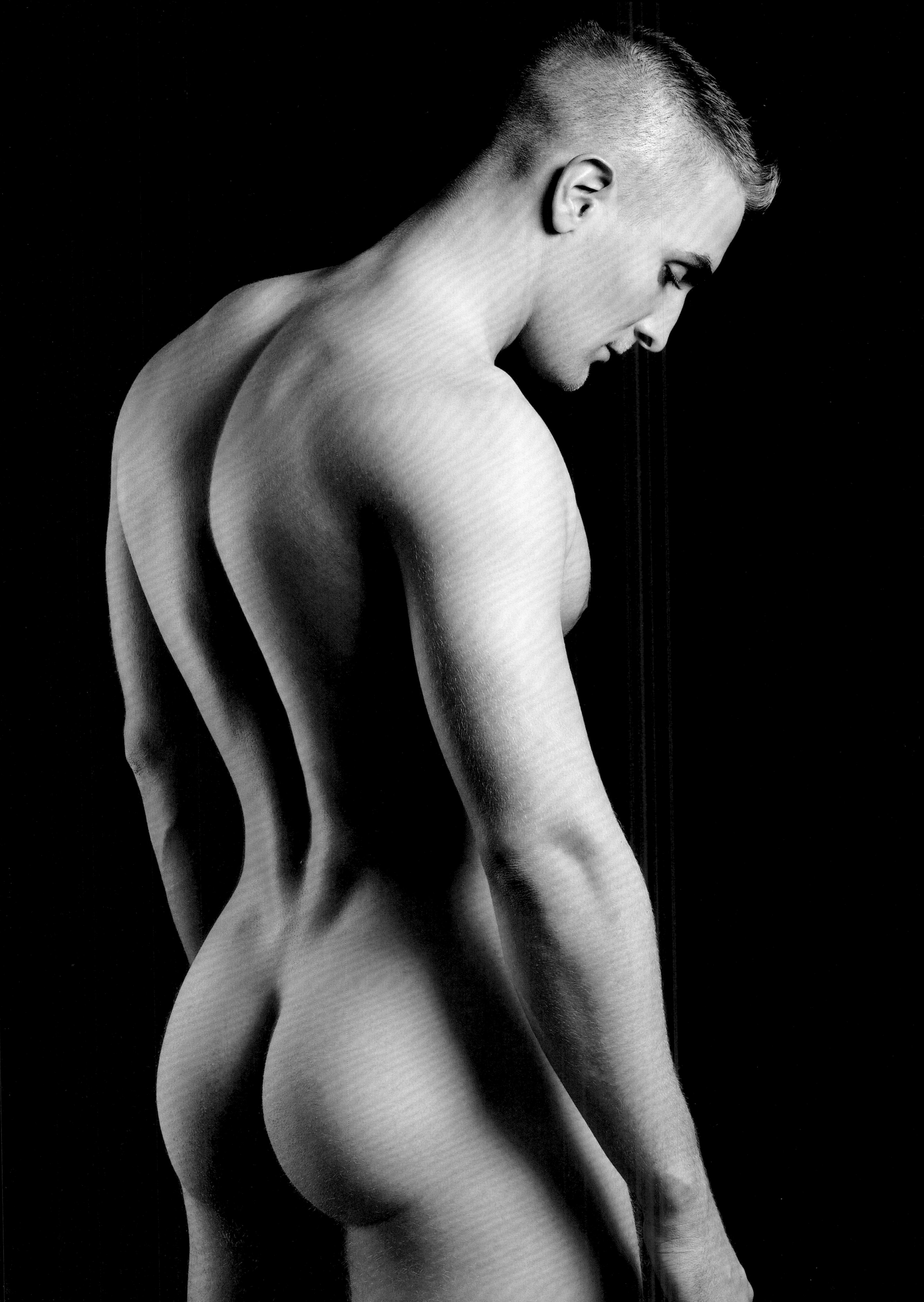

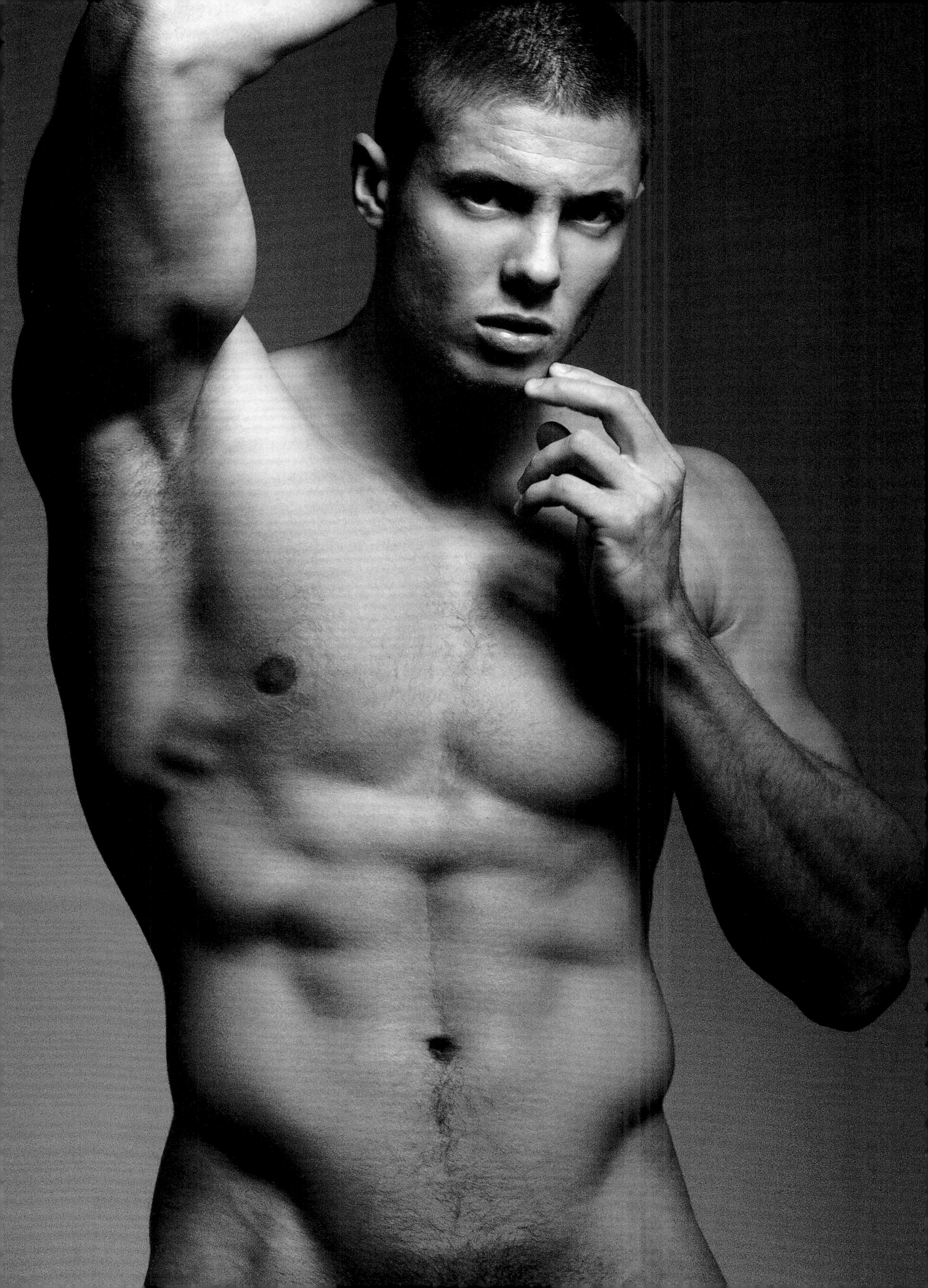

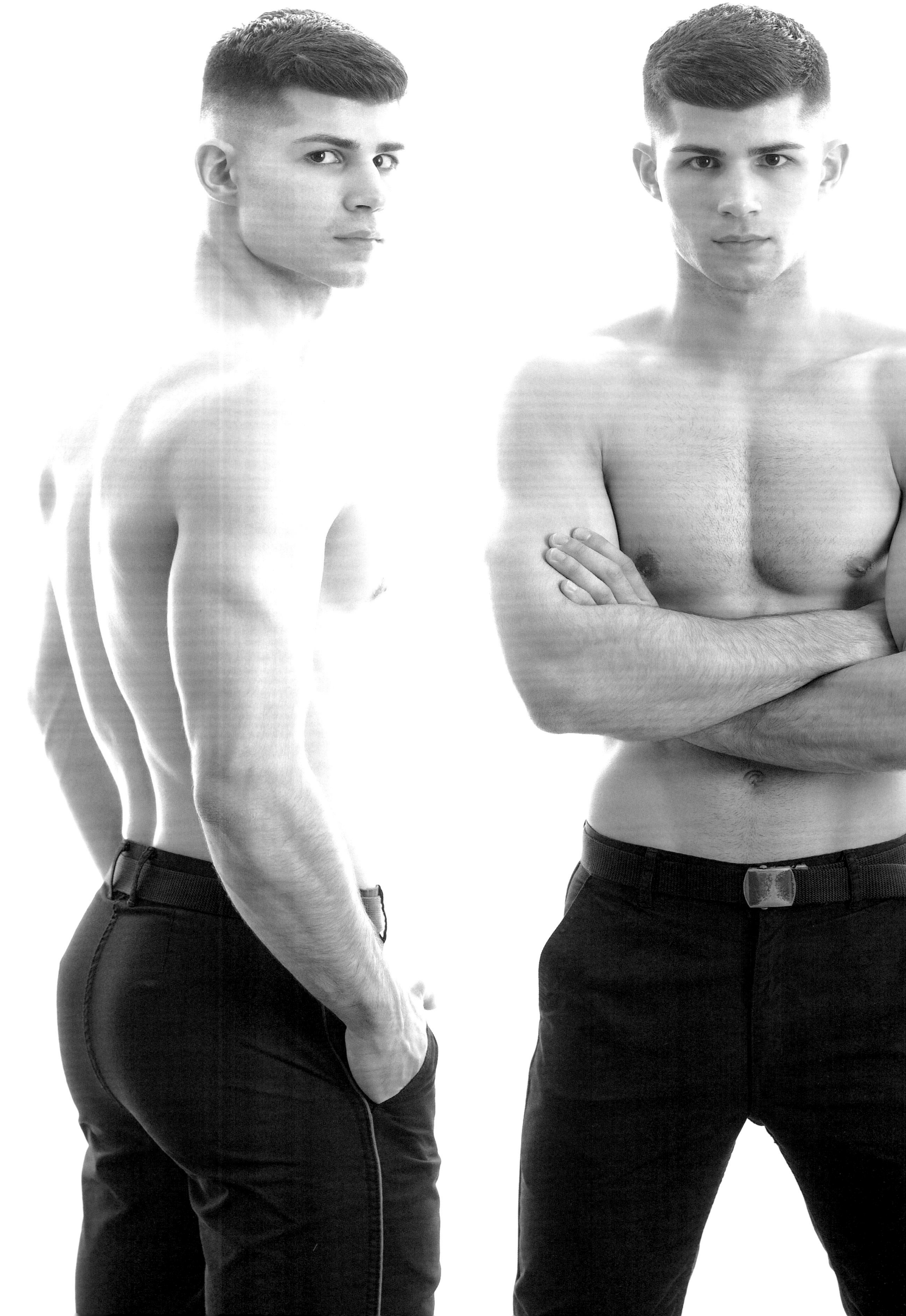

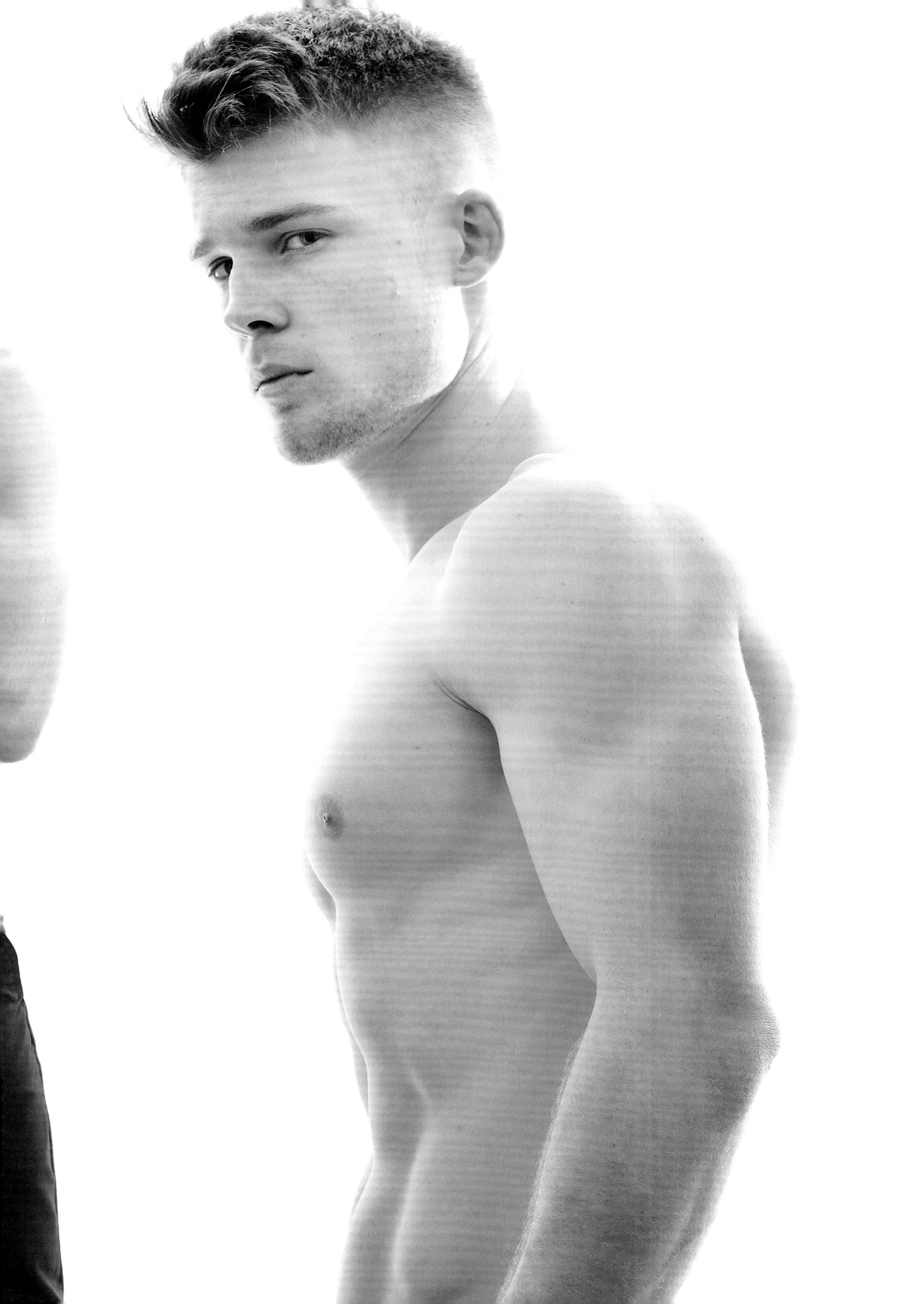

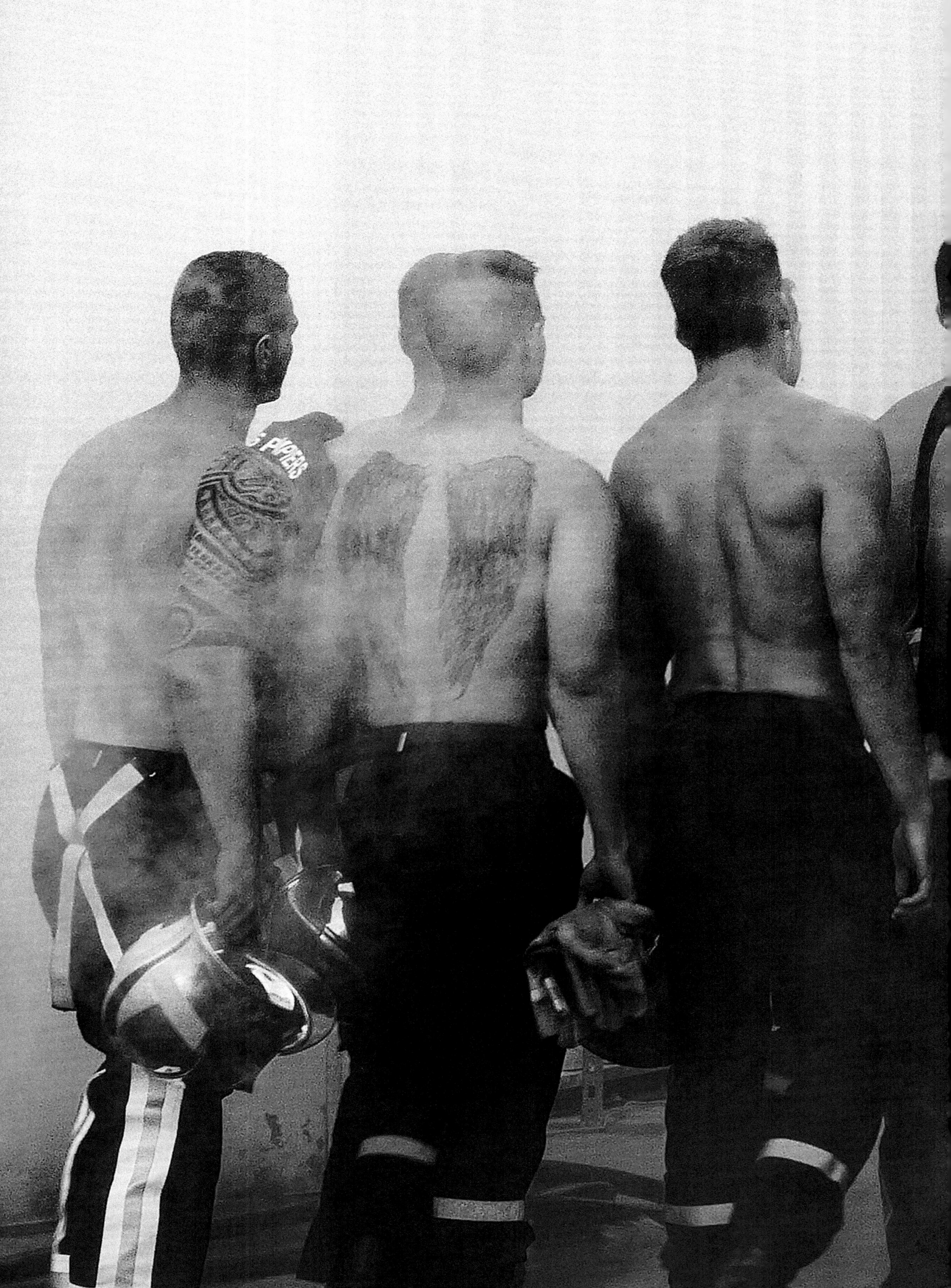
PIPERS

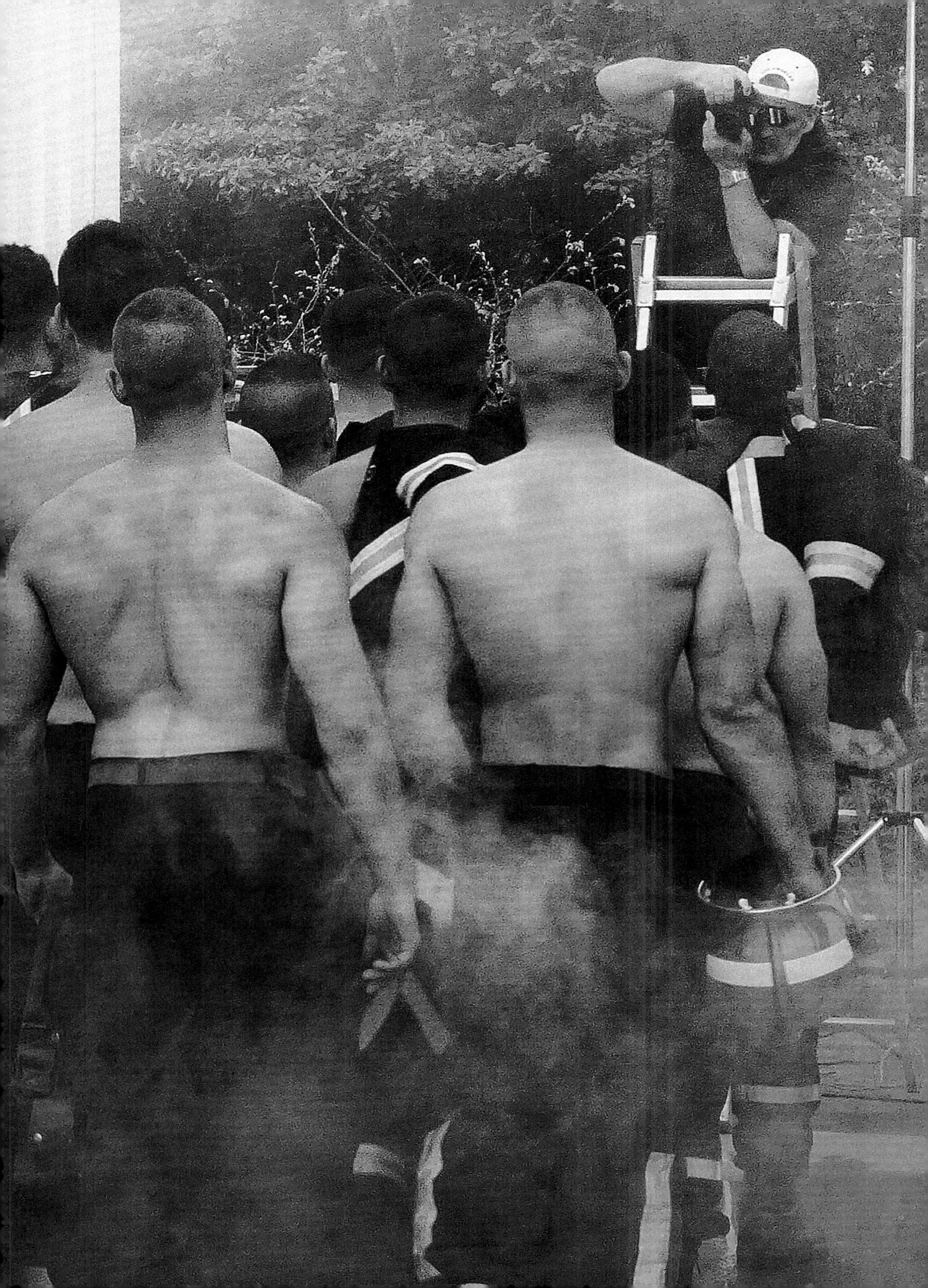

Acknowledgments

To Georgio
To Philippe Duguay and Mike Koepsell
To all the heroes who were injured and killed by fire

I would like to express my gratitude to the firefighters from the associations Pompiers Sans Frontières, Pompiers Entraide Internationale, and Challenge Ludovic Martin for taking part in this beautiful project: Alan B., Alexandre B., Alexis D., Alexis J., Anthony B., Anthony M., Anthony P., Antoine M., Arnaud B., Benoît M., Boris B., Brice N., Brice P., Bruno C., Bruno T., Bryan B., Cédric A., Cédric C., Christopher P., Clément G., Corentin L., Damien B., Florian D., Franck V., Fred S., Gaëtan S., Giovanni D., Guillaume B., Hugo L., Jean-Marc R., Jérémie T., Jérémy J., Jérémy M., Jérémy P., Jonathan B., Jonathan C., Jonathan S., Jules M., Julien A., Kévin A., Kevin P., Killian R., Léo P., Louis L., Lucas B., Ludwig B., Maixent G., Mathias B., Mathias P., Mathieu R., Mikaël F., Nicolas B., Paul B., Pierrick C., Quentin P., Raphaël D., Rémi D., Rémi H., Renaud S., Robin B,. Romain F., Rudy P., Simon D., Simon G., Simon L., Thibaud P., Thomas F., Thomas P., Valentin P., Victor C.

I wish to thank the members of Pompiers Sans Frontières; Pompiers Entraide Internationale; and the Challenge Ludovic Martin; Anthony Frémondière— deputy director—and Jean-Stéphane Camerini— owner—of the Old Course Cannes Golf Links; Esther and Manu Goretta; Nicolas Bigot, Théo, Guillaume, and all the R2 Paris Vendôme team; Navarro, La Villette studio; Aurélie, Béatrice, Dominique, Virginie, and all the Saint-Symphorien Intermarché team; Victor and the Saint-Symphorien stadium; Fabrice; all the Salaprod Paris team; Jeff; Michel Lévêque, Paul Reynaud, Gilles Moreau, Christophe Marguez de Gimaex; the Puy-Sainte-Réparade swimming pool team; Au-delà Plongée; and the Aix-en-Provence Creps.

Special thanks to Antoine Martin and his parents, Charles Boitier, Mathilde Poncet, Denis Taranto, Paul Hagnauer, Serge Montesinos, Louis Bataille, Max Guazzini, Inès Fourny, Ludovic Barthe, and Alain Bailloux.

I had the privilege of meeting wonderful people who were especially receptive to the project: Jean-Jacques Baudouin-Gautier, Gaëlle Lasse, Vincent Barbare, Aurélie Starckmann, Marie-Anne Jost, and Charlotte Becchio. They gave me the means required to develop my vision for the calendars. We built real trusting bonds along the way, allowing me complete artistic freedom. And the result is a profound homage to firefighters in the form of a beautiful almanac that one would be proud to hang on one's wall.

I am thankful to Rizzoli for giving me the opportunity to create this book, which is a compilation of my very best pictures of firefighters.

I would like to express my deep appreciation to Caroline Vasserot, who helped me put my thoughts into words during the writing of the introduction.

With loving thoughts and all my gratitude to my parents, Renée and Georges Goudon, my family, my loved ones, and my friends who have supported me since the beginning and have helped shape me:

Isabelle Beynel, David, Alexandre and Henry, Eli Almany Bradshaw, Dimitri Sarasin, Caroline Saslawsky and Avner, Isabelle Gueye, Valérie and Hervé Paruit, Jean Poderos, Gilles Marini and family, Barbara Machen, Shahrad Tehranchi and family, Marc Dansou, Frederick and Amandine Malahieude, Baptiste Mayeux, Johann De Nebehay, Luc Bellone and family, Etienne Billaud, Clément Becq, Greg Rossi, Clément Grossi, Robin Delépine, Raphaël Smolin Froissart, Adrien Espinosa, Clo and Lucien, Christophe Mallet, Jeremy Parisi, Orphée Petigenet, Robert Piotrowsky, Frédéric Hestin, Kevin Gehrig, Marius, Sebastian Valla, Nicolas Vrban, Joel West, Antoine Brasseur, David Hauschild, Nat Kelly Cole, Thomas Villa, Florent Sourice, Robert Conrad, Jean-Mathieu Vidal, Aymeric Priou, Yannick Lopez, Fabrice Quattrone, Fabien Loaec, Gilles Couturier and Linda Salas Vega, Les Koepsell's, Patrick Leonard and Guillaume Ortega, Laura Favali, Florent Aonon, Sophie Vonlanthen and family, Fabien Desmons, Valérie Caritoux and Ricardo, Léna Lutaud and Marc-Emmanuel Vuaillat, Isabelle Barbedienne and Franck Merienne, Célia and Benjamin Cornil Vial, Régine, Claude and the Perez family, Stéphanie, David, George and Victoria, Julia, Sébastien, Elise, Raphaël and Gabriel, and Sébastien. I love you.

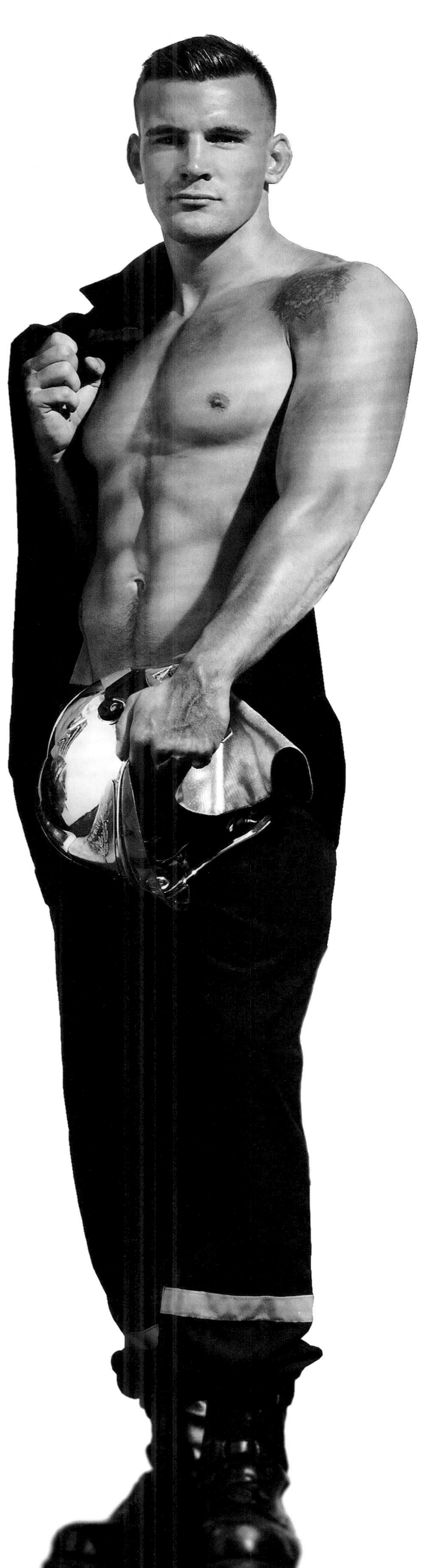

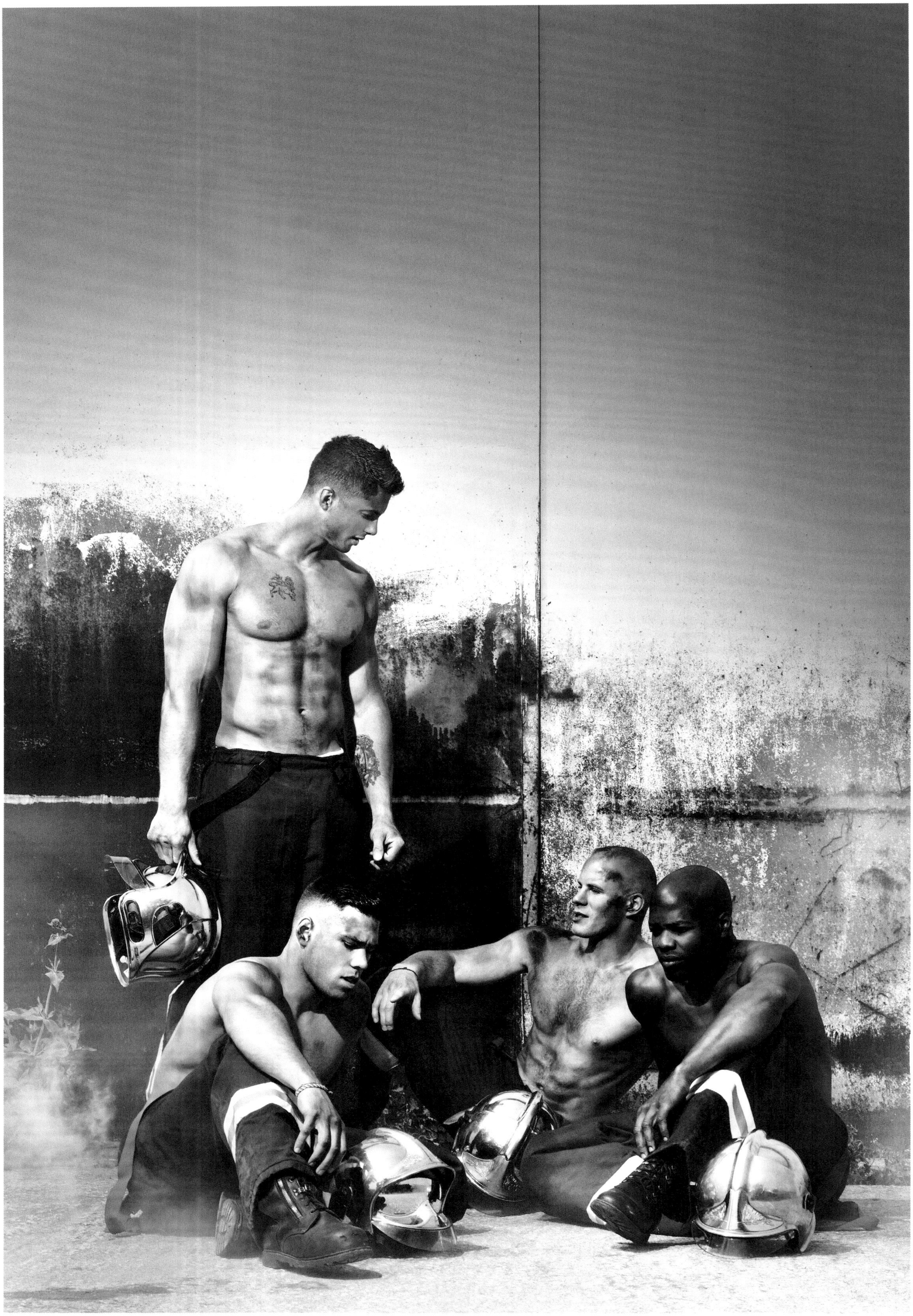

Credits

Production and logistics assistant: Caroline Vasserot
Photography assistant: Côme Bardon
Assistants: Sébastien Paquet, Jonathan Simonnet,
Fred S., Gaëtan Bordat, Florian Secomandi,
Bryan Bérard
Technical advisors: Clément Grossi, Thomas P.,
Jonathan Simonnet
Hair and makeup: Elika Bavar, Aziza El Badaoui,
Katia Ren

Shooting locations: Aix-en-Provence, Annecy,
Antibes, Arcachon, Calanque de la Vesse, Hostens,
Jas de Bouffan, La Dune du Pilat, Lac d'Annecy,
Lac de Biscarrosse, Le Puy-Sainte-Réparade,
Moussonvilliers, Paris, Roanne, Romagnat,
Saint-Symphorien, and Tourouvre.

Behind-the-scenes photograph pp. 138–139:
Caroline Vasserot

Instagram.com/fredgoudonphotographe

On Fire: The Firefighters of France

First published in the United States of America in 2021 by
Rizzoli International Publications, Inc.
300 Park Avenue South
New York, NY 10010
www.rizzoliusa.com

Photography © Fred Goudon. All rights reserved.

Publisher: Charles Miers
Editorial Director: Catherine Bonifassi
Editor: Victorine Lamothe
Production Director: Maria Pia Gramaglia
Managing Editor: Lynn Scrabis

Editorial Coordination: CASSI EDITION
Vanessa Blondel, Lili Doillon, Marie-Charlotte Pulcini

All rights reserved. No part of this publication may be reproduced,
stored in a retrieval system, or transmitted in any form or by any
means, electronic, mechanical, photocopying, recording,
or otherwise, without prior consent of the publisher.

ISBN: 978-0-8478-6852-0
Library of Congress Catalog Control Number: 2020946822
2021 2022 2023 2024 / 10 9 8 7 6 5 4 3 2 1
Printed in Italy

Visit us online: Facebook.com/RizzoliNewYork
Twitter: @Rizzoli_Books
Instagram.com/RizzoliBooks
Pinterest.com/RizzoliBooks
Youtube.com/user/RizzoliNY
Issuu.com/Rizzoli

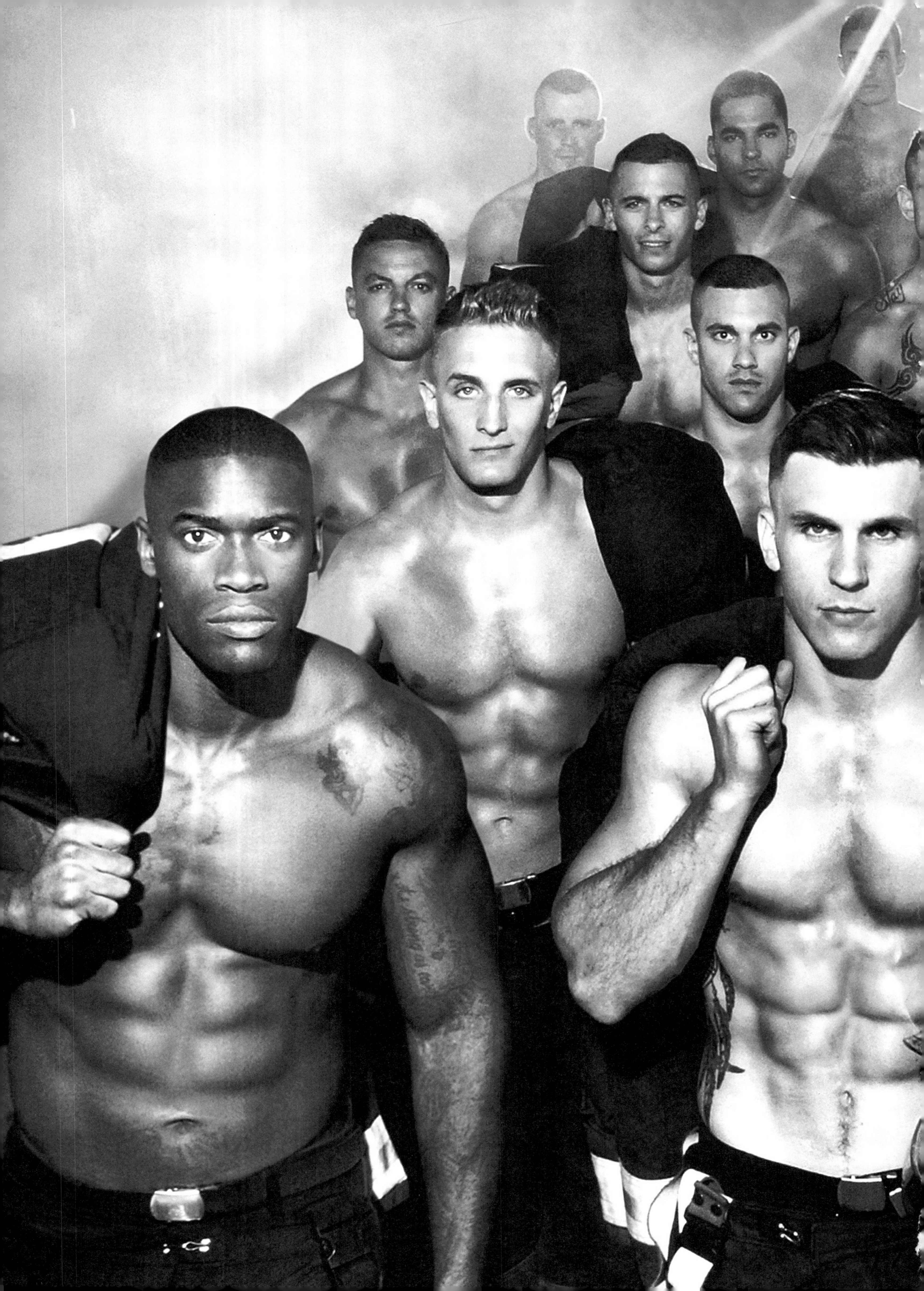